THE Complete
Philosophy FILES

'Accessible, entertaining . . . it's philosophy in action rather than philosophy in aspic . . . It's precisely the maverick combination of passion, rigour, patience and sedition that makes Law such an engaging writer and teacher.' *The Guardian*

'It is much more of a genuine introduction to philosophy than the seemingly more serious efforts of writers such as . . . Alain de Botton' *Times Educational Supplement*

'Readers puzzled by life will enjoy Stephen Law's *The Philosophy Files*. He takes a number of big questions . . . and examines them in a bright and mercifully non-facetious way. Curious philosophers of any age will find some basic problems dealt with in a way that genuinely illuminates them.' Philip Pullman in *The Times*

'The best introduction to philosophy that I've read for ages' Tim Lebon in *Practical Philosophy*

'An outstanding introduction to philosophy. Stephen Law is an exceptionally talented writer.' Nigel Warburton

'Superb . . . if you ever thought that philosophy for kids would be a turn off, check this out, sit back and enjoy the ensuing debate' *Amazon.co.uk*

'How did I arrive at philosophy? At the age of 17 I fell 65 feet head first off a cliff. Some say I never really recovered. I was thrown out of sixth form and never did get any A-Levels.

'After a number of dead-end jobs I ended up working as a postman in Cambridge for four years. While I was a postman I read a lot. One book led me to another and eventually I ended up reading nothing but philosophy books. I found that philosophy books addressed those really big questions that had always bothered me and that most other disciplines just skirt around or ignore.

'I managed to gain a place at The City University, London to study for a degree in philosophy. I got a first and that enabled me to get funding to go to Oxford University where I obtained my doctorate. I have held a number of lectureships at Oxford colleges and I'm currently a Lecturer in Philosophy at Heythrop College, University of London.

'I have lots of interests outside philosophy. I still live in Oxford where I play drums in local jazz and Latin bands. And I like to climb, especially in the Alps.'

THE
Complete
Philosophy
FILES

Including

The Philosophy Files

and

The Philosophy Files 2

Stephen Law

Illustrated by Daniel Postgate

Orion
Children's Books

ORION CHILDREN'S BOOKS

This edition first published in Great Britain in 2011 by Orion Children's Books
Originally published as two separate volumes:
The Philosophy Files
First published in Great Britain in 2000
by Orion Children's Books
The Philosophy Files 2
Originally published as *The Outer Limits*
First published in Great Britain in 2003
This edition published in 2017 by Hodder and Stoughton

14

A CIP catalogue record for this book
is available from the British Library.

ISBN 978 1 44400 334 5

Printed and bound in Great Britain by Clays Ltd, Elcograf S.p.A.

The paper and board used in this book are
made from wood from responsible sources.

Orion Children's Books
An imprint of
Hachette Children's Group
Part of Hodder & Stoughton
Carmelite House
50 Victoria Embankment
London EC4Y 0DZ

An Hachette UK Company
www.hachette.co.uk

www.hachettechildrens.co.uk

For Tilda and Anoushka

Lots of people helped me with this book. Sophie Walker (age 13) gave me some very valuable comments. I would also like to thank these adults: Taryn Storey, Justine Burley, Mick O'Neill, Miranda Fricker, Geoff Mees and Janice Thomas. Special thanks are due to my mum, Maureen.

Contents

Big Questions

Here I am climbing a mountain.

One reason I like to climb is that, while I sit taking in or paying out the rope and my partner is climbing, I can look at the scenery and think.

What do I think about? Well, being so far up above everything can give you a quite different view of the world. Rather than being caught up in my day-to-day life, I usually end up thinking about questions like these: Where did the universe come from? Is there life after death? Does God exist? What makes things right or wrong? and: Could my whole life have been a dream?

These are *philosophical* questions. They are some of the biggest and most exciting questions that have ever been asked. Mankind has been grappling with them for thousands of years.

I'm sure you've asked such questions yourself. If you have, then this book is for you.

Of course, some religious books claim to have the answers to these and other philosophical questions. But it's important to realize that this is *not* a religious book. It's a philosophy book. It's a book that encourages you to question and figure things out for yourself.

The book is made up of eight chapters or *files*. Each file looks at a different philosophical question. You *don't* have to start at the beginning of the book. You can jump in wherever you like, depending on which question first grabs your attention.

And remember, the important thing in philosophy is to think for yourself. You certainly don't have to agree with me about everything. In fact, you may find that I have made mistakes and taken a wrong turn here and there.

Many philosophical questions can be a bit frightening to think about. That's one reason why some people don't like to think about them – they like to stay where they feel safe. But if you are anything like me, you will enjoy the challenge, excitement and sense of vertigo that thinking philosophically can bring. So get ready for a journey to the outer limits of thought. For we are about to open ...

The Philosophy Files!

File 1

Should I eat meat?

The story of Errol, the explorer

Errol was an explorer. He loved to sail
the seas looking for new lands.

On one of his trips up to the north, not
far from where the ice begins, Errol
discovered a small, mountainous island
covered in forest. He decided to leave his
crew behind on the ship and to go ashore in a
rowing boat, quite alone.

Errol took with him some supplies: lemonade and sandwiches.

That night he slept beside the sea in a hammock suspended
between two large pine trees.

The next day, Errol started to walk into the forest. After an
hour or so, he began to see signs of human life. There were
clearings in the forest and burnt areas that looked like they had
once been camp fires. This made Errol very excited. He thought
he was about to discover a new tribe.

Eventually, after several hours, Errol came to
a larger clearing. And there, in the middle
of the clearing, were three strangely
dressed people.

The three strangers wore purple vests and odd red hats shaped
like upside-down triangles. They stood in silence, looking him
up and down. It seemed as if they had been waiting for him.

Errol raised his hand as a sign of friendship. At this, the three
strangers started talking to each other. To his great surprise, Errol
found that he could understand what they were saying, for they
spoke a language quite similar to a language spoken on another
nearby island, a language he already knew.

And then, to his horror, Errol began to understand what the
three strangers were planning. This is what they said:

'He looks nice and big, enough for everyone, don't you think?'

'Yes. Such firm muscle. He should taste very good.'

'But I would like the brains. I always get the brains. They're
the best bit.'

'OK. You can have the brains. Let's get on with it, then.'

The three strangers were *cannibals*: people who eat other
people. They started to walk towards Errol. Only now did Errol
see that they carried clubs, knives and ropes in their hands.

Errol tried to run, but they were too quick for him. When he
came to, he found himself quite naked and trussed up like a
turkey. They had suspended him from a long pole. Under the
pole were logs and kindling ready for a fire

It looked like they were planning to barbecue him.

Errol turned his head to get a better look around him. He now saw that he was in a large room. Surrounding him were many more of the strangely dressed people. They stared back at him in silence. Some were licking their lips.

Then a woman stepped forward. She was carrying a big knife.

'Wait!' said Errol.

Everyone gasped. They were surprised that Errol could speak their language.

'Please don't eat me,' said Errol.

'Why should we not eat you?' asked the woman with the knife.

'Because it's wrong. Don't you see?' said Errol.

'No. I don't see. Why is it wrong?'

'You don't need to eat me, do you? You all look jolly well fed to me. Eat something else. Some roots, or grain, or a bird or something.'

The woman looked puzzled. 'But we like eating people. They taste good! Why shouldn't we eat them?'

'Well, why don't you eat each other then?'

'But none of us wants to die. So it is better that we eat you, instead.'

'But I don't want to die! I am a living thing! I am enjoying my life! Don't you see? It is very wrong to end my life just so you can enjoy eating me.'

Some of the others were nodding.

'Perhaps he is right,' said one of them.

3

Errol thought he was beginning to convince them not to eat him. But then the woman with the knife bent down. She put her hand into Errol's rucksack and pulled out a bottle of lemonade and a brown paper bag. Out of the paper bag fell a half-eaten sandwich.

'What is this, then?'

'Er. That's my lunch.'

'What is it?'

'It's a sandwich. A beef sandwich.'

'This beef was part of a living animal?'

'Er. Yes. I suppose it was.'

'It was a living thing. It enjoyed life. It didn't want to die. Yet it was killed so you could enjoy eating its flesh.'

Errol could see what she was getting at.

'Yes, But that's just an *animal*. It's all right to eat animals. But not humans. Humans are different.'

'But humans are animals too. Why is it wrong to eat human animals, if it's not wrong to eat non-human animals?'

Errol wasn't sure what to say to the cannibal woman's question.

'It just is. Don't you see?'

But they couldn't see. 'No. We don't understand. Please explain.'

What Errol needed to come up with was some *reason* why it is OK to kill and eat a cow, but not OK to kill and eat a human animal.

You know what? Errol couldn't think of a good reason. So they killed him and cooked him. Then they ate him. After they had eaten Errol, the cannibals went through his things. They found some rather nice chocolate-covered mints. So they sat around eating the mints and chatting.

The big question

The question the cannibals asked Errol was: *Why is it wrong to kill and eat human animals, but not wrong to kill and eat non-human animals?*

Of course, many people agree with Errol that, while it is very wrong indeed to kill and eat a human, there is nothing wrong with killing and eating other sorts of animal.

But there are also many people who believe that, if it is wrong to kill and eat humans, then it must be wrong to kill and eat non-humans too. They would say that it is *always* wrong to kill an animal just so we can enjoy eating it, no matter what sort of animal it is.

Now I eat meat. But should I? Am I doing something morally wrong? If I believe that it is wrong to kill and eat humans (and I *do* believe that is wrong), but not wrong to kill and eat non-humans, it seems I must come up with some difference between humans and non-humans that justifies my treating them so differently.

But *what is that difference?* That's my big question for this chapter. It's the question Errol couldn't answer.

Vegetarians

As I say, there are many people who believe it is wrong to kill *any* sort of animal just so we can eat it. Many of these people are *vegetarians*. They eat only vegetables, fruit, beans, nuts, grain and so on, plus certain animal products like milk, cheese and eggs.

5

Some people go even further: they don't eat or use any animal products at all. They don't even wear leather shoes. These people are called *vegans*.

Other reasons for being a vegetarian

Not *all* vegetarians give up meat just because they think it morally wrong to kill an animal just so we can enjoy eating it. There are other reasons why people become vegetarians.

Here is one of them. Many people think that a chicken farm looks like this:

But in fact most of the chickens we eat are raised in conditions much like this:

This sort of farming is sometimes called *factory farming*, because it involves mass-producing animals in much the same way that a car factory mass-produces cars.

Chickens raised in this way often never see the sky. They never see a tree. They only ever see the thousands of other chickens all around them.

SHOULD I EAT MEAT?

This seems to many vegetarians to be a pretty cruel and unpleasant way to treat other living creatures. They also claim that the mass production of other sorts of animal for food is often also pretty unpleasant.

So here is another reason many vegetarians give when asked why they don't eat meat. They say that, while it may be wrong to slaughter animals for their meat, it is doubly wrong to raise and keep them in the cruel and barbaric way that we do. We shouldn't do it.

However, in this chapter, I am just going to focus on just this reason vegetarians give for not eating meat: *It is morally wrong to kill an animal just so we can enjoy eating it.* I shall call those who give up meat for at least this reason 'moral' vegetarians. Let's now get a bit clearer about what 'moral' vegetarians do and don't object to.

The case of Zoe the hunter

Much of the meat we eat is produced by farms and factories. But there are a few exceptions.

This is Zoe, a tough and wily hunter who lives in the woods.

Zoe never eats meat except the deer she has shot and killed herself. She hunts only wild deer. There are plenty in the woods where she lives. Zoe makes sure she always gets a clean, painless kill. The animal doesn't suffer at all. And she always shoots mature animals that have had a fairly long and happy life.

Is Zoe wrong to do what she does?

True, the deer Zoe eats are not produced through cruelty and suffering as factory-farmed chickens are alleged to be. So there wouldn't be that particular moral reason not to kill and eat them.

But the 'moral' vegetarian would say that Zoe is *still* doing something morally wrong. For they say that it is always wrong deliberately to bring to an end the life of a conscious living thing – a creature capable of enjoying life – just so that someone can enjoy the taste of its flesh.

The case of Harry's road accident

What about this case? Harry is a careful driver. But one night he had a road accident. He accidentally ran over and killed a wild deer in his car while driving home at night. There was nothing he could do. The deer just ran right out in front of him.

Would it be OK for Harry to eat this deer? After all, the animal was killed accidentally.

Actually, those vegetarians who are vegetarians solely because they believe it wrong to slaughter an animal just so we can enjoy eating its meat wouldn't object to Harry eating the deer. They would say it was a shame that the deer was killed. But they wouldn't say Harry had done something morally wrong. The point is, Harry didn't *deliberately* kill the deer so that it could be eaten. Its death was an accident.

So it's worth remembering that 'moral' vegetarians needn't say that it's *always* morally wrong to eat meat.

The plane crash cannibals

There is one animal that we are pretty much all agreed it would be wrong to kill for its meat: the human animal. Almost no one thinks it morally acceptable to kill humans so that we can eat them (except for those cannibals that ate Errol, of course).

But actually, I think most of us would think it OK to eat human meat if the person had been killed accidentally and it was a matter of either eating human meat or starving to death. Sometimes this does happen.

A few years ago there was an aeroplane crash high up in the Andes.

The survivors were left stranded high up on a mountain in all the snow and ice. They were miles from anywhere. No one came to rescue them. After a while, what little food they had ran out. They began to starve. If they didn't eat, they would die.

So the plane crash survivors ate the bodies of the other people who had died in the crash. That's how they managed to stay alive. It was a pretty *revolting* thing for them to have to do. But I don't think it was morally wrong. And of course, the 'moral' vegetarian needn't object either. (By the way, I have heard it said that human meat tastes a bit like chicken and that the forearm is the best bit.)

So far, we have looked at the cannibal's question: why is it wrong to kill and eat humans for their meat, but not wrong to kill and eat non-humans? We have also looked at 'moral' vegetarians who argue that it is always wrong deliberately to kill an animal capable of enjoying life just so that we can eat it.

Is the 'moral' vegetarian right? I'm not sure. I have to admit: I find it very difficult to explain why it isn't morally wrong to kill and eat non-humans if it is morally wrong to kill and eat humans.

Let's now look at some of the arguments used to defend eating meat.

A restaurant argument

Not long ago I was at a restaurant with Aisha and Carol: two friends of mine.
Carol was eating a burger.

Carol and Aisha ended up having an argument about the morality of eating meat. The argument went like this.

Carol: Mmm. This burger is delicious!
Aisha: That's terrible! That was a conscious living thing, Carol. And its life was ended just so you could enjoy eating its muscles and other bits mashed up and grilled in a bun. What a waste.

Carol: But I *like* meat. Why shouldn't I eat meat if I want to?

Aisha: Because it's *wrong*, Carol. It's wrong to kill a living thing capable of enjoying life just so that you can enjoy eating it. You could have had a veggie burger instead, like me. They are just as nice.

Carol: No, they're not. They're all mushy and taste weird. I prefer the real thing.

Carol carried on eating her burger. But Aisha sat watching her. She looked very disapproving. After a while, Carol got fed up with Aisha looking at her like that. Carol started trying to defend eating meat.

Carol's first argument: it must be OK because almost everyone thinks it is

Here is Carol's first argument.

Carol: Look, Aisha. Most people agree with me, not with you. They don't think there is anything particularly wrong about eating meat. They don't feel bad about it. If there really was something morally wrong with eating meat, then people *would* feel bad about it, wouldn't they? So there can't be anything wrong with it.

Aisha wasn't convinced.

Aisha: I agree that most people in this country don't think it wrong to kill animals just so we can enjoy eating their flesh. But just because they are in the majority doesn't make them right. After all, not so very long ago there were many countries where the majority thought that *slavery* was morally acceptable. They thought certain races of people were inferior and that people of these races could therefore

11

be used as slaves by the rest of us. Nowadays, we see that slavery is very wrong. So the majority were simply mistaken about what is wrong. The majority may be mistaken about the morality of eating meat, too.

I agree with Aisha. Just because most people think it OK to kill and eat animals doesn't make it right. Perhaps one day – in, say, two hundred years' time – we will look back on how we treat animals and be horrified, just as we are now horrified by slavery. Perhaps we will then see that what the majority of us now find morally acceptable is actually very wrong indeed.

Carol's second argument: it is natural to eat meat

Carol didn't give up. She came up with a second argument to defend eating meat.

Carol: Look, Aisha, it is *natural* for us to eat meat. We are *designed* to eat meat.

Carol opened her mouth and showed Aisha the two pointed teeth that come down from the corners of her mouth.

Carol: See these two teeth? These are *canine* teeth. You have them too. They are *designed* for eating meat. All meat-eating creatures have them. I'm just doing what comes naturally.

But Aisha didn't think that was any reason not to be a vegetarian.

Aisha: So what? So what if it comes naturally to us to eat meat? That doesn't make it *right*, does it? Many of the things that come naturally to us are morally wrong. What about fighting and murdering each other? That sort of behaviour also seems to come quite naturally to us humans. But that doesn't mean it is morally acceptable. We don't *need* to eat meat. We can get by quite well on a vegetarian diet. So we shouldn't eat meat. What you are doing is *wrong*.

Again, I think Aisha is right: just because it comes naturally to us to eat meat doesn't mean that it is morally acceptable.

Some people would perhaps also argue that not only is it natural for humans to eat meat, it is unhealthy for us not to. We need meat to keep us healthy. But it is unclear whether this is true. There are many millions of vegetarians all over the world. Jains, Buddhists and Hindus don't eat meat. And Jains, Buddhists and Hindus all seem pretty healthy.

In any case, even if it were true that we need to eat some meat to keep us in the peak of condition, we don't need to eat nearly as much meat as we do. And even if a bit of meat is required for perfect health, that doesn't mean that we should eat it. We could develop food supplements instead: tablets that contain what it is that we are missing out on by not eating meat. Even if such tablets could not be made, that still wouldn't mean that it was morally acceptable to eat meat. Perhaps we should just put up with being slightly less healthy than we might otherwise be. Maybe that is the price we have to pay for doing the right thing.

But, as I say, it isn't at all clear that being a vegetarian is less healthy than eating meat.

Carol's third argument: animals are bred to be eaten

Carol sat chewing in silence for a while. She certainly didn't think that what she was doing was wrong. So she tried a third argument.

Carol: OK, Aisha, you are concerned about conscious living things, right?

Aisha: Yes. I don't think a living thing capable of enjoying life should be deliberately killed just because we feel like eating it.

Carol: But this animal that I am eating was *bred* to be eaten. It only had a life because we bred it.

Aisha: That's true, I suppose.

Carol: We meat eaters gave life to the animal. So, in a way, we did the animal a favour. True, we brought its life to an early end so that we could eat it. But still, a life existed that would not have existed if we didn't eat meat. So, on balance, breeding animals for slaughter is a *good* thing, not a bad thing.

Aisha: No. You are wrong. Look, suppose that there are some Martian creatures who are farmers. These farmers breed humans. The Martians are quite considerate farmers. They breed humans on a planet – planet Earth – where the human animals can lead happy, fulfilled lives. Just like the cows in a field, we humans don't realize we're being bred.

Carol: Why are the Martians breeding us humans?

Aisha: Because they like to eat us! You know when humans sometimes just disappear? Actually, they are abducted by Martians. They are eaten. The Martians come over here in their flying saucers to stock up on meat in just the same way that we drive over to the supermarket.

SPECIAL OFFER – TWO HUMANS FOR THE PRICE OF ONE!

There is nothing a Martian likes
better than to tuck into a nice,
juicy humanburger at the end of
a long day.

Carol: Yuk. That is *horrible*! Honestly, I'm eating. Couldn't you at least
wait till I finish?

Aisha: So you find that horrible, do you?

Carol: Yes, I do.

Aisha: Well, take a look at yourself. There you are eating an animal that
has been bred and killed just so you could enjoy the taste of it in a
bun. Why is that any less horrible? I think it is *just* as horrible.

Carol: No, it isn't.

Aisha: You said that it was OK to eat animals because they are bred to
be eaten. Well, in my story the Martians breed us to be eaten too. So
what's wrong with the Martians eating us?

Carol's fourth argument: animals are stupid

Carol: OK. I admit the fact that animals are bred to be eaten doesn't by
itself make it right to eat them. But animals are different to us. They
are less intelligent than us. They don't have feelings like we do. They
have no sense of right or wrong. That's why it's OK for us to kill and
eat them.

What do you think about this argument? Does the fact that
animals aren't as smart as us, aren't as emotionally sophisticated
as us, don't have any sense of right or wrong and so on, mean
that it is OK for us to eat them? Aisha certainly didn't agree.

Aisha: So it's all right to eat things that are less intelligent than us? It's all right to eat things that don't have all the same sorts of feelings as us?

Carol: Yes.

Aisha: Well, suppose that, perhaps because of some sort of illness, many human babies are born different to the rest of us. They aren't as intelligent. They are only as intelligent as a fairly intelligent animal: a pig, say. They cannot learn language. Like pigs, they can feel happy or sad, excited or calm and so on. But they can't feel a sophisticated emotion like pride in a new job. They don't even know what a job is. Nor have they any sense of right or wrong.

Carol: The poor things.

Aisha: Well, don't feel too bad for them. These babies are perfectly healthy, happy individuals. They are capable of living long and happy lives. So how should we treat these human beings, do you think?

Carol: We would probably give them lots of care and attention. We would probably employ people to help them lead the most fulfilled and enjoyable lives possible.

Aisha: But why not *kill and eat them*? After all, you said that it was OK to eat animals because they are less intelligent and sophisticated than us. But so too are these humans. So why shouldn't we kill and eat them too?

Carol was absolutely revolted by the thought of eating these humans. But she was more than just revolted. She saw that it would be morally very wrong to kill and eat them.

16

The problem was that Carol was beginning to find it difficult to explain *why* it would be morally wrong to kill and eat these humans if it isn't morally wrong to kill and eat the animals we eat. For these humans are no more intelligent or sophisticated than are those animals.

Carol: Look, Aisha. It's just a fact that humans are more important than animals. Our needs and desires come first. That is just the way it is. Human beings are more important than animals.

Aisha: But why are they more important, Carol? You haven't given me any good reason why they don't deserve the very same sort of moral consideration as us human animals. And if you can't explain why they aren't deserving of equal consideration, then your claim is just a prejudice. It seems to me that you are prejudiced against non-human animals in the same way that some people are prejudiced against women or against other races of humans.

Carol winced. She didn't like to think of herself as being prejudiced.

Aisha: And in any case, even if it *is* true that human animals *are* more important, that doesn't justify our killing and eating other sorts of animal. It doesn't mean we have the right to do just what we like to them. It doesn't mean it is morally OK for us to slaughter them just because we like the taste of their flesh.

Carol now felt quite guilty. So did I. For I had just eaten a burger too. My conscience was starting to bother me. Like Carol, I hadn't really thought about the morality of eating meat before. I felt that Aisha was probably wrong about it being immoral to eat meat. But I couldn't see why she was wrong.

Pets

I had also started thinking about
pets. Carol has a dog. It is a very
cute dog: Tigger.

Now a dog is an animal like any other. Yet Carol would be
absolutely horrified at the thought that we might kill Tigger and
eat him. In fact, Carol has had to spend a lot of money on Tigger
keeping him alive. Tigger swallowed a plastic pen top which got
stuck inside him. The vet had to operate to remove the pen top.
The operation cost a fortune. Carol was very upset when she
thought Tigger might die. Aisha and I had to go round and
comfort her while the operation was taking place. Luckily,
Tigger survived. He's fine now.

Now a dog is a very intelligent and emotional creature. But
apparently it is no more intelligent or emotional than a pig.
That's what friends who have kept pigs tell me, anyway.
Apparently, pigs are very bright, affectionate creatures. Some
varieties of pig can even make quite good pets.

In some countries – China, for example – dogs are eaten.
They eat dogs just as we eat pigs. And why not? There really is
no difference, except perhaps that dogs look a bit more cuddly
to us.

I couldn't help thinking how Carol would react if she were
told that it was Tigger that she had just eaten. Carol would
certainly feel it would be morally wrong to kill and eat Tigger.
But then why wasn't it morally wrong to kill and eat that cow
that she had just eaten?

I thought it probably best not to ask Carol why we shouldn't
eat Tigger.

Carol's fifth argument: animals eat animals

Carol, Aisha and I all ordered ice-creams. While we were eating them, Carol had another attempt at defending herself.

Carol: Animals eat each other, don't they? Cats eat mice and birds. Tigers eat gazelle. Foxes eat chickens. So if animals eat each other, why shouldn't we eat them too?

Aisha: Animals don't know any better. They don't know right from wrong. They have no sense of morality. So they can't be held morally responsible for what they do, any more than new-born babies can. But we adult humans *can* be held morally responsible. Eating meat is wrong. Once we see that, we should stop doing it. If we don't stop doing it, that makes us bad people.

I have to say I now felt very guilty about having eaten meat. So did Carol. But should we have felt guilty? Was Aisha justified in attacking us as she did? I'm not sure. I have to admit, her arguments do seem very powerful.

How could Carol and I have defended ourselves against Aisha? Why is it OK to kill and eat non-human animals, but not human animals?

It is the species that matters

Some people claim that it is the *species* one belongs to that is important, so far as what it is morally acceptable to kill and eat is concerned. It is morally wrong to eat members of the human species. It is not morally wrong to eat the members of other animal species.

But *why* is it wrong to eat the members of the human species, but not other species? Isn't this just a prejudice of ours? Or can this claim be justified? Some try to explain why it is wrong to eat members of the human species but not other species by

saying that humans *as a species* are more intelligent and emotionally sophisticated than other animal species. Even if some
particular human being happens not to be as intelligent or
emotionally sophisticated as the rest of us (like one of the babies
in Aisha's example), it is still wrong to eat that particular
human. It is wrong because they are members of the human
species, and humans *as a species* are far more intelligent and
emotionally sophisticated than are other animal species. The pig,
on the other hand, is a relatively stupid and unsophisticated
species. So it is OK to eat pigs.

I have worries about this view, too. One of my worries is
illustrated by the case of the smart pig.

The case of the smart pig

Suppose there was a talking pig,
like the pig in the film *Babe*. I
know that there aren't really
talking pigs. But just suppose
that, by some miracle, such a pig
was born.

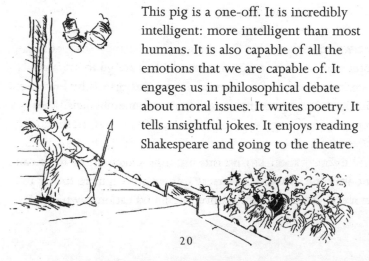

This pig is a one-off. It is incredibly
intelligent: more intelligent than most
humans. It is also capable of all the
emotions that we are capable of. It
engages us in philosophical debate
about moral issues. It writes poetry. It
tells insightful jokes. It enjoys reading
Shakespeare and going to the theatre.

It gets invited to dinner parties.

Would it be morally acceptable to kill and eat this pig? We have not yet been given any reason why it would be wrong to eat it. For it is a member of a species the *normal* members of which are pretty stupid and unsophisticated compared to normal human beings. It is a member of the pig species.

Yet surely it *would* be wrong to eat this particular pig. In fact, it seems to me that this pig would be a *person*, despite not being a human person. And it would surely be wrong to kill and eat a person.

So my worry is this. If it is morally OK to eat animals which are members of species the *normal* members of which are fairly unintelligent and so on, then it should be morally acceptable to kill and eat this pig. But clearly it would *not* be morally acceptable to kill and eat this pig.

Are we bigots?
Some philosophers argue that many of us are guilty of *species discrimination* or *speciesism*. Species discrimination is a bit like sexual discrimination (sexism) or racial discrimination (racism). It is an example of bigotry: unreasoned prejudice against those who are different.

We discriminate against other animal species in many ways: one way is that we think that it's morally acceptable to kill and eat those other species, but not to kill and eat our own species.

But there is no justification for our discriminating against other species of animal in this way. The discrimination is unfair and immoral. Speciesism is no more morally acceptable than is sexism or racism. Just as we now see that sexism and racism are wrong, so we will hopefully one day come to see that speciesism is wrong too.

That is how some philosophers argue, at least. Are these philosophers right? What do you think?

The 'it's no big deal' excuse

Some people argue that 'moral' vegetarians are making a big fuss about very little. Take a look at the world. People are tortured and killed every day. Children are forced to work long hours in appalling conditions for just a few pennies. Some even starve. There are so many terrible moral injustices that cry out for our attention. Even if we admit that killing other animals so that we can enjoy eating their flesh is morally wrong, it's just one wrong among countless many. So isn't it rather narrow minded of 'moral' vegetarians to focus on just this one issue?

I think this is a very poor argument against 'moral' vegetarianism. Of course, many 'moral' vegetarians are concerned about all these other issues too. Just because one is concerned about one thing doesn't mean one can't be concerned about anything else.

Really, people who argue in this way are just trying to excuse themselves. They are saying, 'OK, I admit I am doing something morally wrong. But look at all the other bad things people do! Set against all these other moral wrongs, my eating meat is rather insignificant, isn't it?'

Of course, if this were an acceptable defence, then you could excuse all sorts of terrible things in much the same way: from stealing a book through to murdering someone. How would you feel about someone who tried to excuse themselves for having

murdered someone they didn't like by saying, 'It was just one
little murder! That's all! Thousands happen every year!

Perhaps a better way for meat eaters to try to excuse themselves is to say that, compared to other immoral acts, killing
animals for food is pretty low down on the scale of badness.
Some things are more wrong than others. At the top of the scale
is killing thousands or millions of people, like Hitler or Pol Pot.
Further down the scale is deliberately killing one person. Further
down still is killing someone accidentally through stupidity
(such as running them over while drunk). Further down from
that is stealing someone's life savings. Then there is stealing
some sweets from a shop. Near the bottom of the scale is, say,
picking an apple from a neighbour's tree without asking them
first. Now on this scale of wrongs, surely eating meat is pretty
low down? Even if we admit that killing other animals so we can
enjoy eating them is morally wrong, surely it isn't *that* wrong.

In fact, isn't there something rather offensive about 'moral'
vegetarians who make such a big deal about animal exploitation
and suffering? Isn't human exploitation and suffering far more
important?

Are we as bad as the slave owners?

How good an excuse is the 'It's no big deal' excuse? Most vegetarians would say: not very. Here's why.

Perhaps, in two hundred years' time, people will look back at our treatment of animals today and be quite horrified. Perhaps they will say to themselves: how did we not see that breeding billions and billions of animals per year in barbaric conditions and then slaughtering them just so that we could enjoy the taste of their flesh was an *absolutely monstrous* thing to do? How did we not see that what we were doing was not terribly morally wrong?

Looking back at slavery, we find it very hard to see how people back then didn't realize that how they were treating other human beings was very wrong. In fact, some treated their slaves no better than their animals, sometimes worse. They whipped them, tortured them and kept them in appalling conditions. Some slave owners deliberately crippled their slaves when they tried to run away.

How could those slave owners not see that their behaviour towards these other human beings was wrong? Yet the slave owners *didn't* see it. Most of the slave owners thought of themselves as upright, moral citizens.

So maybe we are like the slave owners. Perhaps we are simply blind to the wrongness of what we are doing. Because we are surrounded by many other people who also think it OK to treat animals as we do, we find it difficult to see that what we are doing is wrong.

I have tried to explain why I am suspicious about the claim that, while eating meat is morally wrong, it isn't *that* wrong. Perhaps it really is very wrong indeed. Perhaps the only reason it doesn't *seem* that wrong is that the majority of other people around us feel quite comfortable with the idea.

And in fact we haven't yet seen any reason to suppose killing other species of animal for their meat isn't very wrong indeed. Indeed, we haven't yet seen any reason to suppose it isn't just as bad as killing human animals for their meat.

Carol's final argument: shouldn't Aisha be a vegan?

Let's go back to Carol and Aisha's argument. I felt that Aisha had definitely been getting the better of the argument up to now. But then Carol came up with a much better argument that stopped Aisha in her tracks. This is what Carol said:

Carol: That was great ice-cream.

Aisha: Mmm. I love ice-cream.

Carol: So Aisha, tell me: *why isn't it morally wrong to eat ice-cream?* After all, ice-cream is made from milk, which comes from cows. And cheese comes from cows too. You had cheese on your veggie burger.

Aisha: But cows aren't *killed* to make cheese and ice-cream.

Carol: But aren't they sometimes kept in quite miserable conditions?

Aisha: I don't know. Perhaps they are.

Carol: Look. Even if they are well looked after, don't they still have to have calves before they can make milk?

Aisha: Yes. I suppose that's right.

Carol: So what happens to all those calves then? Half of them are male, so they are no good for milking.

Aisha: Er. Yes.

Carol: They are *killed*, aren't they? They would have to be. Otherwise we would be up to our necks in bulls.

Aisha: Umm. I suppose you are right.

Carol: Well then. Here you are lecturing me about eating my burger. But it's only because I had a burger that you could have that ice-cream and that cheese on your veggie burger. You are a hypocrite! Also, I bet you are wearing leather shoes, aren't you?

Aisha: Yes.

Carol: And where did the leather for your shoes come from? Another dead animal. So you see, you are just as responsible for the deaths of all these animals as me, despite the fact that you don't eat meat!

It is true that, in order to continue to produce milk, cows need to become pregnant once a year. Only about a quarter of their calves go on to provide milk. The rest are killed. And even those cows that are used for milk are slaughtered at 3–7 years (cows can live for much longer than this). So milk production certainly does require that a great many animals be killed.

I was quite impressed by Carol's argument: if Aisha really was convinced about the immorality of killing animals, then it seems she should also give up milk and cheese and ice-cream. She should give up leather too. She should wear plastic or cotton shoes.

As I explained at the beginning of this chapter, some people – called *vegans* – do go this far. They give up all animal produce. If Aisha were convinced by her own arguments, it seems she should become a vegan. Yet Aisha never did become a vegan. To this day, she still wears leather shoes. She still eats cheese, milk, eggs and ice-cream.

Still, all Carol has shown, at best, is that Aisha is a bit of a hyprocrite. All she has shown is that, if it is wrong to kill and eat animals for their meat, then it's also wrong to kill them for their milk, eggs, leather and so on. Notice that Carol hasn't shown that it is morally acceptable to kill and eat other species of animal. She still hasn't given us any reason to suppose that killing animals for meat, milk, eggs and leather isn't *very wrong indeed*.

Should I eat meat?

I have tried to look at the arguments for and against vegetarian-ism and veganism as fairly as I can. I have not tried to push you one way or the other. I want you to think carefully about the arguments and make up your own mind.

I eat meat. But I have to admit, I find the moral arguments for not eating meat to be very powerful. If it is morally OK to kill and eat other species of animal just because we like the taste of their flesh, then why is it OK? If we cannot justify treating other species so very differently from our own, then it seems we really are guilty of speciesism.

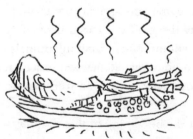

File 2

How do I know the world isn't virtual?

Jim's game
Here's Jim.

DIE, MONSTER SCUM!

Jim is playing a computer game. The game is called *Dungeons and Monsters*. To win the game you have to run around inside a maze of dungeons, kill all the monsters and collect all the treasure. As you can see, Jim loves the game. Especially killing the monsters.

I had better warn you now: something nasty happens to Jim. But we'll come to that later. First, I need to explain about *virtual reality*.

Virtual reality
The dungeons, gun, monsters and treasure in Jim's game aren't real, of course. They form what is known as a *virtual reality*: a world created by a computer. A virtual reality is made up of a *virtual environment* within which can be found *virtual objects*. In Jim's game, the dungeons and corridors are the virtual environment. The gun, monsters and treasure are virtual objects.

You will probably have come across a virtual reality yourself.

Perhaps you have played a computer game in which you drive a car round a race track or fly a plane through the sky. The cars, race track, planes and so on that you see in these games are all virtual. They don't actually exist.

Wearing a virtual reality helmet

Usually, when you play one of these games, you watch the action on a sort of TV screen. But there are now other ways of experiencing virtual reality.

In fact, computer scientists have developed *virtual reality helmets*.

Here's how a virtual reality helmet works. When you put it on, you see a small screen. This screen shows the virtual environment. And the important thing about the screen is that, when you move your head about, what you see changes just as it would if you really were in such an environment. For example, if you turn your head to the left, you see what's to the left of you in the virtual environment. Look down and you see what's on the floor of the virtual environment. Spin round and you see what's behind you, and so on.

The helmet also contains little loudspeakers – one for each ear – so that you can hear what is going on inside the virtual reality. Again, these speakers change what you hear depending on which way you are facing. So with the virtual reality helmet on, it looks and sounds as if the virtual environment is actually all around you.

29

Virtual hands and legs

It's also possible to reach out and pick up virtual objects.
Electronic gloves have been developed that control virtual hands.
Put the gloves on and you can move the virtual hands that you
see in front of you when you wear the virtual reality helmet.
With these virtual hands you can steer a virtual car or fire a
virtual laser gun at a virtual alien.

VIRTUAL REALITY   ACTUAL REALITY

In fact, you can even walk around inside virtual reality. The
computer that generates the virtual reality can be wired up to
special sensors strapped to your legs and feet. Walk forward and
the computer detects this and changes what you see and hear: it
makes it seem as if you are walking forward into the virtual
environment.

Suppose we give Jim one of these virtual reality outfits – the
helmet, gloves and leg-sensors – and connect it up to a powerful computer running a version of his favourite *Dungeons and
Monsters* game. Then Jim can play his game, only this time it will
seem much more real to him. This time it will seem to Jim as if
the virtual dungeon is actually all around him. This time it will
seem as if he can actually reach out and touch the walls of the
dungeon with his hand.

Artificial eyes

Let's now look at a different sort of technology: artificial eyes. Unlike virtual reality, this technological breakthrough hasn't happened yet. But there seems to be no reason why it *couldn't* happen.

Put your hand up in front of your face and take a good look at it.

What happens when you see your hand?

First of all, light is reflected off your hand into your eyes. A lens at the front of the eye focuses this light on to a surface at the back of the eye, producing an image. Now this surface at the back of your eye is made up of many millions of light-sensitive cells. And when light falls on to one of these cells, it produces a tiny electrical impulse. The pattern of electrical impulses caused by the image of your hand falling on to the cells then passes along a bundle of nerves (called the optic nerve) that runs from your eye into your brain. That's how you come to see your hand.

NORMAL EYE

BRAIN

EYE SOCKET

IMAGE

IMAGE INFORMATION SENT TO BRAIN

OPTIC NERVE

LENS

EYE

31

But does it have to be a
normal human eye that sends
the electrical impulses down
your optic nerve and into
your brain? I don't see why.
Why couldn't your normal
human eyes be replaced with
little TV cameras instead?

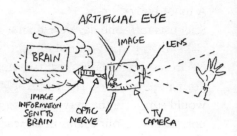

These cameras could do the job that your human eyes do now,
sending down your optic nerves just the same patterns of electrical stimulation that your normal eyes send now. So everything
would look just the same to you. The world seen through artificial eyes would look just like it does through normal eyes.

Having an eye on the end of a stick
In fact, in some ways having little TV camera eyes could be a big
advantage. Suppose you had artificial eyes. They could be
attached to your optic nerves with extra long cables.
Then you could take out an eye and hold it in
your hand. You could stick it round the back of
your head: very useful if you want to know
whether someone is following you.
Or you could have an eye on the end of a stick –
invaluable for finding that coin you dropped
under the sofa.

A robot body

Scientists may one day develop not only artificial eyes, but also artificial ears: little
electronic microphones that take the place of
normal human ears. These microphones
would stimulate the nerves that connect our
normal ears to our brains in just the way our
normal ears do.

So the ringing of a church bell would sound
just the same to someone fitted with artificial ears.

In fact, when you think about it, there seems no reason in
principle why your *whole body* should not be replaced with an
artificial one. You could have a robot body. Here's how.

Your brain is connected to the rest of your body by a system
of nerves. Some of these nerve pathways *send out* electrical
impulses. Others *receive* electrical impulses.

Those nerves that *send out* electrical impulses send many of
them out to the muscles that enable you to move
your body around. For example, when you
go to turn this page, your hand moves
because your brain sends out a pattern of
electrical impulses to certain muscles in
your arm.

The impulses make the muscles move.
And the movement of those muscles moves
your hand. The
nerve pathways that *receive* electrical
impulses receive many of
them from your five
senses: your ears, eyes,
nose, tongue and skin.

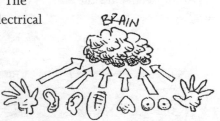

That's what allows you to experience the world around you.

But now suppose this happens: your brain is removed from your old human body and fitted into a new robot body.

Then your old human body is destroyed. But that doesn't matter because your new robot body keeps your brain alive. It also stimulates the nerves running into your brain in just the way they used to be stimulated by your old human body. So your new robot body gives you experiences just like those your old human body gave you. With your new robot body you can enjoy chocolate ice-cream, listen to music, smell the flowers. Everything seems just the same.

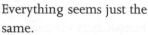

And the patterns of electrical impulses coming out of your brain make your new robot body move around in just the way your normal body did (only now they don't move muscles: they move little electric motors instead). So you can talk and walk just as before.

Surviving the death of your human body

Of course, we can't build ourselves robot bodies just yet. Technology hasn't developed that far. But it certainly seems possible that robot bodies might one day be built, perhaps in a few hundred years' time.

If robot bodies are built, we will be able to survive the death of our normal flesh-and-blood bodies. Suppose your human body accidentally got flattened by a truck. Your brain could be taken out and put in a new robot body instead.

Then you could carry on living, even though your flesh-and-blood body was dead. You would now be part human, part machine.

Robot bodies could probably also be made stronger, more durable and in various other ways better than our ordinary flesh-and-blood bodies. You could have super-human strength. You could be given incredibly sensitive hearing. You could even have X-ray vision.

Perhaps one day, maybe in a thousand years' time, we will *all* be robot super-beings.

Perhaps the only human parts of us left will be our brains.

Having a virtual body

It seems that not only is it possible to have a robot body, it's also possible to have a *virtual body*.

Suppose this happens. A little electrical socket is wired into the back of your neck. This socket is connected up to where the nerves running in and out of your brain join up to the rest of your body. The socket allows you to connect your brain up to an incredibly powerful super-computer. You need only plug a cable connected to the computer into your socket and flip a little switch attached to the back of your neck.

When you flip the switch, all of the electrical impulses coming out of your brain that would go on to move your body about are diverted. They are sent off to the super-computer instead. And rather than receiving electrical impulses from your eyes, ears, nose, tongue and skin, your brain receives them from the super-computer.

Now, suppose this computer is running a virtual reality programme. Here's how it works. You lie down on a bed next to the computer and plug yourself in. Then you reach round to the back of your neck and flip that switch. Of course, the moment you flip the switch, your body goes limp: you've just disconnected your body from your brain.

But that's not how it seems to you. It seems to you that you can still move your body. Suppose you try to wiggle your fingers in front of your face. The computer registers the finger-waggling electrical impulses coming out of your brain. It then sends back to your brain just the sort of impulses it would receive from your eyes and hands if you really were waggling your fingers in front of your face. So this is what you see. It looks and feels to you just as if you are waggling your fingers in front of your face. But of course, the fingers you now see waggling are *virtual* fingers, not real fingers. Your real hands lie quite still on the bed.

In fact, if the computer were powerful enough, it could generate *a whole virtual environment* for you. For example, it could make it seem to you as if you are lying in a wood inhabited by fabulous singing birds and beautiful flowers. You could get up and walk about in this wood. The trees you saw, the birds you heard and the flowers you smelled would not be real, of course. They would all be virtual. And the body it seemed that you now had would be a virtual body not a real one. Your real body would still be lying motionless on the bed.

Switching over to a virtual body might be a pleasant way to spend an evening. After a hard day at work you could relax by switching to a virtual body and exploring a virtual environment. You could invent whatever strange new world you felt like occupying for a few hours.

You could even choose what your virtual body looked like. For example, you could choose to look like Elvis Presley and visit a planet made entirely out of marshmallow.

Having seen how you might come to have a virtual body in a virtual environment, let's take a break. I shall now tell you what happens to Jim.

Intermission: a horror story

One day, two Martians – Blib and Blob – arrive on Earth. Blib and Blob are here to study human beings. They decide to make Jim their first subject and set about secretly observing his behaviour.

Blib and Blob are fascinated to see just how much Jim loves his computer game *Dungeons and Monsters*. They observe that Jim devotes every spare minute of his time to playing the game. Jim's father cooks Jim's tea. 'Come and get it, Jim!' he shouts up the stairs. The Martians notice that Jim has to be asked six times. They also notice that, after Jim has gulped down his food, he always runs straight back upstairs and starts playing the game again.

Blib and Blob also observe that every time a new version of the *Dungeons and Monsters* game is brought out, Jim is desperate to get hold of a copy. For the two months before Christmas, Jim's every other sentence is: 'Mum, Dad, *please* can I have the new *Dungeons and Monsters* game for Christmas?'

After making all these observations, Blib and Blob decide that what would make Jim happiest would be if he could be left permanently to play the most realistic version of *Dungeons and Monsters* imaginable. And so they decide to make Jim happy.

It is Christmas morning. Jim begins to wake. The first thing he notices is his bed. It feels hard and cold, like stone. And it smells kind of strange too. Sort of dank and musty. Like mushrooms. And he can hear a dripping noise.

Jim slowly opens his eyes. He finds himself in a long, stone corridor. The corridor is lit by torches hanging from rusty metal brackets. There are passages off left and right. Jim turns to look behind him. He sees that the corridor stretches back into the shadows in just the same way.

This corridor seems vaguely familiar to Jim. Then he remembers: it looks just like the one in *Dungeons and Monsters*. Only this corridor seems real. He can reach out and run his fingers down the cold, slimy walls.

Then Jim's blood runs cold, for he hears a howl. It is a howl Jim has heard a thousand times before. Only this time the howl doesn't come out of the little loudspeakers next to his computer. This time the howl comes from out of the shadows at the end of the corridor. This time the howl is real. And so too are those shuffling footsteps. Jim knows what's coming. With his heart pounding in his ears, Jim staggers to his feet. He starts to run.

Jim's parents are puzzled. They have bought Jim a new computer programmed with the very latest *Dungeons and Monsters* game. So why hasn't he rushed downstairs to open his present as usual? His parents climb the stairs and slowly open his bedroom door. They peek inside.

'Jim? Are you awake?' The room is quiet. The curtains are still drawn. And Jim's bed is empty.

The bedroom is lit by an eerie light. Jim's parents turn to see that the light is coming from a computer screen down on the floor. But it is not Jim's own computer they are looking at. As their eyes begin to adjust, they can just make out that the flickering screen is attached to a large grey box.

In fact, this grey box is a Martian super-computer. Blib and Blob have been busy. They built this computer to run the most realistic version of *Dungeons and Monsters* you could possibly imagine. They built the computer specially for Jim.

'AAARGH!!!' Jim's parents scream in horror. As the image on the screen flickers brighter for an instant, filling the room with light, they see that there in the shadows behind the computer is *a human brain floating in a glass vat.*

It is Jim's living brain. And it is fully conscious. Blib and Blob came in the night and removed Jim's brain. They destroyed the rest of Jim's body and placed his brain in this life-supporting vat of liquid. Then they connected his brain up to their computer. Jim now has a virtual body in a virtual environment: the environment of *Dungeons and Monsters*. Jim is now playing the most realistic version of *Dungeons and Monsters* imaginable. Only he can't stop. And he can't tell it's not real.

Jim's parents' eyes turn to the image on the computer screen. It's Jim! They see him being chased down a narrow corridor by a huge monster. 'My poor Jim!' cries his mother. But of course it is quite pointless to shout. All Jim can hear is the howling monster hot on his heels. Jim will never hear his mother's voice again.

In shock, Jim's parents watch as he tries to shake off the monster. Eventually, he makes a desperate lunge into some shadows. He crouches motionless, daring not even to breathe. The monster stops. It sniffs briefly at the damp air. And then it is gone. For now.

Jim's parents can bear to watch no longer. They turn away from the screen. Only then do they notice that a card has been left tied to the computer with a red ribbon. Trembling, they move closer. Finally, in the flickering glow from the screen, they make out the message written on the card in a strange, spidery scrawl. The message reads:

Are YOU a brain in a vat?

A pretty ghastly story, don't you agree? Jim ends up trapped
inside a horrible virtual reality so life-like that he can't tell it's not
real. And the Martians thought they were doing him a favour.

Stories about brains in vats are very interesting to philosophers.
They are particularly interesting to those philosophers who are
interested in the question: *what, if anything, can we know about the world
around us?* This is the question we are now going to look at.

Here's a slightly different brain-in-a-vat story — a story about
you. Suppose that last night Blib and Blob came to your house
while you were sleeping. They drugged you and whisked you
off to Mars in their flying saucer. They removed your brain from
your body, floated it in a glass vat of life-supporting
fluid, and connected it up to a super-computer.
Your body was then destroyed.

It is the super-computer that now
controls all your experiences. Snap your
fingers. When you go to snap your
fingers, the computer monitors the
impulses leaving your brain: the impulses
that would have gone on to move your fingers if you still had
some. The computer then stimulates the nerve endings that used
to be connected to your eyes, fingertips, ears and so on, so that it
seems to you that you see, feel and hear your fingers move and
hear the snap. But in fact you don't have real fingers any more.

You have only virtual computer-generated fingers.

The computer that creates these experiences is incredibly advanced. It copies your normal environment down to the very last detail. So everything seems to you just as it would if what you were experiencing was real. Your virtual bedroom seems exactly like your real bedroom. Your virtual parents act just like your real parents.

VIRTUAL PARENTS

REAL PARENTS

Your virtual street seems just like your real street.

Now the big philosophical question this story raises is: *how do you know you're not a brain in a vat?* How do you know the world you see around you isn't virtual? Perhaps Martians really *did* come last night. Perhaps they really *did* take out your brain and connect it to a super-computer. If they did, could you tell? No. It seems not, because everything would now seem exactly the same to you.

Perhaps you've ALWAYS been a brain in a vat

Here's an even more frightening thought. Perhaps you have *always* been a brain in a vat, right from birth. Perhaps planet Earth doesn't exist. Perhaps the things with which you seem so familiar – your house, your neighbourhood, your friends and family – are no more 'real' than are the places and characters in Jim's *Dungeons and Monsters* game. Perhaps they were made up by Martian computer programmers. Perhaps these Martians are studying your brain to see how it reacts to the world that they have invented.

In other words, perhaps the only reality you have ever known is a virtual reality. Could you tell? No. It seems not.

How do you know you're not a brain in a vat?

Now of course, you don't really believe you're a brain in a vat. In fact, like me, you believe you're not a brain in a vat. But the question is: do you know that you're not a brain in a vat? Do you know that the world you seem to see around you is real ?

The answer seems to be: no, you don't know. You may believe the world you see is real. And perhaps it is true that the world you see is real. But even if it is true, it seems you don't know that it's real. In order to know something, you surely need some reason to believe that it is true. And you have no reason at all to believe that it is a real world that you see and not a virtual one, for everything would seem exactly the same to you even if it were virtual. So, amazingly, it seems you don't know you're not a brain in a vat!

In fact, it seems you don't know anything about the world out there. For all you know, the hands you see in front of you, this book you seem to hold in your hands, that tree you seem to see outside your window, even planet Earth could all be virtual.

What is scepticism?
The argument that we have just looked at – the argument that you don't know anything about the world around you – is called a *sceptical* argument. Sceptics claim that we don't really know what we think we know. The claim that you don't know anything of the world about you is called *scepticism about the external world*.

Scepticism against common sense
Of course, the common sense view is that we *do* know about the external world. In fact, if you were to say, 'I don't know that trees exist', especially while looking at a tree in broad daylight, other people would think you had gone mad.

But according to the sceptic, you would be quite right. You *don't* know that trees exist. Common sense is wrong.

Other examples of common sense being wrong
The sceptic's argument can make some people quite angry. That we do know that trees exist is one of our most basic beliefs – as I say, we feel it's just common sense. There are many beliefs that we would be quite happy to give up were someone to show us we must be wrong. But when it comes to our most basic common sense beliefs – such as the belief that we know that trees exist – we are not at all happy about giving them up.

Indeed, having our most basic beliefs challenged can be a very uncomfortable experience, especially when we can't see how to defend them. So some people get very cross. They say that the philosopher is talking complete rubbish. 'That's just plain *stupid!*' they shout. 'Of *course* I know that trees exist.' And they walk off in a huff.

But the philosopher can point out that there are many other cases where common sense has turned out to be wrong. For example, it was once the common sense view that the Earth is flat. People thought it just obvious that the Earth is flat. After all, it looks flat, doesn't it? Sailors even used to worry about sailing over the edge.

Now, some people got very angry when this common sense belief of theirs was challenged: 'Don't be *ridiculous!*' they shouted. 'Of *course* the Earth is flat!' And they stomped off.

But we now know that the Earth isn't flat. Common sense was wrong.

Here's another example of how common sense can be wrong. Take a look at this sheet of paper. It has two sides: this side . . .

. . . and this side. Now ask yourself: could there be a piece of paper that had only *one side*? Most people would say: *of course* not. Any sheet of paper just *has* to have two sides. That's just common sense.

But actually common sense is wrong about this. If you take a strip of paper like this:

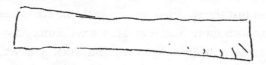

. . . give it a half-twist . . .

. . . and then join the two ends together to form a loop . . .

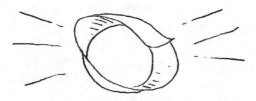

. . . you will find that you now have a piece of paper with *only one side*. The strip *looks* like it still has two sides, but when you pick one side and follow it around the loop, you find that what look like two different sides are actually the same side.

So common sense has turned out to be wrong about many things. Perhaps common sense is also wrong about our knowing that trees exist.

What the sceptic ISN'T claiming

It is worth getting clear what our sceptic isn't claiming, so we
don't get confused.

First, the sceptic isn't claiming to know that you or they are a
brain in a vat. They are claiming only that *no one can know one way or the
other* whether or not they or indeed anyone else is a brain in a vat.

Secondly, they are not *just* claiming that you cannot be
absolutely certain that the world you see is real and not virtual. They
are claiming much more than that. They are claiming that you
have *no reason at all* to believe that it is a real world you see, not a
virtual one.

Thirdly, they are not going so far as to claim that no one can
know *anything at all*. After all, they are themselves claiming to
know *something*: that no one can know about the external world.

An ancient puzzle

So we are faced with a difficult puzzle. On the one hand, the
common sense view is that we do know that trees exist. We
really don't want to give up this common view (actually, I'm
not sure we *could* give it up, even if we wanted to). On the other
hand, the sceptic has an argument which seems to show that the
common sense view is wrong: we *don't* know that trees exist.
Which view is correct?

Although I have dressed it up in modern clothing, this puzzle is actually very old. In fact, it is one of the best-known philosophical puzzles. Even today, at universities all over the world, philosophers are working on this puzzle. And they still aren't agreed about whether the sceptic is right. I must admit: I just don't know whether or not the sceptic is right.

Down through the centuries many philosophers have tried to deal with scepticism. They have tried to show that common sense is right: we do know about the world out there after all. Some of their attempts at defeating the sceptic are very clever. But do any of them actually work? Let's now take a look at one of these attempts.

Ockham's razor

The sceptic presents us with two theories or *hypotheses*. The first hypothesis – the common sense hypothesis – is that you are not a brain in a vat: the world you see around you is real. The second hypothesis is that you are a brain in a vat: the world you see is merely virtual.

The sceptic says that you have no more reason to believe the first hypothesis than you do to believe the second. Both hypotheses are equally well supported by the evidence of your senses. Everything would seem just the same to you either way. So you don't know that the first hypothesis is true and the second false.

Now, we may agree with the sceptic that how things seem to you is *consistent* with both hypotheses. But, as I explain below, it doesn't follow from this that how things seem equally *supports* both hypotheses.

There is a famous philosophical principle which says that when you are presented with two hypotheses, both of which are otherwise equally supported by the evidence, it is always reasonable to believe the *simpler* hypothesis. This principle is called *Ockham's razor*. It seems a very plausible principle.

The two boxes example

Here's an illustration of how Ockham's razor works. Suppose you are shown a box with a button on the side and a light bulb on top. You see that, whenever the button is pressed, the light comes on. Otherwise the light stays off.

Now let's look at two competing hypotheses, both of which explain what you see.

The first hypothesis is that the button and bulb are linked by a circuit to a battery inside the box. Press the button and the circuit is completed. That lights up the bulb.

The second hypothesis is more complicated. It says that the button is attached to an electrical circuit linking a battery to a second light bulb *inside* the box. When the button is pressed, this internal light bulb comes on. A light-sensor inside the box then detects this and connects a *second* electrical circuit linking a *second* battery to the bulb you see on the outside of the box. That lights up the outside bulb.

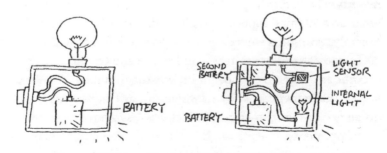

Now, which of these two hypotheses is more reasonable, do you think? True, both hypotheses are equally *consistent* with what you have seen: on both hypotheses, the light will come on when and only when you press the button. But it seems wrong to say that both hypotheses are equally *reasonable*. Surely it is more reasonable to believe the first hypothesis than it is to believe the second, because the second hypothesis is *less simple*: it says there are *two* electrical circuits in the box, not one.

Can we use Ockham's razor to defeat the sceptic? Perhaps. You might say that of our two hypotheses – the hypothesis that it is a real world that you see and the hypothesis that it is merely virtual – the first hypothesis is simpler. For while the first hypothesis says there's just *one* world, the second hypothesis in effect says there are *two*: there's an actual world filled with Martians, a super-computer, a vat and your brain, within which is created a second virtual world containing virtual trees, houses, people and so on. So, given that the first hypothesis is simpler, that means it's more reasonable.

Therefore the sceptic is wrong: it *is* more reasonable to believe it is a real world that you see, not a virtual world, despite the fact that how things seem to you is equally consistent with both hypotheses.

A worry

What do you think about this reply to the sceptic's argument? I certainly have some worries about it. One worry I have is this: *is* the hypothesis that it is a real world you see really the simpler hypothesis? That rather depends on what is meant by 'simpler'. In fact, while there are ways in which the first hypothesis is simpler, there are also ways in which it's less simple.

For example, someone might say that the second hypothesis is simpler because it needs *far fewer real physical objects*: just the Martians, your brain in a vat and a super-computer. There is no need to suppose that planet Earth with all its trees, houses, cats, dogs, mountains, cars and so on also really exists.

Or someone might say that the second hypothesis is simpler

because it needs *far fewer real minds*. If your friends, family, neighbours and so on are merely virtual, then so too are their minds. The only real minds the second hypothesis needs are your mind plus those of the computer operators.

So it isn't obvious that the first hypothesis really is simpler. In fact, you might argue that it is actually the second hypothesis that is simpler and so more reasonable. It's actually more reasonable to believe you are a brain in a vat!

Am I an island?

If the sceptic is right (and I'm not saying they *are* right), then each of us is in an important way detached from the world around us. You know nothing about the world out there. You have no reason at all to believe that you inhabit a world of trees, houses, cats, dogs, mountains and cars. And you have no reason at all to think that you are surrounded by other people. For all you know, your entire world – including all the people in it (including even *me*) – is merely virtual.

That is quite a scary thought. It forces you to think of yourself in a very different way. Someone once said, 'No man is an island.' But if the sceptic is right, there is a sense in which this is false. Each of us is stranded on our own desert island, unable to know anything of the world that lies beyond the horizon of our own sensory experiences. We are closed off from the world beyond. And we are closed off from each other. We are prisoners within our own minds.

The sceptic paints a very lonely picture.

Yet in another way scepticism makes no difference at all. Scepticism leaves our day-to-day lives untouched. Even the sceptic continues with his or her daily routine. They feed the cat. They do the washing up. They go off to work. They meet a friend for a coffee. Not even the sceptic can really stop themselves believing that the world they see is real, despite the fact that they believe they have no *reason* to believe it's real. It seems we are natural born believers: we just can't help ourselves.

But *is* the sceptic right? I'm just not sure. What do you think?

File 3

Where am I?

Matilda

Meet my Aunt Matilda.

As you can see, Matilda is now quite old: seventy-five years old, in fact. Over the years she has changed a great deal. She has changed physically, of course. She now has white hair when once her hair was brown. She now needs a stick and glasses. A very long time ago, when Matilda was a baby, she weighed just a few kilograms. Now she weighs over 80 kilograms.

Take a look at Matilda's photo album.

When you look through this album, you can see many of these physical changes taking place.

Of course, Matilda has changed mentally too. Her store of memories has increased over the years. She has also forgotten many things. During her childhood, her intelligence and personality developed very quickly. And even over the past few years, her personality has continued to change a little. For example, she no longer loses her temper when she can't finish a crossword.

But despite all these physical and psychological changes to Matilda over the years, it is still one and the same person that we are presented with in each photograph. It is still Matilda.

Personal identity

Let's now look at the question: what links that two-year-old, that five-year-old, that ten-year-old, that twenty-five-year-old, that fifty-year-old, that seventy-five-year-old and of course Matilda as she is today together as a single person? What *makes* them one and the same person?

This is a question about *personal identity*. More generally, what we want to know is: in what does the identity of any given person essentially consist? This is a question that philosophers have been asking themselves for over two thousand years. And as we shall see, it is a very hard question to answer.

Actually, you might think the answer to my question is pretty obvious. Clearly, the two-year-old, five-year-old, ten-year-old and so on in the photographs all share the *same living body*.

Of course, I don't mean that it is the *same lump of matter* each time. For the matter in Matilda's body has changed as she has become older. Each living body is composed of millions of cells, and these cells are gradually replaced.

But the same living organism continues on through all these changes. And this, you may think, is what determines the identity of a person. What makes that two-year-old, that five-year-old, that ten-year-old, and so on, all one and the same person – Matilda – is just the fact that they all share the same living body: the one she still has to this day.

But I am not so sure this 'obvious' answer is correct. In fact, the imaginary case I shall now describe seems to show that it isn't correct.

The brain swap case

Here are Fred and Bert.

Fred and Bert live on opposite sides of town and have never met. Fred is a five-foot-eight, slim redhead. Bert is six-foot-six, bald, and very fat indeed. Bert also has a wooden leg.

One night, two Martians – Blib and Blob – break into Fred's home while he is sleeping. Blib and Blob drug Fred. Then, with their highly advanced surgical skills, they open up the top of Fred's head. Using complex scanning devices, they record precisely how Fred's brain is connected up to the rest of his body. Then they remove his brain.

Blib and Blob then fly Fred's brain across town in their flying

saucer. There they meet up with Flib and Flob, two other Martian scientists. Flib and Flob have been performing the exact same operation on Bert. The two teams of Martians exchange information about how the two brains were originally connected up. Then Flib and Flob fly off to Fred's house, where they install

Bert's brain in Fred's body. And Blib and Blob install Fred's brain in Bert's body.

The Martians put Fred's and Bert's skulls back together and sew up their scalps. They use a special technique to heal up the scars so they can't be seen. Then they carefully remove any trace of their having been at either house. Finally, they leave.

Morning comes. The person in Fred's bed wakes up and looks around. He doesn't know where he is. 'This isn't my bedroom,' he thinks. He walks past a mirror and catches sight of himself. He gets a shock. He seems to have completely changed in appearance. He thought he was fat, but now he is thin. He thought he was six-foot-six, but now he is five-foot-eight. He feels sure he used to be bald, but now he has lots of bright red hair. He seems to remember having brown eyes, but now his eyes are blue. He thought he had a wooden leg, but now he has two normal legs. 'What's happened to me?' he asks himself.

There is a knock at the door. The person with Fred's body goes to answer it. It's the postman. 'Oh, hello Fred,' says the postman. The postman thinks it is Fred because it's Fred's body that he sees in front of him. But the person with Fred's body replies, 'I'm not Fred! I'm Bert! What's going on?'

Of course, the person who wakes up at Bert's house gets a similar surprise.

Where do Fred and Bert end up?

Now ask yourself: *where do Fred and Bert end up?*

When I consider this story, it seems right to me to say that what has happened is that Fred now has Bert's body and Bert now has Fred's. Fred and Bert have *swapped bodies*. For the person with Fred's body has Bert's brain. So he has all Bert's memories. He also has all Bert's personality traits: he has Bert's taste for meat pies, his hatred of classical music, his short temper, his mean streak, and so on. He even *believes* he is Bert. But then surely the person with Fred's body *really is* Bert. For doesn't he have everything that's essential so far as being Bert is concerned?

Now let's go back to our original question: what makes this two-year-old, this ten-year-old,

this twenty-five-year-old

and this seventy-five-year-old
one and the same person? Our first answer was: the fact that they all share the same living body: the one that Matilda still has to this day. But it now seems that *this answer cannot be right*.

What the brain swap case seems to show is that a person need not necessarily end up where their body ends up. In the brain swap case, Fred doesn't end up where his body ends up. Fred ends up with Bert's body and Bert ends up with Fred's.

Of course, in the normal course of things, brain swaps never happen. People do usually end up where their bodies end up. But the brain swap case seems to show that it is at least *possible* for people to swap bodies.

So Matilda has actually ended up with the same body. But she needn't have. If at some point her brain had been moved to a different body, then she would have ended up with that different body.

An objection

Some (though certainly not all) philosophers are convinced by such brain swap arguments. They take them to show that having a particular body is inessential so far as personal identity is concerned.

But perhaps you are unconvinced by the argument. Perhaps you don't believe that the person with Bert's body will be Fred. One reason you might object is that you might believe the person with Bert's body will not be very Fred-like after all. You might argue like this. Suppose Fred was a very good runner. Suppose he had won gold medals at the Olympic Games.

Running was Fred's whole life. Now the person in Bert's body finds himself with a very fat, unfit body and a wooden leg. He can't run at all. Understandably, this affects his personality greatly. Instead of being happy and outgoing, he may become very depressed, perhaps even suicidal. But then surely he isn't really Fred, for Fred is a happy and outgoing person.

I don't agree. I don't think this shows it would not be Fred who now has Bert's body. Of course, it's true that finding himself with such a different body might make Fred feel very depressed. But I think it would still be Fred that was depressed. Forget the brain swap case for a moment. Suppose instead that in the normal course of things Fred loses a leg, loses his hair and suddenly puts on 20 kilograms in weight due to an illness.

This too would make him very depressed. But surely, it *would* still be Fred. Just because Fred becomes very depressed doesn't mean it isn't still Fred.

Of course, if this did happen to Fred, we might well say that Fred 'isn't the same person any more'. We might say that he 'isn't the person he used to be'. But we wouldn't mean by this that the person we are now presented with is not Fred. We would just mean that he had changed a lot. Indeed, wouldn't we be admitting that it is still Fred by saying that Fred 'isn't the person he used to be'?

So I have to say I don't agree with this objection. Just because the person with Bert's body feels very depressed whereas Fred previously was happy and outgoing doesn't show that it isn't Fred who now has Bert's body.

The brain scanner case

Perhaps you still aren't convinced. You might say that the body is relevant to personal identity, but it is not the whole of the body that is relevant, just a bit of it. The relevant bit is the brain. You might agree that Fred and Bert swap bodies. But of course they don't swap brains. Fred and Bert still end up where their brains end up. So, you may say, the brain swap case doesn't show that it isn't the brain that determines where the person ends up.

I agree that the brain swap case doesn't show that it isn't the brain that determines where the person ends up. However, let's now change the story slightly. Suppose that the Martians *don't* swap your brains around. Rather, they use a *brain scanner* instead. The brain scanner works like this. The machine is wired up to two helmets.

BRAIN SCANNER MK1

61

When these helmets are placed on two heads, the machine records exactly how the two brains inside are wired up, how all their neurones are spliced together, how all the chemicals are balanced, and so on. All this information is stored in the machine. Then, at the press of a button, this information is used to restructure each brain just as the other was structured.

It seems that a person's personality, memories and other psychological attributes are fixed by how their brains are structured. So by swapping round the way the brains are structured, the brain scanner *also* swaps round all these psychological attributes.

Now suppose that, instead of swapping Fred's and Bert's brains around, Blib and Blob simply use this brain scanner instead. They restructure Fred's brain as Bert's was structured and restructure Bert's brain as Fred's was structured. Notice that the two brains stay where they are. They are simply reorganized.

By reorganizing the two brains, Blib and Blob swap round the two sets of memories and personality traits. Fred's memory and personality traits move from his body over to Bert's and Bert's move over to Fred's.

BRAIN SCANNER MK1

After having performed this swap on an unconscious Fred and Bert, the Martians place the person with Fred's body back in Fred's bed and the person with Bert's body back in Bert's bed.

Of course, the result will be just as it was in the brain swap case. The person who wakes up in Fred's bed the next morning will have Bert's personality and memories. So again, he will be shocked by his appearance, will think he is Bert and so on.

Now ask yourself: where do Fred and Bert end up? Surely, Fred ends up with Bert's body, and Bert with Fred's, just as in the brain swap case. But if that is right, then *a person doesn't have to go where their brain goes*. In the normal course of things, people do end up where their brains end up. But it seems that it is at least *possible* for persons to swap round their *entire* bodies, including their brains.

In fact, what the brain scanner case seems to show is that what determines the identity of a person is where the relevant memories and personality traits end up, not where their body or indeed any part of it ends up.

Is a person like a rope?

We have arrived at the view that what is relevant so far as personal identity is concerned is having the right memories and personality traits. What makes the person in Fred's body Bert is that he has Bert's memories and his personality traits. It does not matter that he no longer has Bert's body.

If that is right, then what makes the two-year-old, ten-year-old, twenty-five-year-old, fifty-year-old and seventy-five-year-old in the photographs in Matilda's album one and the same person is the fact that these individuals share the same memories and personality traits. That is what ties them all together as a single person. It may as a matter of fact be true that Matilda has one and the same living body throughout, but that is not what *makes* the two-year-old, ten-year-old, and so on, all Matilda. There is no reason in principle why Matilda should not swap bodies with someone else, just as Fred and Bert did.

Of course, in order for this seventy-five-year-old:

THE COMPLETE PHILOSOPHY FILES

to be the same person as this two-year-old:

they do not have to have *all* the same memories. That would be ridiculous. At the age of seventy, there are things Matilda remembers having done that she hasn't yet done at the age of two. There are also plenty of things she has done that she has completely forgotten about.

What seems to be important, so far as personal identity is concerned, is that there be the right sort of *continuity* to the memories and personality. Obviously, a person doesn't have to have exactly the same memories and exactly the same personality throughout their life. But there has at least got to be some sort of *overlap*.

Here is an example of such an overlap. Matilda's memory is very poor. She can remember nothing of when she was two years old or even when she was five years old. Still, she can remember something of when she was ten years old. Suppose also that, when she was ten years old, she could *then* remember being five, though she still could remember nothing of being two. And suppose that, when she was five years old, she could *then* remember something of when she was two.

So there is an overlapping series of memories linking Matilda as she is now back to that two-year-old, despite the fact that she now has no memory of when she was two.

You might think of Matilda's life history as being a bit like this rope. The rope is made up of overlapping fibres, all of which are much shorter than the rope itself. Some fibres reach from the beginning to a third of the way down its length, other fibres reach from a quarter to three-quarters down its length, other fibres stretch only the length of the final third. None of the fibres poking out of one end of the rope can be found poking out of the other end. Still, all these fibres form a single rope because of the way the fibres overlap. Similarly, Matilda's memories and personality traits now are quite different from those she had as a two-year-old. Still, this two-year-old

and this seventy-five-year old
are both Matilda because there is an overlapping series
of memories and personality traits linking them together.

Reincarnation

If what makes a person you is their possessing the right personality and memories, whether or not they have the same physical body, then it seems that when someone dies they might come back later with a different body. Perhaps this never actually happens. The point is that it *could* happen.

To come back to life with a new body is to be *reincarnated*. Some religions claim that we are all reincarnated.

One way in which you might be reincarnated is if we used the brain scanner I talked about earlier to scan your brain shortly

65

before you died, and then later on used it to restructure someone else's brain so that your memories and personality traits
were transferred over to their body. It seems you would be
brought back to life with a different body.

So science may one day allow us to be reincarnated. Of
course, it would hardly be fair for you to take over the body of
another person. For what happens to them? But perhaps a new
body might be made for you either by cloning or by some other
process. Then you might live for centuries. When your old body
wore out, you could change it for a new one, much as you
might change an old, broken-down car for a new one.

The soul

Some people, especially religious people, believe that each of us
has a soul. A soul is a very peculiar sort of thing. We aren't
talking about a physical thing made out of physical stuff. We
are talking about something non-physical. Indeed, a soul is a supernatural thing – the thing which many believe goes up to heaven
when one's physical body dies.

Now, your soul, if you have one, is apparently connected
up to your physical body. It controls your physical body. But
it can be separated from your body. In fact, your soul can exist
without any physical body at all.

Of course, if each person is really a soul, then it would be possible in principle for people to swap bodies. Your soul could come to be connected up to a different physical body instead.

However, it's important to realize that, by suggesting that you might swap bodies with someone, I'm certainly not suggesting you have a soul. Certainly, if we have souls, then body swaps are possible. But it does not follow that if body swaps are possible, then we have souls.

I'm suggesting that all that's required for persons to swap bodies is that certain psychological properties (such as being bad-tempered or being able to remember the war) be switched from one body to the other. You don't have to move any physical part of one body over to the other, not even the brain. But neither do you have to move some sort of non-physical, supernatural, soul-stuff thing over from one body to the other.

In fact, as I shall now explain, even if there are such things as souls, it doesn't seem to be the fact that a particular person has your soul that makes them you.

The soul swap case

Suppose that you and I each have a soul, and that these two souls will swap round in two minutes' time. However, everything else – including all our memories and psychological traits – will remain in place. My soul will come to have your body, memories and personality traits. Your soul will come to have mine.

Notice that after the swap everything will seem exactly the same not only to everyone else, but also to us (wherever we end up). For the person that ends up with this body will have the memories and personality that go with this body. So even if you end up with this body, you won't remember any swap. For you won't remember any of your own past, only mine.

Suppose this soul swap happens. Where do you and I end up? If we say that the person is the soul, and so the person goes where their soul goes, then we must say that the person with your body, memories and personality traits is now me. And the person with my body, memories and personality traits is now you.

But this can't be right, can it? Surely, the person with your body won't be me, despite the fact they have now got my soul. For they are nothing like me. They have none of my memories. Their personality is quite different to mine. When asked who they are, they give your name. If we ask them about their relatives, they talk about your relatives. It certainly won't be easy to convince this person that they are not who they think they are.

In fact, this sort of soul swap could be happening all the time and no one, including the people involved, would be any the wiser. Perhaps your soul and mine did just swap round five minutes ago. What difference would it make? No one would notice. Not even us!

Isn't it more plausible to say that, even if there are such things as souls, it is the person with all your memories and personality traits that is you, whatever soul they might happen to have? In that case, it seems that not only is the body irrelevant so far as our question about personal identity is concerned, so too is the soul.

Three theories

We have now looked at three different theories about personal identity.

The first theory we looked at was that it is the living body that determines the identity of a person. On this theory, a person necessarily ends up where their body ends up. Let's call this theory the *Body Theory* of personal identity. The brain scanner case seems to show that the body theory is wrong: it is possible for people to swap bodies.

We also looked at the theory that each person has an immaterial soul and that this is what determines their identity. On this theory, a person necessarily ends up wherever their soul ends up. Let's call this the *Soul Theory* of personal identity. It seems that, even if there are such things as souls, it would be possible for persons to swap souls, which means that the soul theory cannot be right either.

So far, the theory that seems most plausible is the theory that it is memory and personality traits that determine personal identity. Let's call this the *Stream Theory* of personal identity. On the Stream Theory, what links the two-year-old, five-year-old, ten-year-old, and so on, that appear in Matilda's photo album together as a single person is the fact that there is a stream of memories and personality traits linking them together. They are psychologically continuous with each other. If this psychological stream were to pass from one body to another, or even from one soul to another (if there are such things), then so too would Matilda.

The Mars 'Transporter' Case and the Two-Of-You Problem

I have tried to make the Stream Theory seem as plausible as

possible. But I must now reveal that there is a serious problem
with it. I shall call this problem the *Two-Of-You Problem*.

In order to help explain the Two-Of-You Problem, let's take a
look at another science fiction, an example I call the *Mars
'Transporter' Case*.

Suppose Martian scientists develop a machine that can scan a
human body (or any physical object, for that matter) and then
produce a copy that is indistinguishable down to the last atom.
You are presented with this machine. You are asked to step into a
cubicle and press the red button to start the machine. You do so.
There is a zap. Your original body is instantaneously vaporized.
But just before it is destroyed, it is scanned and all the information needed to produce a duplicate body is transmitted to Mars
where there is a similar machine. The machine on Mars then
produces a duplicate body. This all takes but a second or two.

Of course, the person who steps out of the cubicle on Mars is
not only physically just like you. They are also psychologically
continuous with you. They have all of your personality traits.
They have all of your memories. When asked who they are, they
give your name. They seem to remember having just stepped
into the machine on Earth and pressed the red button.

Now, if we accept the Stream Theory of personal identity, then we must say that the person on Mars *really is you*. For that person is psychologically continuous with you. What we have here really is a *transporter*. The machine can transport people from Earth to Mars, and back again if they so wish. Perhaps you find this plausible. Perhaps you would be happy to step into the machine and press the red button, thinking that you will be whizzed off to Mars.

But I'm not so sure. Suppose we change the story slightly. Suppose that instead of producing *one* duplicate body on Mars, we programme the machine to produce *two*. Two people get out of the cubicle on Mars, both of whom are psychologically continuous with you. One might say that in this case the psychological stream divides. It branches into two.

This story lands the Stream Theory in deep trouble, for it says that because both people are psychologically continuous with you, so both people *are* you. Both are one and the same person as you. But they *can't* both be one and the same person as you, for it would then follow that they are one and the same person as each other, which clearly they are not: there are *two* of them, not one. They may be *exactly similar*, but they are not *one and the same person*. So it seems the psychological stream theory can't be correct.

The Single Stream Theory

We have seen that the possibility of the psychological stream dividing raises a big problem for the Stream Theory. Can the theory be altered to deal with this problem?

71

Some philosophers have suggested that we need only add on a further condition to solve the problem. The condition requires that there be *no dividing of the psychological stream*. It says that if at some point the psychological stream does branch into two, then neither of the later individuals is identical with the earlier one. At the moment the stream divides, two new people come into existence, and the original person is no more. However, if there is no dividing of the stream – if there is only one later individual psychologically continuous with the earlier individual – then the later and earlier individuals are one and the same person.

Let's call this the *Single Stream Theory* of personal identity.

The duplicator gun

One problem the Single Stream Theory has to deal with can be brought out by two more thought experiments.

Suppose that Martian scientists develop a scanning machine that can scan bodies from a great distance and then duplicate them. Let's call it the *duplicator gun*. I leave my front door and start to walk down the street. Unknown to me, the Martians, who are flying out in space, then aim the duplicator gun at me and press the starting button. The machine instantly reads off exactly how I am physically put together and produces an atom-for-atom duplicate of me in a cubicle on board their space craft. Of course, the duplicate that steps out of the cubicle on the space craft is psychologically continuous with me. It seems to him just as if he stepped out of my front door and started walking down the street when suddenly the street turned into a Martian space craft. Back on Earth, the person with my original body reaches the end of the street and turns the corner. He is oblivious to what has happened.

In this story, my psychological stream branches into two. There are now two individuals who are psychologically just like the earlier me: the individual who reaches the end of the street and turns the corner; and the individual who steps out of the cubicle on the space craft. So where am I? According to the Single Stream Theory, *neither* of these two individuals is me. As the duplicating gun is fired, the original me disappears and two new people come into existence. Neither the person that steps out of the cubicle on the space craft *nor the person that reaches the end of the street* is Stephen Law. Stephen Law has *ceased to exist*.

But isn't this absurd? How can the Martians make me cease to exist just by producing a copy of me? Surely, whether or not the Martians make a copy of me as I walk down the street, it's still *me* that reaches the end of the street and turns the corner? But that is just what the Single Stream Theory denies. So it seems the Single Stream Theory must be wrong.

Here is another difficult case for the Single Stream Theory. Suppose that no one reaches the end of the street to turn the corner. The Martians fire the duplicator gun and produce a copy just as before, only this time, just as the duplicate starts to materialize, I step off the kerb and a passing truck squashes my body flat (I forgot to look).

Where am I now? Do I still exist? According to the Single Stream Theory, I do still exist. In fact, I am transported to the space craft. For in this story, exactly one later individual is psychologically continuous with the earlier me: the person who steps out of the cubicle on board the space craft. Therefore, according to the Single Stream Theory, the person on board the space craft is me.

But again, isn't this absurd? Surely I am dead. The fact that the Martians happened to make an exact copy of me the instant before my body is flattened by the truck doesn't alter this fact. There may be a person just like me on the space craft. But that person isn't actually me.

So the Single Stream Theory runs into problems because it has some rather absurd-sounding consequences. Perhaps these problems can be dealt with.

But perhaps they can't be dealt with. Perhaps what these last two science fiction cases involving the duplicator gun show is that having a certain living body is not irrelevant so far as personal identity is concerned. Perhaps we were too easily persuaded by the brain swap and brain scanner cases. Regarding the first story about the duplicator gun, doesn't it seem right to say that the person who reaches the end of the street is me because he is the same living organism that left my house? It does not matter that a copy of that living organism has been produced elsewhere. In the second story about the duplicator gun, doesn't it sound right to say that the person on the space craft isn't me because they are not the one and the same living organism as the one that left my house? Unfortunately, that living organism is no more: it was flattened by a truck.

So we are presented with two conflicting sets of intuitions. On the one hand, our intuitions about the brain swap case and brain scanner case are that having a certain living body is completely irrelevant so far as personal identity is concerned. On the other hand, our intuitions about the two stories involving the duplicator gun are that having a certain living body is very relevant indeed so far as personal identity is concerned. Which of these conflicting sets of intuitions are we to trust? I must admit: I am very confused.

The issues we have been discussing are brought out in my last science fiction story, set out below. The story ends with me facing a terrible dilemma. I shall leave you to decide what I should do.

Holiday of a lifetime?

Blib and Blob come and visit me one day. They set up their Martian 'transporter' (which we talked about earlier) in my front room, and explain to me how it works. They demonstrate by using it to 'transport' Blib from a cubicle on one side of the room to one on the other side of the room and back again. 'See!' says Blib. 'It's completely reliable!'

Blib and Blob explain that they have set up similar cubicles all over the universe at their favourite holiday destinations, and they offer to let me use them to tour the universe. I need only step into the cubicle in front of me, dial in my first destination, and press the red button.

'What an incredible opportunity,' I think. I step in, dial in my chosen destination (I decide to visit a spaceship hovering over the rings of Saturn), and press the button. From there I spend months travelling to all sorts of exotic destinations. I have the time of my life.

But one day, while I am sitting on a beach on a beautiful deserted planet way over on the far side of the Galaxy, I start to think more carefully about the Martian 'transporter'.

A niggling doubt starts to eat at me. I'm not so sure I want to step back inside the cubicle from which I emerged a few hours ago, select a destination, and press the red button again. For I'm not so sure it really is a transporter after all. Blib and Blob might have convinced themselves that it is a transporter. But perhaps they have fooled themselves. Perhaps, every time someone steps inside and presses the button, that person is just *killed*. For the living organism that steps inside and presses the button is instantly vaporized. The organism that is produced elsewhere is just a copy of the original.

And then a horrible thought strikes me. If that is true, then *Stephen Law died months ago*. He killed himself when he stepped into the first cubicle and pressed the button. I am not Stephen Law

(though I thought I was). I am merely someone just like Stephen Law. In fact, I have only been in existence for a few hours: the few hours since I stepped out of that cubicle over there.

So what should I do? Should I remain here alone, stranded for ever on the far side of the Galaxy? Or should I step into the cubicle, dial in home, and press that red button? If I do, will the person who steps out of the cubicle on Earth really be me? Or will he merely be a copy? Will I return home? Or will I die? What do you think?

File 4

What is real?

The world around me
Here's my study.

As you can see, I'm working on a computer. On my desk is a
bowl full of apples. There are also some Tibetan singing bowls
that I bought when I visited India. Beside the desk is a bookcase
full of books. There's a fireplace with some rather dusty dried
flowers in it. And on the other side of the room is a window.
You can see some trees and clouds and the sun shining outside.
Beyond them are the spires of Oxford.

Now most people, if you were to ask them: *what is reality?*
would probably say that reality is what I'm experiencing all
around me right now. The world of desks and chairs, trees and
clouds: that's reality; that's the real world.

But not everyone would agree with this. In particular, Plato
wouldn't agree. According to Plato, what I see around me are
actually just shadows. The real world is hidden from our five
senses. It cannot be seen, touched, heard, smelled or tasted.

So what is this hidden world like? According to Plato, it is
quite wonderful.

It contains everything that is essential and perfect. It has always been there and will always be there. It is the place from which we came. And it is the place to which we go when we die.

Plato also says that, if we want knowledge, it is to this world beyond the shadows that we must look. Our five senses cannot give us knowledge of how things *really* are. So how do we find out how things are beyond the shadows? As we shall see, Plato argues that the only way to genuine knowledge is through the use of reason.

This chapter is about Plato's world beyond the shadows. Does it really exist?

Plato

Who was Plato?

Plato was born nearly two and a half thousand years ago, in Ancient Greece. He is perhaps the most famous of all philosophers. In fact, Plato is considered by many to be the father of philosophy.

A good place to start with Plato is with a story – a story first told by Plato all those years ago (I've changed the story a bit, but it's essentially the same).

Plato's story of the cave

There is a cave. And at the very bottom of this cave are kept some prisoners. The prisoners are kept chained up, facing a wall.

They are never allowed to turn and see what is behind them. So the prisoners spend their entire lives looking only at the wall.

Then, one day, one of the prisoners – let's call him 'Alf' – is released. He is made to turn around and look up.

At first, Alf is blinded by a brilliant light. It hurts his eyes. But after a while Alf's eyes start to adjust.

As his eyes become accustomed to the light, Alf begins to see that up above the prisoners and behind them is a fire. It was this fire that first blinded him. And between the fire and the prisoners is a path, like this:

The path is used by the jailers. Alf can see that, as the jailers walk along the path carrying objects, the objects they carry cast shadows down on to the wall in front of the prisoners.

Now, Alf has never seen a real object before. When he was a prisoner, he could only see the shadows that were cast on to the wall. So, like all the other prisoners, he ended up supposing that these shadows were the real objects. He mistook what he saw on the wall for reality.

But now Alf can see how he and the other prisoners had been fooled. He now understands that what he had earlier taken to be the real world was merely a parade of shadows. He realizes that the *real* world had been hidden from him.

A little later, some of the jailers lead Alf from the cave into the sunlight outside. The brightness of the light again blinds him at first. But gradually Alf's eyes adjust. Finally, he recognizes the sun.

Now, Alf is a kind man. Not surprisingly, he feels very sorry for the other prisoners he left behind in the cave. So he decides to return down into the depths to tell them what he has seen, to explain to them how things *really* are. He feels sure they will want to know all about his journey into the real world.

But then Alf reaches the bottom of the cave, his eyes are no longer accustomed to the dark. He stumbles. He bumps into things. So the other prisoners think that Alf's journey has made him blind.

Then things get worse. When Alf starts to explain to them how things *really* are, they don't want to listen. They are happily engrossed watching the shadows in front of them. The tell him to shut up. They act just like a grumpy person acts when their favourite TV programme has been interrupted.

But Alf won't give up. He wants to help them. So he carries on trying to tell them all about the hidden world up above them. Then the prisoners get really angry. They start shouting at him. 'Just *go away!*' they yell. 'Stop pestering us with your stupid talk! *We* can see perfectly well how things are – it's *you* that's blind!'

And when Alf *still* won't give up, the prisoners throw rocks at him. They drive him away. And so the prisoners waste away their lives watching shadows. They never do find out the truth.

The world beyond the shadows

You've probably guessed that Plato's story about the prisoners in the cave is not just a story. Plato is trying to tell us something. But what is he trying to tell us?

Well, *we* are the prisoners in the cave. And the things we see around us are those shadows on the cave wall. Just like the prisoners in the cave, we are taken in by the shadows. We mistake the shadows for reality. We suppose that what we can see is the real world. But the real world cannot be seen.

Souls

Plato also argued that each of us has a *soul*. He argued that it is to this real world that the soul goes when we die. So death is really nothing to be afraid of. When you die, your soul doesn't stop existing. It carries on. It goes to a much better place.

Heaven

A number of religions talk about *Heaven*. Heaven is where we are supposed to go when we die (at least if we have been good).

Now, Plato's idea of a perfect world – the real world that lies beyond the shadows – certainly does sound a bit like this modern idea of Heaven, doesn't it? And that's not entirely a coincidence. Over the centuries religious thinkers have read Plato and borrowed from his ideas. The modern idea of Heaven – in particular, the modern Christian idea of Heaven – has been shaped in part by Plato's ideas.

C.S. Lewis and the Shadowlands

Plato's thinking has influenced our thinking about the world right up to the present day. In particular, Plato's philosophy has had an important part to play in shaping western philosophy, religion, art and literature.

Let me give you one example. You may have heard of C.S. Lewis. C.S. Lewis was a Christian. He wrote children's books about a land called Narnia. The best-known book about Narnia is called *The Lion, the Witch and the Wardrobe*.

The final book about Narnia is called *The Last Battle*. In its closing pages, Narnia comes to an end. The land is covered by sea and the sun is put out. All the good creatures from Narnia pass through a door into an extraordinary new land.

Finding themselves in this new land, the children whom the Narnia stories are about wonder where they can be. Parts of the new land seem like the Narnia they remember, only far more wonderful. And parts of it seem like the England they remember, only, again, far more wonderful.

Then one of the characters in the story explains to the children that the Narnia and England that they remember were not the *real* Narnia or the *real* England. They were just *shadows* of the real world in which they now find themselves. This real world has always existed and will always exist, and is as different from the old Narnia and the old England as a real object is different from its shadow.

Finally, on the very last page of *The Last Battle*, the children wonder how they could have ended up in this wonderful place. They are afraid they might be made to leave. But then it is explained to them that they are actually all dead – they were killed in a railway accident. They have now passed over from what C.S. Lewis calls the *Shadowlands* into the real world where they will live happily ever after. Their old lives were but a dream: this is the morning.

As you have probably guessed, C.S. Lewis borrowed this idea of the real world beyond the shadows – the real world to which we go when we die – from Plato. In fact, if you read *The Last Battle* carefully, you will discover that near the end of the story one of the characters actually tells the children that it's all in Plato.

An invisible world

So Plato believes that *this* world – the world that you and I are experiencing right now – isn't the real world. These are merely the Shadowlands, as Lewis calls them.

The world we see around us might seem like the real world, but it's not.

The real world is invisible. It lies beyond what we can see, touch, hear, smell and taste.

But why did Plato suppose that these are merely the Shadowlands, that the real world lies beyond? What's the philosophy, the argument behind these extraordinary views? That's what I shall now explain.

The form of beauty

Here are five beautiful things:

They are: a beautiful flower, a beautiful person, a beautiful mountain, a beautiful sunset and a beautiful garden. Of course, these five beautiful things are different in many ways (for example, the person has hair and the mountain doesn't). Still, each is beautiful.

But what is *beauty itself*? While each of these things may be a beautiful thing, it seems that none is beauty itself. Beauty itself seems to be something else – a *further* thing that exists in addition to all the particular things that there are.

Plato calls this further thing – beauty itself – the Form of beauty. He says that what makes particular beautiful things beautiful is the fact that they share this Form.

Other Forms

According to Plato, it's not just beautiful things that share a common Form. Beautiful things are just one type of thing. There are many other types of thing. Take chairs, for example.

Chairs are a type of thing. So, despite their many differences, there is something that all chairs have in common – the some-thing that *makes* them chairs. According to Plato, this 'something' is another Form: *the Form of the chair*.

This Form of the chair exists in addition to all the particular chairs that there are.

There are many other sorts of Form, according to Plato. For example, large things (such as elephants, mountains and Giant Redwood trees) are a type of thing. To them corresponds the Form of largeness. Actions that are just (an example of a just action would be when a judge and jury fairly punish someone for a terrible crime) are yet another type of thing. To them corresponds the Form of justice. And so on.

In fact, if we follow Plato's reasoning here, it seems there must be a Form for *every* type of thing there is. There must be a Form of the flower, a Form of red things, a Form of the rabbit, a Form of the house, a Form of the cheeseburger, even.

So what are Plato's Forms like?

The Forms are perfect

First of all, the Forms are perfect. Take beauty, for example. Any beautiful thing that you might experience will not be *perfectly* beautiful. It could always be more beautiful than it is. But the Form of beauty — beauty itself — is quite perfect. For there can't be anything more beautiful than beauty itself, can there?

All the things we see around us are imperfect. All are flawed. All will break or wear out or go mouldy. Take beds, for example. Any particular bed that you might happen to see will not be perfect. It could always be more comfortable. It will eventually wear out or break. But, again, the Form of the bed is quite perfect. Each Form is the one and only perfect example of things of that type.

The Forms are invisible

Secondly, *the Forms are not the sort of thing that one can see, touch, smell, hear or taste.* Nothing that we can experience is ever perfect. So the Form of the chair, being perfect, is not something that we can experience. We can see particular, imperfect chairs, of course, but the Form of the chair is invisible.

The Forms are more real

Thirdly, the Forms are *more real* than are the particular things that we experience around us. For those particular things depend for their existence on the Forms.

Take a look at the tree in my back garden. Throughout the day this tree casts many shadows. It is also reflected in puddles and in windowpanes.

These fleeting images of the tree are distorted and imperfect copies of the tree. They depend for their existence on the tree being there. Without the tree there can be no shadows or reflections of it.

Similarly, without the Form of the tree there can be no particular trees. Those trees we see around – including that tree in my garden – depend for their existence on the Form of the tree: they are imperfect shadows or reflections of this Form.

And the same goes for all the other objects we see around us. They are not the *real* objects. The real objects are the Forms, of which the objects we see are but fleeting shadows or reflections.

The Forms are eternal and changeless

According to Plato, the Forms are *eternal*. They have always been there and always will be there. While particular beautiful things may come and go, beauty itself remains.

The Forms are also *changeless*. Of course, the world around us is changing all the time. Chairs and tables warp, bend and break. Plants and animals grow, wither and die. The weather varies from day to day. The seasons come and go. Mountains eventually tumble into the sea. Everything is shifting. But according to Plato, the Forms never change.

You might wonder about this. Take beauty, for example. Don't we consider different things beautiful at different times? For example, our current ideal of a beautiful person is someone who is thin, but not so long ago heavier people were considered more beautiful.

Fashions change. What at one time might be considered beautiful later generations may find vulgar or even downright ugly. So if there is a Form of beauty, doesn't it change over time?

Not according to Plato. He thought that while fashion may change, beauty itself does not. *Real* beauty is always the same. It's only our ability to recognize it that varies.

The supreme Form

So there you have it: the world we see around us is not the real world. The real world is a hidden world of perfect, changeless and eternal Forms.

But there is one last Form that we still need to put into place. There are many Forms. So the Forms themselves are a type of thing. So there must also be a Form of the Forms.

What is the Form of the Forms like? Well, what do all the Forms have in common? They all exist and they are all perfect. So the Form of the Forms is the Form of *existence and perfection*.

Plato called this supreme Form the *Form of the Good*.

The arrangement of the Forms

According to Plato, then, the Forms are arranged like this:

At the very top of the pyramid is the Form of the Good. Below the Form of the Good are all the other Forms: the Form of beauty, the Form of the chair, the Form of the table, and so on. And below these Forms are the particular objects that we see around us: particular beds for example.

Just as the particular chairs, tables, beautiful things and so on gain what existence and perfection they have from their corresponding Forms, so these forms in turn get what existence and perfection they have from the Form of the Good. So ultimately

all existence and perfection flows down from
the Form of the Good.

In Plato's story about the cave, the Form
of the Good is represented by the sun
shining outside the cave.
Just as we sometimes think of the sun
as being that from which everything
ultimately comes (because it makes night
and day, controls the seasons and the weather,
makes the plants grow on which animals in turn feed,
and so on), so the Form of the Good is that to which everything
ultimately owes its existence.

God

Plato's idea of the Form of the Good – the Form from which all
existence and perfection flows – sounds much like the modern
idea of God, doesn't it? Many modern religions – in particular,
Christianity, Islam and Judaism – suppose that God has precisely
this role. God is that to which everything owes its existence and
from which all perfection comes.

Again, this similarity is not completely accidental. This is
another example of how Plato's ideas have helped to shape
religious thinking right up to the present day.

Where does knowledge come from?

We experience the world around us by using our five senses –
sight, touch, taste, smell and hearing.

But, as we have seen, Plato argues that the world we experience in this way is not the real world. The world that we experience is merely a shadow world.

This is one reason why Plato says that our senses cannot provide us with genuine knowledge. According to Plato, our senses can only deceive us. *Genuine* knowledge is knowledge of the true reality, the world that lies beyond what our five senses reveal. Genuine knowledge is knowledge of the Forms.

So how do we come by knowledge of the Forms, if not by our senses? According to Plato, real knowledge comes through doing *philosophy*. Real knowledge comes through the use of *reason*, through *thinking and reflecting*. Those who want real knowledge must ignore the senses. They must close their eyes, put cotton wool in their ears, sit in their favourite armchair and think.

Of course, Plato admits that it is very difficult for philosophers to turn people away from the world of the senses, to convince them that the world we see around us is a mere shadow world. For it does *seem* so real.

The world of the senses can also seem so enticing. We learn to love our senses and the pleasures they bring us: the taste of ice-cream, the sound of music, the sight of a beautiful tree. But, according to Plato, there are rarer, higher pleasures – the pleasures that only philosophy can bring. Compared to these higher pleasures, the pleasures of the senses are very crude and measly indeed.

Still, most of us are captivated by our senses. We reject the philosopher who tries to turn us away from the world of the senses and towards the unseen Forms. That's what Plato was trying to warn us about at the end of his story about the cave. We are like the grumpy prisoners who threw rocks at Alf when he tried to turn them away from the shadows and towards the real world.

Science

You might find Plato's views about knowledge rather surprising. For nowadays we think of *science* – physics, chemistry, astronomy and the rest – as being one of the best routes to knowledge. Science rests ultimately on our five senses: on sight, hearing, touch, smell and taste. Scientists make *observations*. They watch, listen, prod, sniff. Sometimes they even lick. They perform experiments and carefully examine the results. It is upon all these different observations that they base their scientific theories.

Now *surely*, you may think, isn't this sort of *scientific* method one of the best methods of finding out what the world is really like? So isn't Plato wrong to say that our senses cannot give us true knowledge?

Perhaps you are also thinking to yourself: how could someone discover anything of any importance by sitting in their favourite armchair with their eyes shut? Isn't this the *last* way in which we could find out anything about reality? So, again, isn't Plato wrong to say that quiet reflection is the only way to true knowledge? Isn't it quite obvious that no genuine knowledge can be had without the use of the five senses? Surely reason alone is blind. Aren't our senses our only real window on to reality?

It may be that Plato is wrong about the senses not being able to give us knowledge. But perhaps there is *something* to what he says. Perhaps it's at least true that some of the most important questions are questions our senses cannot help us answer. Have a look at the following argument.

An argument

Some of the questions that are most important to us are questions that ask: *what-is-X?* For example, we want to know: what is *justice?* The question: what is justice? is obviously a very important question. We want our society to be just. For example, we want it to have just laws. We want courts to hand out just punishments: punishments that are deserved and that fit the crime (for example, it would hardly be just to execute someone for stealing an apple from their neighbour's tree, would it?). So it is very important that we know what justice is. If we don't know what justice is, we won't know how to build a fair and just society.

Other important *what-is-X?* questions are: what is *good?* what is *courage?* what is *beauty?* and so on.

Now Plato argued that, if you don't yet know what good is, or what courage is, or what beauty is and you want to find out, it is impossible to find out by observing the world around you.

Take beauty, for example. There may be many beautiful things around you. So why can't you find out what beauty is by observing those things? The problem is this: if you don't *already* know what beauty is, *you won't be able to tell which of the things around you are beautiful.* You won't be able to recognize beauty.

Here's another example (which I just made up – it's not from Plato). Take a look at these different objects:
Suppose I tell you that some of these objects are blibblies and

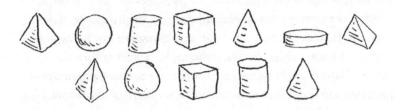

some of them are not. Now, you don't yet know what a blibbly is, do you? You have no idea what it is to be a blibbly. Could you find out what it is to be a blibbly by observing these different objects? No. Obviously not. For you don't yet know which of them are blibblies.

Of course, if I now tell you that something is a blibbly if and only if it is a cube, then you will know which of these objects are blibblies. Now you can tell that just the middle two objects are blibblies. But of course, observing the blibblies won't be of any help now because you *already* know what a blibbly is.

It seems, then, that when it comes to answering the question: what is a blibbly? observing the world around us can't help. Neither, it seems, can it help us answer the questions: what is justice? what is beauty? and so on.

Does this argument convince you? Is Plato right to say that the senses can't help when it comes to answering such questions as: what is justice? and: what is beauty? What do you think?

The soul and knowledge of the Forms

As I have already mentioned, Plato believes that each of us has an immortal soul. One reason why the soul is important in Plato's philosophy is that he uses it to explain how we come to have knowledge. As we have just seen, according to Plato, true knowledge comes not from the senses but through the use of reason. But that raises the question: how can reason give us knowledge of the Forms?

Plato's answer to this question seems to be: by somehow reminding us of the Forms. Through reasoning we recollect what we have somehow always known. Our souls existed before our physical bodies were born. Our souls were at that time presented with the Forms. And what knowledge we have of the Forms is actually remembered from back then.

That means, for example, that you are able to recognize beauty now only because you experienced the Form of beauty before you were born. That's also how you are able to recognize a tree. Before you were born, your soul experienced the Form of the tree.

Then, when you see a tree now . . .

. . . it reminds you of the Form.

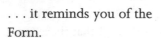

That's how you recognize it's a tree.

Now that I have explained Plato's theory of Forms to you, let's look at two of the best known criticisms of it.

Criticism 1: the Form of the bogey

Plato paints a glorious picture. His perfect, eternal world beyond the shadows certainly sounds wonderful. In fact, it sounds like heaven. Plato certainly seems to think of it as being very heavenly.

Now one of Plato's arguments for the Forms seems to be this. Whenever there are things that form a *type* of thing (such as beautiful things or chairs or whatever) there is always a further thing – a Form – that exists in addition to them. Let's call this argument the *Extra Thing Argument*.

However, there is a problem. Some types of thing are pretty revolting. Take bogeys, for example – they are a type of thing. So by the Extra Thing Argument there must also be a Form of the bogey. There must be *a perfect eternal and changeless bogey*.

But that can't be right, surely? The perfect bogey doesn't sound very heavenly, does it? Do we really suppose that the real, heavenly world beyond the shadows contains such disgusting things? I guess not. Certainly, Plato himself didn't seem very keen on the idea.

So the problem is this. Either Plato has to accept that there is a Form of bogey (which it seems he wouldn't accept) or else he must admit that the Extra Thing Argument is no good. He can't have it both ways. And if the Extra Thing Argument is no good, then it can't be used to show that *any* Forms exist.

Criticism 2: too many Forms

One of the most famous criticisms of Plato's theory goes like this.

As I say, Plato seems to use the Extra Thing Argument. Take these beds, for example:

Beds form a type of thing. So, by the Extra Thing Argument, there must be an *extra* thing – the *perfect* bed – that exists in addition to them all, like this:
This form is the thing that all particular beds have in common.

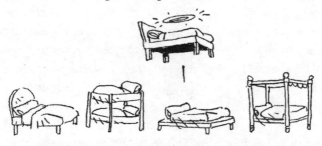

But now the original beds plus the Form *also* form a type. They too are all beds, so they all have something in common too. So by the Extra Thing Argument we must now add a *second* Form of the bed, like this:

But of course, the original beds plus the two Forms now also form a type. They too are all beds. So by the Extra Thing Argument there must be a third Form of the bed, like this.

There must also be a fourth Form of the bed, and a fifth, and a sixth, and a seventh. The Extra Thing Argument applies again and again without end. So if the Extra Thing Argument is any good there must actually be an infinite number of Forms of the bed. But that is ridiculous.

Of course, the same problem arises for all the other Forms too. The problem is that Plato can't stop at just one Form for each type of thing. In each case, the Extra Thing Argument seems to require that there be an infinite number of Forms for each type of thing.

If, on the other hand, we deny that there are an infinite number of Forms for each type of thing, as Plato surely would, then we must accept that the Extra Thing Argument is no good. In which case it can't be used to show that there is even one Form for each type of thing.

Do we live in the Shadowlands?

We have now looked at two criticisms of Plato's theory of Forms, both of which seem to be quite good criticisms. But some philosophers argue that these criticisms don't really work. It is also worth remembering that Plato himself knew about these criticisms and wasn't convinced by them. Plato stuck with his theory (as, of course, have very many other philosophers, religious thinkers, writers, artists and others down through the centuries).

Has Plato convinced you? Is what we see around us the real world? Or are these merely the Shadowlands? What do you think?

I must admit that I am not convinced by Plato's arguments. Still, I have to admit that Plato touches on a feeling that I and many other people seem to have, a feeling that there is more to life, more to reality, than just this. We feel that the *essential* thing – the *important* thing – is hidden.

We feel that, if only the curtain could be pulled back, we would see something wonderful. We cannot see, touch, hear, smell or taste this 'something', but still we feel it is there.

File 5

Can I jump in the same river twice?

Aisha's amazing philosophical 'discovery'

Not long ago Aisha and Carol went down to the river near
where they live. They went for a swim. Then they sat at a picnic
table and ate their sandwiches.

Aisha was looking at the river and thinking to herself. Suddenly
she became very excited.

Aisha: I've just made an amazing philosophical discovery!
Carol: What is it, then?
Aisha: You can't jump in the same river twice!
Carol: Don't be silly! Of course you can.
Aisha: I'm not being silly. Look, suppose you jump into that river over
    there . . .

101

Splosh. Then you get out. And then you jump back in a second time. The river will have changed in many ways between you jumping in the first time and you jumping in the second, right?

Carol wasn't sure about this.

Carol: Erm. Why?
Aisha: Well it's obvious. Water will have flowed down the river. So the river won't contain exactly the same water. And things will have moved about in the river. The reeds will have moved.

The fish will have swum around . . .

The mud on the bottom will have been churned about a bit . . .

That sort of thing. The river will have changed.

Carol agreed that the river will have changed in these different ways.

Aisha: Well then, if the river has changed, then it is *not the same*, is it?
Carol: I suppose not.
Aisha: And if it's not the *same* river, then there are *two* rivers, not one.

There is the river you jump into the first time. And then there is a second, different river that you jump into the second time. Don't you agree?

Common sense

Carol wasn't sure she did agree.

Carol: Er . . . no. That's not right. *Of course* you can jump into the same river twice. I mean, that's just common sense.

Aisha: Common sense? Pah! What does common sense know? Common sense has been shown to be wrong about many things. A few hundred years ago it was the common sense view that the sun goes round the Earth. That's what everyone believed. If you had said that the Earth goes round the sun, people would have thought you were mad. But the sun *doesn't* go round the Earth, does it? The Earth goes round the sun.

Carol: Yes. Of course.

Aisha: Well, then. Common sense *can* be wrong, can't it? And common sense is also wrong about it being possible to jump in the same river twice. In fact, I've just *proved* that common sense is wrong. I think I may be a genius!

Jumping back in very quickly

Carol sat silently. She helped herself to another sandwich. Then she had a thought.

PHILOSOPHER OF THE YEAR

Carol: Wait a minute. What if I were to jump in, get out and then jump in again *really, really quickly?* Then it would still be the same river, wouldn't it?

Aisha: No, I'm afraid not.

Carol: Why not?

Aisha: Because the river will still have changed, even if only a tiny bit. It's changing all the time. Even after just a tiny bit of a second it has changed. So it won't be the same when you jump in the second time, even if you do jump in very, very soon after jumping in the first time.

Carol took a bite of sandwich and pulled a face. She was now getting very frustrated. In fact, Carol was now so frustrated that she started to speak with her mouth full, spraying crumbs everywhere.

Carol: Yeth. But there jutht *aren't* two wiverth, are there? I mean, the river you jump into first doesn't *dithappear*, does it?
Aisha: Yes, it *does* disappear! It's amazing, isn't it? The second there's a change, the river is gone! It no longer exists! It is replaced by a *new* river. And the second there's another change, no matter how tiny, that river is gone too, to be replaced by a third river. And so on. You see, in each case, once there is a change, no matter how small, the river is different. It's not *the same*. And if it's not the same river, then it must be a new river that takes the old river's place.

Aisha pointed over at the river flowing gently past them.

Aisha: Look at that river. What you are actually looking at are very many rivers – *millions and millions* of rivers, in fact – each one existing for but a moment, each immediately being replaced by another river very slightly different to it.

Carol: Oh, honestly! That's just mad. You're *bonkers*!

Aisha: I'm *not* bonkers! I've made an amazing philosophical discovery! OK, I admit it's not common sense. But common sense can be wrong. In fact, that's *why* my discovery is amazing: it *shows* that common sense is wrong.

'I can see that the river doesn't disappear'

Carol still wasn't convinced.

Carol: This is utterly ridiculous! Look! You can *see* that the river doesn't disappear! What I see with my own two eyes shows me you're wrong.

Aisha admitted that the river doesn't *seem* to disappear. But she thought the fact that the river didn't *seem* to disappear didn't prove anything:

Aisha: Look Carol, think about your TV set.

When you look at the moving picture on the screen, what you are actually looking at is lots of still images which appear one after the other. But because each image is so similar to the one before and because they come and go so quickly, it looks as if there is just one picture which moves.

Carol: Yes. I know about that.

Aisha: Well, the same is true of this river. We are actually looking at many rivers none of which change. But because each river is so similar to the one before and because the rivers come and go so quickly, it *looks* as if there is just *one* river that is changing.

Aisha wondered whether she had convinced Carol.

Aisha: So, Carol, do you *now* agree with me that the river you jump into the second time is a second, different river?

Carol: I suppose so.

Actually, Carol didn't really agree at all. Carol just said she agreed because she couldn't see what was wrong with Aisha's argument. But she still felt there must be something wrong with the argument.

What do you think? Do you agree with Aisha or with Carol?

Aisha and Carol go bowling

Carol spent that night tossing and turning.

She was thinking about Aisha's argument. Finally, after a lot of thinking, Carol changed her mind. She decided that Aisha must be right after all. For no matter how hard she tried, Carol just couldn't see anything wrong with Aisha's argument. In fact, Carol even came up with a similar argument of her own.

Next day Carol and Aisha decided to go ten pin bowling. They met up at the bowling alley. Soon they had their bowling shoes on and were about to play their first game.
As they played, Carol explained her new argument to Aisha.

Carol: Aisha, I have also made an exciting philosophical discovery.
Aisha: What is it, then?
Carol: You cannot meet one and the same *person* twice.
Aisha: Why not?

Carol picked up a ball and aimed it carefully at the pins. Then she released the ball. Aisha watched as Carol's ball rumbled along and noisily knocked over all the pins.

Carol: Wipeout! Well, it's just like in the case of the river. You said that the river is not the same the second time you jump in. And if it is not the *same* river, then there are *two* rivers, not one. Right?
Aisha: Yes. That's right.
Carol: Now, when you meet a person and then you meet them again later they too will also have changed in various ways, won't they?
Aisha: I guess so.
Carol: The person you meet the second time will be different in various ways. So they won't be the same. And if it is not the *same* person you meet, then there are *two* people that you meet, not one!

Aisha was quite impressed. She picked up a bowling ball.

Aisha: Actually, I think you're right! You know, I hadn't thought of that!
Carol: Yes. In fact, the person you meet the first time must *disappear!* The second there's a change, they are gone for ever. They are replaced by a new person. And the second there's another change, that person is gone too, to be replaced by a third person. In each case, once there is a change, no matter how tiny, the person is different. They are not the same. So a new person must take the old person's place.

Aisha put her bowling ball down again. She had started to worry about what Carol was saying.

Aisha: But hang on. That means that you aren't the person I was talking to yesterday.
Carol: Actually, *you* didn't exist yesterday, so *you* weren't talking to anyone yesterday! Neither of us existed yesterday! So that conversation yesterday was had by *two other people entirely!*
Aisha: That can't be right, can it?
Carol: Yes. It *is* right! It seems we have made another amazing discovery! In fact, here's a second reason why I can't jump into one and the same river twice. Not only will it not be one and the same river that's jumped into the second time, the person who jumps into it *won't be me. I* won't exist anymore. The person who jumps in the second time is a brand new person.

Aisha looked stunned. Carol picked up a bowling ball and started to aim it at the pins.

Carol: Actually, I have just made an *even more* amazing discovery. Even the people who started *this* conversation just two minutes ago don't exist now. In fact, because we are changing all the time, *even the person that started this sentence is not the same person as the person now finishing it.* In fact . . .

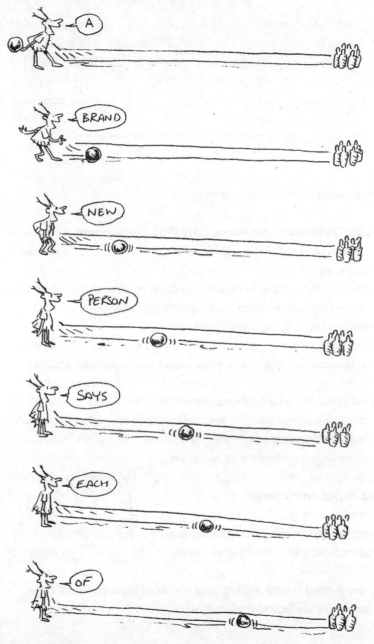

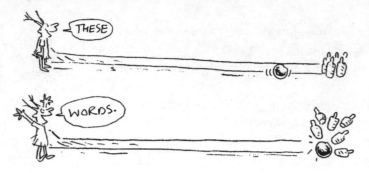

Now Aisha started to feel very unsure.

Aisha: That certainly *is* amazing, Carol. Actually, that seems just a bit *too* amazing. It's *downright ridiculous.* Haven't we made a mistake somewhere?

Carol: You're not going to go back to boring old common sense now, are you? Common sense can be wrong. It's been wrong before. You said so yourself. Don't you remember?

But Aisha now felt that they must have made a mistake somewhere.

Aisha: Yes, I know I did. But now I'm not sure we should be so quick to give up common sense. To say that neither of us existed one minute ago or even just a second ago *can't* be right, surely? We *must* have gone wrong somewhere along the way.

The toffee-apple incident

Aisha said she was hungry, so they both walked over to the toffee-apple stall and bought a toffee-apple each.

Aisha gulped her toffee-apple down straightaway. Carol stood holding hers while it cooled down a bit.

Suddenly, just as Carol was about to take her first bite, Aisha grabbed Carol's toffee-apple from out of her hands and bit a huge chunk out of it.

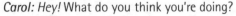

Carol: Hey! What do you think you're doing?
Aisha: What's the problem?
Carol: You just ate *half my toffee-apple*! That's the problem!
Aisha: No, I didn't.
Carol: Yes, you did! I just saw you!
Aisha: Actually, you're wrong.

Carol looked like she was about to explode, so Aisha thought she had better explain.

Aisha: Look, *I* didn't eat your toffee-apple. For if your argument is correct, *I* didn't exist two moments ago, did I?
Carol: Er . . . Well, no.
Aisha: Right. So the person who ate your toffee-apple was another person entirely.

Aisha gave Carol back the remains of the toffee-apple.

Aisha: And in any case, *you* haven't missed out on anything because the person who was about to bite into that toffee-apple before it was grabbed *wasn't you. You* have only existed for a tiny fraction of a second.
Carol: You're just being stupid!
Aisha: I'm just pointing out that if your argument is correct, then *I* haven't done anything wrong. So why are you blaming me?

Actually, Aisha is quite right. If Carol's argument is correct, then the person who stole the toffee-apple isn't the person now standing in front of her. In fact, the person who stole the toffee-apple *no longer exists*. But that can't be right, can it? Not even Carol *really* believed that the person who stole the toffee-apple had ceased to exist.

Two puzzles

There are two puzzles facing Aisha and Carol. The first puzzle is this. On the one hand, it seems obvious that you *can* jump into one and the same river twice over – that's the common sense view. On the other hand, it seems Aisha has an argument that shows that you *can't* jump into one and the same river twice. The river will have changed. So it won't be the same. And if it isn't the same river, then, amazingly, it seems there must be *two* rivers, not one.

There is a similar puzzle about how you could meet the same person twice. On the other hand, the common sense view is that you can meet the one and the same person twice over; on the other hand, Carol's argument seems to show that you can't.

How are we to solve these two puzzles? Should we give up the common sense view? Or is there something wrong with the arguments that seem to show that common sense is wrong? But if there *is* something wrong with these arguments, then *what is* wrong with them? What do you think?

Heraclitus

These puzzles are very old. They may even be two and a half thousand years old. Heraclitus, a philosopher who lived in Ancient Greece, is often supposed to have claimed that one cannot jump into the same river twice.

If that is what Heraclitus claimed, then perhaps it was an argument like Aisha's that led him to that conclusion.

I introduce myself

Let's get back to Aisha and Carol. They were now looking rather crossly at each other. Carol ate the rest of her toffee-apple in silence.

Now I also happened to be at the bowling alley that day. So I decided to walk over and say hello.

Me: I couldn't help overhearing what you two were saying. You know, about not being able to jump in the same river twice or meet the same person twice.

Carol: Sorry. We were shouting a bit, weren't we?

Me: Well, anyway, I'm afraid I'm not very good at bowling.

Aisha: Yes. We noticed you falling over earlier on.

Me: But I think I can help you with your philosophical puzzles.

Carol: How?

Me: Well, you seem to have got yourselves into a bit of a muddle. I think I can sort it out for you.

Aisha: What muddle? What do you mean?

Two sorts of sameness

I started to explain that the words 'the same' are actually used in two different ways. They are used to talk about two quite different sorts of sameness.

Me: To get unmuddled you need to distinguish between two sorts of sameness.

Aisha: I don't follow. What two sorts of sameness?

113

Me: Let me explain. Take a look at these two bowling balls.

I pointed to two bowling balls lying on the floor nearby.

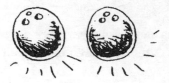

Me: Those two balls are not *the same ball*, are they? There are two balls in front of us, not one. Right?

Aisha: Of course.

Me: So here is a sense in which the balls are *not the same*: they are not *one and the same ball*. The number of balls is two, not one.

Aisha: I agree.

Me: Yet there are also many ways in which these two balls *are* the same. Both balls are round. Both are black. They weigh the same. They're both made out of the same kind of stuff. The two balls are the same in many of their *qualities*, aren't they?

Aisha: Yes. Of course.

Me: Now, when two things *share the same qualities* we philosophers say that they are *qualitatively* the same.

Aisha: I see.

Me: These two balls aren't qualitatively *exactly* the same in *all* their qualities, of course. There are many small differences between them, mostly too small for the eye to see. But there seems no reason why there couldn't be two balls that were exactly the same in all their qualities, does there?

Carol: No. I guess not.

Me: Now think. Suppose there are two balls that are qualitatively exactly the same in every respect. They share all the same qualities: both are black, they weigh the exact same amount. In fact, the two balls are exactly the same right down to the last atom.

These two balls are still not *one and the same ball*, are they?
There are still *two* balls, not one, aren't there?

Carol: Yes. There are two balls.

Me: Right. So here is a sense in which two balls that *are* qualitatively exactly the same are still *not* the same. They are not one and *the same* ball. We philosophers often say that they are not *numerically* the same, because the number of balls is two, not one.

Aisha: I see. You are saying there are two sorts of sameness: qualitative sameness and numerical sameness.

Me: Exactly!

Carol: You are saying that bowling balls can be qualitatively the same without being numerically the same. Even if two balls share all the same qualities, there are still *two* balls, not one.

Me: Precisely!

Numerical sameness without qualitative sameness

In fact, not only can you have things which are qualitatively the same but not numerically the same, you can also have things that are numerically the same but not qualitatively the same, as I now explained.

Me: Here's an example of numerical sameness without qualitative sameness. Suppose we take that black bowling ball and paint it white.

Once the ball has been painted it's not *qualitatively* the same as it was before, is it?

Carol: No. One of its qualities is different. It's white, not black.

Me: Exactly. So it is not *qualitatively* the same. But it is still *numerically* the same ball. There is just *one* ball, not two, despite the fact that it has changed colour.

Carol: Right.

Me: Here's another example. Suppose I see a tasty cake on a plate in front of me.

I pull off a small bit of cake and eat it.

Is it now the same cake that's sitting on the plate in front of me?

Carol: The cake is and isn't the same. It's *numerically* the same cake. But the cake isn't *qualitatively* exactly the same as it was before. It weighs a bit less and it's a slightly different shape: it has a bite out of it.

Me: That's right! The cake is another example of something being numerically the same but not qualitatively the same. Just because I have taken a bite out of the cake doesn't mean the cake now sitting in front of me isn't *numerically* the same cake that was sitting there before.

Aisha: I see.

Where did Aisha go wrong?

I now explained the problem with Aisha's argument.

Aisha argued like this.

WHEN YOU JUMP IN THE SECOND TIME, THE RIVER WILL HAVE CHANGED. SO IT WON'T BE THE SAME. BUT IF IT'S NOT THE SAME RIVER, THEN THERE ARE TWO RIVERS THAT YOU JUMP INTO, NOT ONE.

Can you now see the problem with this argument? Aisha starts by pointing out, quite correctly, that the river you jump into the second time won't be *qualitatively* exactly the same as it was before. For it is of course true that between jumping in each time the river will have changed qualitatively in some respects: things will have moved about, the water will have flowed along, and so on. Of course, this is hardly an amazing philosophical discovery, is it? It's just a pretty obvious and rather boring fact about rivers.

On the other hand, the claim that you can't jump into numerically the same river twice is a much more exciting claim. It is the claim that Aisha ends up making. She ends up saying that there are two rivers that you jump into, not one. It certainly would be amazing if Aisha could show that you can't jump into numerically the same river twice.

The problem is, of course, that Aisha has shown no such thing. Aisha's argument is a bad argument. It only looks convincing while we fail to notice that Aisha is using the words 'the same' in two different ways. Yes, the river won't be qualitatively exactly the same as it was before. But just because the river is not qualitatively the same as it was before does not mean it's not numerically one and the same river.

Of course, Carol's argument that you cannot meet one and the same person twice is also a bad argument and for exactly the same reason.

The solutions to the puzzles

So between us we solved the two puzzles.

The first puzzle was this. On the one hand, common sense says that you can jump into one and the same river twice. On the other hand, Aisha has an argument that seems to show that you can't jump into one and the same river twice: there must be two rivers, not one. We either had to find something wrong with Aisha's argument or else give up the common sense view.

We can now see that here is one philosophical puzzle that does have a solution. There is something wrong with Aisha's argument. So we can stick with the common sense view after all – at least until someone comes up with a better argument than Aisha's.

Of course, Carol's puzzle about how one could meet one and the same person twice is also solved in much the same way.

Tripped up by words

After I had explained to Aisha and Carol where they had gone wrong, we all bought milk shakes.

Carol now felt quite relieved. The two puzzles had really been starting to annoy her. But Aisha felt slightly disappointed.

Carol: But that means that neither of us had *really* made an amazing philosophical discovery after all, doesn't it?

Me: Yes. I'm afraid so.

Aisha: I thought I was a philosophical genius. But it turns out I was just confused!

Me: That's right. You were *tricked by language.* Sometimes, when it seems to us that we have made an amazing philosophical discovery or that we face a difficult philosophical puzzle, all that's really happened is that we have been tripped up by words.

Aisha: How were we tripped up?

Me: Well, you didn't pay enough attention to how certain words are *used.* You overlooked the fact that the expression 'the same' is used in more than one way.

Carol: I see. I heard Aisha use the words 'the same' and didn't notice she was using them differently each time.

Me: That's right. Aisha started off by saying that the river isn't qualitatively 'the same', but then ended up by saying that therefore the river isn't numerically 'the same'. Once you spotted that Aisha was using the words 'the same' in these two different ways, you saw that her argument didn't work.

A moral

There's an interesting moral to my story about Aisha and Carol. The moral is this. Sometimes, when it seems to us that we have made an amazing philosophical discovery or that we face a difficult philosophical puzzle, all that's really happened is that we have been tricked by language.

Of course, I'm not saying that *all* amazing philosophical 'discoveries' are really just a result of our having been tricked by language. But whenever you come across such a philosophical 'discovery' it's always worth bearing in mind that you *might* have been tricked by language.

Wittgenstein's philosophy

Actually, a very famous philosopher, Ludwig Wittgenstein, argued that *all* philosophical puzzles are a result of our having been tricked by language. According to Wittgenstein, what always leads us into philosophical trouble is the fact that we overlook differences in the  way that language is used. He argued that the way to remove any philosophical puzzle is to look closely at these differences in use.

Our two puzzles about jumping in the same river and meeting the same person certainly fit Wittgenstein's view about philosophy. We've now seen that both resulted from our being tricked by language. In each case we overlooked the fact that the expression 'the same' was being used in two different ways.

That's what caused all the trouble. Once we saw that the expression 'the same' was being used in two different ways, the puzzles disappeared.

But is Wittgenstein right to say that *all* philosophical puzzles are a result of our overlooking differences in the way words and other signs are used? Is he right to say that the way to remove *any* philosophical puzzle is to look closely at the different ways in which language is being used? That is something that philosophers disagree strongly about.

What do you think?

File 6

Where do right and wrong come from?

Horrible Harriet
Meet Harriet.

Harriet is a schoolgirl. But she's
not a very nice schoolgirl. She hits
other schoolchildren and steals their
lunch money.

She tears up library books and breaks the other children's
bikes. In fact, Harriet makes the other pupils' lives quite miserable.

Murderous Murphy
Of course, we all do things that are wrong. Often we feel guilty
about the bad things we have done. We feel that we should try
to be better people than we are. Certainly there are many things
that I have done that I feel pretty guilty about and that I wish I
hadn't done. And I am sure the same is true of you, too. No one
is perfect.

While many of the things that Harriet has done are wrong, there are things that are worse. Take Murphy, for example. Murphy is a cowboy. He is also a murderer. Murphy shoots and kills defenceless travellers so he can steal their money. Here's Murphy killing some poor unarmed cowboy who was on his way back home to his family.

Killing another person is of course considered to be one of the very worst things that a person can do.

Morality

By saying that some of the things that Harriet and Murphy have done are wrong I am talking about the morality of what they did. Harriet and Murphy ought not to have done what they did.

Of course, morality is not just about what we ought not to do. It is also about what we ought to do. It is about doing the right thing. Suppose Mr Black borrows Mr Brown's Big Bouncer.

But while Mr Black is riding on the Big Bouncer, he gets a bit carried away and punctures it.

123

What should Mr Black do? He thinks about throwing the Big Bouncer back into Mr Brown's garden when Mr Brown isn't looking and running off before he finds out. But Mr Black does the right thing. He admits to Mr Brown that he punctured the Big Bouncer. He agrees to fix it up.

Repaying debts, helping people in trouble, telling the truth – these are other examples of doing the right thing.

When we talk about morality – about right and wrong – we are talking about how we ought to live our lives. Most of us feel that it is morally wrong to lie, cheat, steal and kill. We feel we ought to be honest and trustworthy. We feel we ought to treat other people with respect.

Morality and the law

It is important not to get morality – right and wrong – muddled up with the law. Of course, morality and the law do often coincide. For example, stealing and killing are both morally wrong. They are also both against the law. But morality and the law *need* not coincide.

Take the *apartheid* laws in South Africa not so long ago. These laws separated black people from white people. They treated black people as second-class citizens. Black people weren't allowed to vote, for example. They were only allowed to live in certain poor, run-down areas. Many things in South Africa were for whites only.

But while it might have been against the law for black people to live in certain areas or use certain things, it wasn't *morally wrong* for them to do so. In fact, in South Africa it was the *law* that was wrong. So just because something is illegal doesn't mean it is wrong.

There are also things that are morally wrong that aren't against any law. For example, suppose Toby, a handsome and greedy young man, is told by one of his friends at a party that the sick-looking woman over there is very ill and will soon die.

Toby is also told that the woman is a bit dim, but very nice and immensely rich. And she has no living relatives. So, despite actually finding the woman rather ugly and dull, Toby spends the evening pretending to find her fascinating and beautiful. Why? Because Toby wants to trick the woman into marrying him. He wants to trick her into leaving him all her money.

Now, most people would say that Toby's behaviour is morally very wrong indeed.

But of course, what Toby is doing isn't *illegal*. Even if Toby did manage to trick the woman into marrying him, he wouldn't have broken any law. So what's morally wrong isn't always illegal.

Is it always wrong to kill?

We all think that killing is wrong. But is killing *anything* wrong? What about a sheep, a flea or a blade of grass? Of course, most people would say that there's nothing wrong with killing these sorts of thing. They would say that it is only other people that we shouldn't kill.

But is it *always* wrong to kill another person? Think about this case. Suppose you are a rancher in the old Wild West. Murderous Murphy breaks into your house. He dusts himself down, points his two six shooters at you and your family, and says that he is going to kill the lot of you and steal all your money.

Suppose you have a gun hidden in your hand. And suppose the only way to stop Murderous Murphy killing you all is to shoot him dead. What would you do? I'm sure you would say that you would shoot Murderous Murphy dead. In fact, I'm sure you would say that that was the *right* thing to do.

126

So it seems it isn't always wrong to kill another person. While we all agree that killing another person is wrong, most of us don't mean that it is always, in every case, wrong. We mean only that generally speaking killing is wrong. There are exceptions.

It seems there are also exceptions to other moral principles. Take, for example the moral principle that it is wrong to lie. If Murphy asked you if there was anyone else worth robbing living nearby and you knew that there was, would it be wrong to lie to him? I don't think so.

Perhaps you can think of other moral principles to which there are exceptions. For example, are there cases in which it wouldn't be wrong to steal?

Where does morality come from?

We have been talking about morality, about right and wrong. Now we come to my big philosophical question. My question is: *where does morality come from?* People give a number of different answers to this question. We are going to look at three of them.

One answer is: *morality comes from us. We* are the source of morality, of right and wrong. Our description of some things as 'right' and others as 'wrong' does no more than reflect how we think or feel about them. Things aren't right or wrong independently of what we might happen to think or feel about them.

Another quite different answer to the question: where does morality come from? is: *morality comes from God*. It is God who lays down what is right and what is wrong. So even if none of us felt that what someone did is wrong, it would *still* be wrong if God says it's wrong.

A third answer to the question: where does morality come from? is: *things are right or wrong anyway*, whatever we might happen to think or feel about them or even what God might happen to think or feel about them.

What do you think?

Which of these three answers would you give? Do you think that morality reflects only how we think or feel about things? Or do you think that morality comes from God? Or do you think that things are right or wrong *anyway*, whatever we or even God might happen to think or feel about them? Let's take a closer look at these three answers to see if we can figure out which (if any) answer is correct.

Let's start with the claim that *morality comes from us*.

Answer number 1: morality comes from us

How could morality come from us? Here are two famous philosophical theories both of which say that morality comes from us.

Morality comes from us: the Feelings Theory

Suppose that Murderous Murphy is drinking at a bar. Another cowboy arrives and orders a beer. Murphy notices that this other cowboy is unarmed. Murphy also notices that the other cowboy has a lot of money in his wallet.

So when the other cowboy finishes his beer and rides off into the desert, Murphy secretly follows him. Then, when Murphy is quite sure no one is watching, he sneaks up behind the other cowboy and shoots him in the back.

Murphy then takes the money and rides off, leaving the cowboy to die in the sand.

Now suppose I see Murphy shooting that poor unarmed cowboy in the back. I say 'What Murphy is doing is wrong!'

WHAT MURPHY IS DOING IS WRONG.

According to what I shall call the Feelings Theory, when I say 'What Murphy is doing is wrong!' I am just saying that I have certain feelings about what Murphy is doing. I am making a claim about myself. I am saying that I disapprove of what Murphy is doing.

This means that if I do disapprove, then what I say is true: Murphy is doing something wrong.

Similarly, if I see someone repaying a debt and I say 'That person is doing something right', then I am saying that I approve of what they are doing.

As you can see, according to the Feelings Theory, morality comes from us. We make things right or wrong by approving or disapproving of them.

Morality comes from us: the Boo-Hoorah Theory

Here's another theory that also says that morality comes from us. Philosophers often call this theory the *Boo-Hoorah Theory*.

As we have just seen, according to the Feelings Theory, when I say that something is wrong I make a claim, a claim about how I feel. According to the *Boo-Hoorah Theory*, on the other hand, I don't make a *claim* about how I feel. I *express* how I feel. Let me explain the difference.

Suppose I am about to watch a pig race.

I bet £5 on Pink Flash at 10–1. So if Pink Flash wins, I win £50.

The race begins. Pink Flash is slow to start. Then one of the other pigs – Honking Harry – pushes Pink Flash over. I am upset about this. I yell, 'Boo to Honking Harry!' Then Pink Flash gets up. He catches up with the other pigs. Finally, with just metres to go, Pink Flash noses ahead. He wins!

I yell out, 'Hoorah for Pink Flash!'

Now, ask yourself, when I yell out 'Hoorah for Pink Flash!' is what I say *true or false*? Of course, it's *neither*. I am not saying something true. But neither am I saying something false. I am not making any sort of *claim*, not even a claim about how I feel.

So what *am* I doing, then, when I say 'Hoorah for Pink Flash!'? I am *expressing* how I feel. I am expressing my happiness. Similarly, when I yell, 'Boo to Honking Harry!' I am again expressing how I feel. I am expressing my disapproval of what Honking Harry did.

Now, according to the Boo-Hoorah Theory, something similar happens when I see Murphy shoot the other cowboy and I say 'What Murphy is doing is wrong!' When I say 'What Murphy is doing is wrong!' it's as if I yell 'Boo to what Murphy is doing!' I am expressing my disapproval of what Murphy is doing.

Similarly, when I say, 'Repaying one's debts is right,' it's as if I am yelling, 'Hoorah for repaying one's debts!' I am expressing my approval of repaying one's debts. In each case I am not making a *claim* about how I feel. I'm just *expressing* how I feel.

So according to the Boo-Hoorah Theory, it's *neither true nor false* that what Murphy is doing is wrong. Indeed, according to the Boo-Hoorah Theory, there is *no fact of the matter* about whether what Murphy is doing is wrong (any more than there's a fact of the matter about whether Hoorah for Pink Flash).

The Vargs

We have just looked at two theories both of which say that morality comes from us: morality does no more than reflect how we *feel* about things. What do you think about these two theories? Is either theory any good?

Like most philosophers nowadays, I have worries about both theories. In order to explain one of my worries, I shall tell you about the Vargs.

This is Planet Varg, where the Vargs live.

The Vargs are intelligent beings like ourselves. And by an amazing coincidence they also speak English. They even talk about things being 'right' and 'wrong'.

But Vargs feel quite differently about *what* is right and wrong. Their most basic moral principle is: *always look after number one!* All Vargs feel very strongly that each Varg ought, as far as possible, to try to get what it wants, even at the expense of other Vargs. So they believe it is right to steal and cheat. In fact, they even believe it is right for one Varg to kill another if by so doing it can get something it wants (this doesn't mean Vargs go round stealing, cheating and killing all the time, of course: they only cheat, steal and kill if they think they can get away with it).

Because Vargs feel that each Varg should always look after itself even at the expense of other Vargs, they feel that charity is wrong. In fact, if ever a Varg feels like being charitable it soon starts feeling guilty.

Some Vargs are even religious: they believe in a god called *Vargy* from whom they suppose their morality comes. On Sunday some Vargs go to Varg-church where they hear sermons on the virtues of selfishness.

Why do I mention the Vargs? Because the possibility of creatures like the Vargs raises a problem for both the Feelings Theory and the Boo-Hoorah Theory.

A problem with the Feelings Theory

Why is the possibility of creatures like the Vargs a problem for the Feelings Theory? The Feelings Theory says that when I say 'What Murphy is doing is wrong!' I make a claim. I claim that I disapprove of what Murphy is doing. As I do disapprove, what I say is true: Murphy *is* doing something wrong.

But of course, a Varg would say 'What Murphy is doing is right!' According to the Feelings Theory, when a Varg says this, it claims that it approves of what Murphy is doing. So, as it does approve, what the Varg says is true too. We are both right! So we can happily agree with each other!

But this can't be correct, can it? For surely, when I say 'What Murphy is doing is wrong!' and the Varg says 'What Murphy is doing is right!' we are *contradicting* each other. Obviously, we can't *both* be right. As we are contradicting each other, the Feelings Theory must be false.

A problem with the Boo–Hoorah Theory

Why are the Vargs a problem for the Boo-Hoorah Theory?

According to the Boo-Hoorah Theory, when I say 'What Murphy is doing is wrong!' I don't make a claim. I merely *express* how I feel. It's as if I yell 'Boo to what Murphy is doing!' Similarly, when a Varg says 'What Murphy is doing is right!' it doesn't make a claim either. It merely expresses how it feels.

Now, according to the Boo-Hoorah Theory, which of us – the Varg or me – is right about what Murphy is doing? Neither! There is no fact of the matter as to which of us is correct! According to the Boo-Hoorah Theory, what I say is no more 'true' than is what the Varg says.

134

But isn't there a problem here for the Boo-Hoorah Theory? For surely, when I say 'What Murphy is doing is wrong!' I don't merely express how I feel. I *do* make a claim. Indeed, I suppose that what I say is *true* and what the Varg says is *false*. I suppose there is a fact of the matter about whether or not killing is wrong. Indeed, I suppose that the Varg is *mistaken* about this fact of the matter.

But if this is right – if when I say 'What Murphy is doing is wrong!' I do make a claim, a claim that is true – then the Boo-Hoorah Theory must be wrong too.

In fact, when you start to think about it, isn't it clear that morality can't come from us? For surely, it's a fact that killing is wrong *anyway*, whatever we or the Vargs might happen to feel about killing. Surely, even if we happened to agree with the Vargs that there is nothing wrong with killing, as a matter of fact killing would *still* be wrong, wouldn't it? But how can this be?

Answer number 2: morality comes from God

We are looking at the question: where does morality come from? So far we have looked at the answer: *morality comes from us*. But it seems that this answer cannot be right. So let's now turn to a different answer.

According to many people, the reason killing is wrong *anyway*, whatever we might have to say about it, is that *God* says it's wrong. Killing is wrong because God disapproves of it.

Morality comes from God.

KILLING IS WRONG.

How do we find out about right and wrong?

So how do we find out what God disapproves of? Many would say: by looking to religion and religious books such as the Bible or the Koran. For example, the Old Testament of the Bible contains the Ten Commandments, a list of ten dos and don'ts which God is supposed to have carved on to two stone tablets for Moses.

One of these Ten Commandments is, of course: Thou shalt not kill.

The Morality-Comes-From-God Argument

So does morality come from God? Are things right or wrong simply because God says so?

I heard a man talking on the radio the other day. This man laid down a challenge to people who don't believe in God. Surely, he argued, if there is no God, then there can be no real morality. If you believe in morality, then you have to believe in God too. Here's the man's argument:

> IF THERE IS NO GOD TO DECIDE WHAT IS RIGHT OR WRONG, THEN WHAT IS RIGHT AND WRONG MUST BE DECIDED BY US. BUT REAL MORALITY ISN'T SOMETHING THAT WE CAN DECIDE. THERE'S AN INDEPENDENT FACT OF THE MATTER ABOUT WHAT'S RIGHT AND WRONG. SURELY IT'S WRONG TO KILL ANYWAY, NO MATTER WHAT WE HAPPEN TO SAY OR FEEL ABOUT IT. AND IF KILLING IS WRONG ANYWAY, THEN THAT CAN ONLY BE BECAUSE THERE'S A GOD WHO SAYS THAT KILLING IS WRONG. MORALITY MUST COME FROM GOD. SO IF YOU BELIEVE IN MORALITY, YOU HAVE TO BELIEVE IN GOD TOO.

Let's call this the Morality-Must-Come-From-God Argument. The Morality-Must-Come-From-God Argument is certainly a very popular argument. I have heard much the same argument from many different people. But is the argument any good?

Suppose God had said killing is right . . .

In fact, the Morality-Must-Come-From-God Argument isn't any good, as I shall now explain.

The man on the radio claimed that killing is wrong *because* God says it is wrong. God actually *makes* killing wrong by saying that it is wrong.

But this means that *if God had instead said that killing is right, then it would be.* But this can't be right, can it? Ask yourself: suppose God had said killing is right, would it have been right?

Surely not. Surely, even if God had said that we *ought* to kill, it would still be wrong to go round murdering people. Not even God can make killing other people right.

The man on the radio argued like this: morality can't come from us, for *we* can't make killing right just by saying so. What the man on the radio failed to notice is that exactly the same is true of God. Killing is also wrong whatever God might have to say about it. So, by the same argument, morality can't come from God either.

Answer number 3: things are right or wrong anyway

We are looking at the question: Where does morality come
from? We have now looked at two different answers to this
question. The first answer was: morality comes from us. The
second answer was: morality comes from God. Neither of these
answers seems to be correct. So let's now turn to the third of the
three answers we are going to look at. The third answer is: *things
are right or wrong anyway*, whatever we or even God might happen
to say about them.

Objective moral facts

Those who say that killing is wrong anyway, whatever we or
even God might have to say about it, are saying
that it is an *objective fact* that killing is wrong.

What is an *objective fact*? Here's an example.
Suppose I believe that there is a pen on the
table behind me.

My belief may be true or it may be false.
Suppose my belief is true. What *makes* it true is
a certain corresponding *fact*: the fact that there
is a pen back there on the table.

MY BELIEF IS TRUE

MY BELIEF IS FALSE

And this fact seems to be an *objective* fact. What I mean is: it's a fact that there's a pen on the table whether or not I or anyone else knows there's a pen on the table, and no matter what I or anyone else might feel about there being a pen on the table. That there's a pen on the table is a fact 'out there' in the world, a fact that is there anyway, whatever anyone might think or feel about it.

Now you might suppose that it's also an objective fact that what Murderous Murphy did is wrong.

I believe that what Murphy did is wrong. And you might suppose that my belief is made true by a corresponding fact: the fact that what Murphy did *is* wrong. You might also suppose that this fact is an *objective* fact: it's out there *anyway*, no matter what I or anyone else (including even God) might think or feel about it. So, even if no one thought that what Murphy did was wrong, it *would still* be wrong.

If there are objective moral facts, then the right answer to the question: where does morality come from? is: *not from us, or from God or from anyone else for that matter.* Morality is 'out there': it's independent of *all* of us.

And this does seem correct, doesn't it? For surely, even if we and the Vargs and God had all decided that there is nothing wrong with killing . . .

KILLING IS RIGHT!

. . . as a matter of fact killing *would* still be wrong, wouldn't it? So it seems that there really are objective moral facts.

How do we detect wrongness?

Still, there are problems with the theory that there are objective moral facts. One very famous problem is: how do we *discover* these facts? Or, to put it another way, how do we *detect* this property – wrongness – that acts of killing or stealing are supposed to have?

In order to explain this problem I shall tell you a story. The story is about two Martian visitors to the Earth.

The Martian visitors

One day, two Martians – Flib and Flob – arrive in my back garden.

Flib and Flob are quite similar

to us. They also have eyes and ears, a mouth and nose, two arms and two legs.

Flib and Flob offer to give me a trip round town in their flying saucer. So we get in and take off. As we fly around we look out of the window at the town below us.

Flib and Flob make the flying saucer invisible so that no one can see us as we skim over the rooftops. We circle round the town and look at the pigeons. Then, as we pass over a narrow street on the outskirts of town, I notice something. I see a young man trying to snatch the purse of a woman who is walking home from the shops. I quickly point this out to the Martians.

'Look!' I say. 'That man is trying to steal that woman's purse. That's wrong!'

But Flib and Flob just look puzzled. Flob says: 'Ah, yes. Wrong. We do not understand your Earthling talk of right and wrong. Please show us the wrongness.'

Where is the wrongness?

'Look!' I say, pointing down at the robber. 'Can't you *see* that this man is doing something wrong?'

But Flib and Flob *can't* see the wrongness of what he is doing.

'No,' replies Flob. 'Our eyes are just like your eyes. But we find your talk of *seeing wrongness* very strange. We just can't see this thing you Earth people call wrongness. Where is the wrongness, please?'

The Martians stare at me, waiting for a reply. I'm not quite sure what they are getting at. So Flob continues.

'We have five senses just like you Earthlings. We too can see and hear. We too can smell and taste things. And we have a sense of touch just like yours. But our five senses do not allow us to detect this thing you call *wrongness*. And we find this very mysterious. What we want to know is: *where* is the wrongness? Please point it out to us. Please explain to us how you humans manage to detect it. By which of your senses do you perceive it?'

Now I begin to see what Flib and Flob are getting at. Certainly, wrongness doesn't seem to be observable in the way that, say, redness is. Redness is something that you can see (you can see the redness of an apple, for example). Wrongness, on the other hand, seems to be invisible.

The DIRS scanner
I look down at the man struggling to pull the woman's purse from her hands. I have to admit, I'm not sure *how* I detect the wrongness of what he is doing. Still, I feel quite sure that the man is doing something wrong. So I have another go at explaining to the Martians the wrongness of what the robber is doing.

'Look! That man is stealing that woman's purse! You can see that, can't you?'

Flob says that they can certainly see that.

'Well, then, stealing is wrong, isn't it?'

Flib and Flob don't understand. Flib asks: 'But where is the wrongness? This further thing you call wrongness is not detected by us when we observe people stealing. Nor does the wrongness show up on any of our scanning equipment.'

Flib points to a huge, gun-like object in the corner of their room.

'This is the DIRS — the Detect-all Infinite Resolution Scanner. It is the most powerful and all-encompassing scanner in the whole universe. There is nothing in the natural world that the DIRS can't detect! But not even the DIRS can detect this thing you call wrongness. We will show you.'

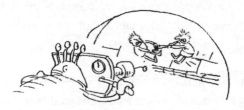

Flib and Flob aim the DIRS towards the robbery taking place on the street.

They press a red button. There is a slight humming noise as the DIRS begins to scan what is going on down below.

'See?' says Flib, pointing at the many dials on the side of the DIRS. 'We just aren't picking up any wrongness. Not a sausage!'

'Please show us the wrongness,' continues Flib. 'We are scientists. We want knowledge. We want a complete theory of the universe. We do not want to miss anything out. But this thing you call wrongness continues to evade us.'

'But the woman is upset . . .'
I decide to have another go at explaining about wrongness. 'Look. That woman down there is very upset. That purse contains all her money. If she loses her purse, then she won't be able to buy things that she needs from the shop. Can't you see how sad and afraid she is?'

'Oh, we know all about that,' says Flib. 'We already know all about those facts: the fact that the man is stealing the woman's money; the fact that that is all the money she has, the fact that the man is making her unhappy and frightened. But you seem to be able to detect an *extra* fact: the fact that what the man is doing is *wrong*. If this extra fact is out there, please point it out to us. We can find no trace of it.'

'Is' facts and 'ought' facts
I scratch my head. 'What do you mean by saying that the fact that what the man is doing is wrong is an *extra* fact?'

Flob explains as follows. 'Look, by saying that someone is doing something *wrong*, you Earthlings mean that they *ought not to* do it, don't you?'

'Yes, that's quite correct.'

'Well, then,' continues Flob. 'The fact that someone is doing something wrong is an entirely different sort of fact to the facts we can observe. Just like you, we *can* observe what *is* the case. We can observe that this man *is* stealing the purse. We can observe that the woman *is* upset. And so on.'

I nod. So Flob continues.

'But the fact that the man down there is doing something wrong is clearly an extra fact on top of all these facts about what is the case. For by saying that the man is doing something wrong you are clearly saying *more* than what he is doing. You are saying that he *ought not to be* doing what he is doing. So you are no longer just talking about what *is* the case.'

I have to agree with Flob. The fact that the man is doing something wrong does indeed seem to be an extra fact on top of all the facts about what is the case.

'So you see,' continues Flob. 'We can observe only what is the case. And all of the facts about what is the case leave entirely open the question of whether that man *ought* or *ought not* to be doing what he's doing. So please explain to us how you detect the extra fact that he *ought not to be* doing what he's doing. How do you detect the fact that what he is doing is *wrong*?'

So how do I detect the wrongness?

I look down. The man is still down there struggling to steal the woman's purse. I look at Flib and Flob. They raise their green eyebrows and look disappointed.

'I'm sorry,' I say. 'I just don't know *how* I detect the wrongness. I don't seem to be able to see it or feel it or taste it or smell it or touch it. But *somehow* I know it's out there.'

The wrongness detector

A famous philosopher called G.E. Moore tried to solve the problem of explaining how we detect wrongness. He supposed that we have a sort of *extra* sense – a sixth sense – on top of our other five. We can't see, hear, smell, touch or taste wrongness. But we *can* detect it using this sixth sense. I shall call this extra sense our *wrongness detector*.

You might think of your wrongness detector as being a bit like an antenna. Just as sailors can use a radio antenna to detect a submarine hidden beneath the waves, so your wrongness detector allows you to detect the wrongness of what someone is doing despite the fact that you can't detect the wrongness with your other senses.

So I detect the wrongness of what the thief down in the street is doing by using my wrongness detector. Why can't Flib and Flob detect the wrongness of what the man is doing? Because they don't have a wrongness detector, of course.

Has Moore solved the problem of explaining how we detect wrongness? No. Not really. Moore has simply said that by some strange mechanism – a wrongness detector – we do manage to detect wrongness. But it remains utterly mysterious how this wrongness detector is supposed to work. So we are still left with a big mystery.

Back to where we started?

We have been examining the view that there are objective moral facts. On the view that there are objective moral facts, wrongness is 'out there'. It's a property that acts of stealing have *anyway*, whatever anyone (including even God Himself) might happen to think or feel about stealing.

We have also seen that there's *a big problem* with this view. If wrongness really were 'out there', then it seems it would be a very *weird*, *undetectable* sort of property. In fact, it seems that if wrongness really were 'out there' then we wouldn't be able to know about it.

So, as I *can* detect when someone is doing something wrong, it seems it can't be an objective fact that what they are doing is wrong.

A big advantage of the view that morality comes from us

Indeed, it seems we are being forced back to where we started. It seems we are being forced back to the position that morality must *come from us* after all. For a really big advantage of the view that morality comes from us is that it very neatly explains why Flib and Flob can't detect the wrongness of what the robber is doing.

Take the Boo-Hoorah Theory, for example. It clearly explains why Flib and Flob can't find the fact that makes what I say true when I say 'That man is doing something wrong!' For according to the Boo-Hoorah Theory, I am just *expressing* how I feel. It's as if I were shouting 'Boo to what that man is doing!' I don't make any claim at all. So what I say is *neither true or false*.

THE COMPLETE PHILOSOPHY FILES

But that means that Flib and Flob are on *a wild goose chase*. They are desperately looking for the 'fact' that makes what I say 'true'.

But of course, *there is no such fact*.

The Feelings Theory also neatly explains why Flib and Flob can't find the fact that makes what I say true. According to the Feelings Theory, when I say to Flib and Flob: 'That man is doing something wrong!' what I say is true. Indeed, what I say is made true by a fact. But of course, what I say is *not* made true by an objective moral fact. It's not made true by a fact about how things are 'out there' on the other side of the window. Rather, the fact that makes what I say true is *a fact about me* – the fact that I disapprove of what the man is doing.

That's why Flib and Flob can't find the fact that makes what I say true: they are looking in the wrong place. They're looking *out of the window*. In order to find the fact that makes what I say true, Flib and Flob must stop looking out of the window. They must turn around and examine *me*.

The big picture

We have taken quite a long and complicated philosophical journey. So you may now be feeling a bit lost. Let's take a step back to see where we've been. Let's get the big picture.

The big philosophical question we have been looking at is this: *where does morality come from?* Does morality *come from us*? Or does it *come from God*? Or are there *objective moral facts*? That is, are things right or wrong *anyway*, independently of whatever we or God or anyone else might have to say about it?

In trying to answer this question we have run up against a problem – a very famous philosophical problem. The problem is that we find ourselves being pulled in two directions at once. On

148

the one hand, it seems that there must be objective moral facts. But, on the other hand, it seems that there can't be objective moral facts.

Why must there be objective moral facts? Because it seems that when we say 'Killing is wrong', we make a claim made true by a fact; the fact that killing really is wrong. And this fact is an *objective fact*: killing is surely wrong *anyway*, whatever we or the Vargs or even God might happen to think about killing. So even if we, the Vargs and God all felt that killing was right . . .

KILLING IS RIGHT!

. . . killing would *still* be wrong.

Why *can't* there be objective moral facts? Well, as Flib and Flob pointed out, if wrongness is 'out there' – if wrongness is a property that killing has *anyway*, whatever anyone might happen to think about killing – then it seems we come up against an unsolvable mystery: how do we *detect* this property? It seems we *couldn't* detect it. In which case we couldn't know that killing is wrong. So, as we *do* know that killing is wrong, it seems it can't be an objective moral fact that killing is wrong.

How do we solve this puzzle? That is something that philosophers are still arguing about even today. I must admit, I am confused. I'm just not sure where morality comes from. What do you think?

File 7

What is the mind?

My mind
This is me.

And this is a brick.

One important difference between me and the brick is this:
unlike the brick, I have a mind.

So what goes on in my
mind? Well, having a typical
human mind means that I
can *have experiences*. For example, I can enjoy the taste of
marmalade and the smell of
fresh coffee.

I can also *make decisions*. For
example I can decide to go
for a walk.

151

Having a typical human mind means I can also *feel sensations* like pain, and *work things out* (such as the answers to a crossword puzzle).

I can also *remember things*, *feel emotions* and *have beliefs* (such as my belief that it is going to rain).

A brick, on the other hand, can do none of these things.

Bat minds

It's not just human beings that have minds, of course. Take bats, for example
It seem that bats have minds too. But it also
seems that a bat's mind must be very different from our own.

Bats use something called *echo-location* to find their way about. The bat emits a very high-pitched squeaking noise. This noise is so high-pitched that we humans cannot hear it.

This noise bounces back off the objects near the bat, producing an echo. The bat has very large, sensitive ears with which to hear this echo. The strength of the echo, the direction from which the echo comes, and the time it takes to return allow the bat to build up a picture of what's around it.

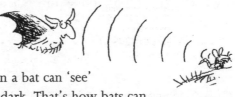

By using echo-location a bat can 'see' even when it is pitch dark. That's how bats can fly at night without bumping into anything.

I wonder what it must be like inside a bat's mind. How does the world seem to a bat when it 'sees' using echo-location? The bat's experience must be very strange indeed. It seems it must be quite unlike any experience that we can have.

The brain

I don't just have a mind. I also have a brain.

My brain is a rather sludgy, grey-coloured organ found in my head, right between my ears.

Atoms and molecules

The brain is of course a *physical object*. It's part of the physical universe. Just like every other physical object, my brain is made out of *physical matter*.

Physical matter is made up of tiny particles called *atoms*. These atoms group together to form slightly larger particles called *molecules*. Every physical object – be it your brain, a peanut, this piece of paper, a desk or even planet Earth – is made out of atoms and molecules.

Cells

A living body is made out of tiny parts called *cells*.

Your body is made out of many *billions* of cells. The cells out of which your brain and nervous system are made are called *neurones*. This is a neurone.

There are about a *million, million* neurones in your brain. That's about as many neurones as there are stars in our galaxy! Each of these neurones is in turn made out of atoms and molecules.

How my mind and brain interact

What does the brain do? Some Ancient Greeks thought the brain was simply an organ for cooling the blood (a bit like a car radiator cools water).

But of course, nowadays we know that the brain has a quite different purpose. We know that the brain is closely connected to the mind. We know that what happens in the brain affects what happens in the mind, and that what happens in the mind affects what happens in the brain.

Many drugs illustrate how what happens in the brain can affect what happens in the mind.

For example, by subtly
changing what's going on in
my brain, a pain-killing drug
can make my experience of
pain vanish.

Scientists have also discovered that by directly
stimulating the brain in different
ways they can produce certain sorts of experience in the mind,
such as visual experiences. For example, they have discovered
that by applying a tiny electrical current to an area at the back of
the brain they can cause a person to experience a flash of light.

So there's no doubt that what happens in the brain can affect
what happens in the mind. And the reverse is true, too. What
happens in the mind can affect what happens in the brain.

For example, a scientist will tell you that when you decide to
turn this page, something
happens in your brain. Your brain
sends electrical impulses down to
the muscles in your arm.
These impulses make the muscles
move, making your hand turn the
page . . .

. . . like that. That movement of your arm was caused by something that happened in your brain.

So scientists have shown that the mind and the brain are closely connected. Still, most of what goes on inside the brain remains a mystery. For the brain is *incredibly* complex. It is buzzing with chemical and electrical activity.

The mind is a private place

Here's a weird fact about minds: they seem to be *hidden* in a very peculiar way. Suppose I take a look at something bright purple: my bright purple pen, for example.

No one else can get inside my mind and have my experience of that colour along with me. Only I can have my experience.

Of course, other people may have experiences that are *just like* mine. If you look at my pen you will no doubt have a similar experience of its colour. But your experience is yours and my experience is mine.

In other words, it's as if my mind has a super-strong wall around it: a wall that prevents others from getting in.

All my experiences, thoughts, feelings and so on are locked away behind this wall.

My mind seems to be like a secret garden, a hidden place within which only I can roam.

Indeed, the inside of my mind seems to be hidden from others in a way that even the inside of my brain is not. Brain surgeons could X-ray my brain, of course.

They could even cut open my skull and look at what's going on in my brain. But it seems that not even a brain surgeon can get inside the realm of my mind. If they were to look inside my brain right now they wouldn't come across my experience of the colour of this pen. They wouldn't find anything bright purple. They would just find lots of sludgy grey stuff.

Exactly the same is true of the mind of a bat. It seems quite impossible for us to get inside a bat's mind and find out what it's like to be a bat. It seems that even if we knew absolutely everything there is to know about what is going on physically inside a bat's brain when it 'sees' an object using echo location, that *still* wouldn't tell us what the experience is actually like for *the bat*, from inside its mind. We still wouldn't know what it's like to experience the world as a bat does.

The big question: what is the mind?

Let's now take a look at my philosophical question for this chapter. My question is: *what is the mind?* What is this thing that is conscious, that thinks, that enjoys experiences, that feels happiness, anger and other emotions, that has hopes and fears, that makes decisions, and so on?

In this chapter we are going to look at two very different answers that philosophers have given to this question.

The first answer is: the mind is somehow *part of the physical world*. How could the mind be part of the physical world? Well, one obvious way would be if what goes on in your mind just *is* what goes on in your brain. Perhaps our thoughts, feelings, emotions, experiences, and so on are nothing more than certain physical processes taking place within our brains. Perhaps the mind just *is* the brain.

The second answer is: the mind is *separate from the physical world*. The mind may interact with the brain, but it is certainly not the same thing as the brain.

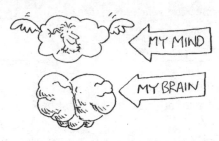

According to this second answer, our thoughts, feelings, emotions, experiences and so on are *something extra*: something in addition to the buzz of activity going on in our brains.

Which of these two answers do you think is more plausible?

Aisha and Kobir

Remember Aisha? Well, she recently met Kobir, a friend of ours. Kobir is a science student. He studies at the university.

Aisha and Kobir decided to go for a coffee in a local café. And, as you will soon discover, they ended up arguing about the mind. Kobir thought that the mind must be physical. But Aisha was convinced that the mind is something extra, something on top of what's going on physically.

Kobir: Mmmm. I needed this.

Aisha: Me too. I love coffee. So tell me, what have you been up to this morning?

Kobir: This morning I went to one of Dr Jones's lectures on the brain.

Aisha asked Kobir what that morning's lecture on the brain had been about.

Kobir: Today Dr Jones explained how all of our experiences of the world are caused by our sensory organs – our skin, eyes, nose, ears and tongue – sending electrical impulses up to our brains.

Aisha: Really?

Kobir: Yes. Here's an example. Take a sniff of this coffee. It smells good, doesn't it?

Aisha: Yes. It's great coffee.

Kobir: Now according to Dr Jones, the experience you have as you smell this coffee is caused by tiny little particles travelling from the coffee up your nose.

160

These particles come into contact with
cells on the inside of your nose.

Those cells then send electrical impulses
up to your brain.
That causes something to happen in your
brain. That's how you finally come to have
that experience you're now having.

Aisha: How interesting!

Kobir: Yes. It is, isn't it? It's fascinating to discover that all our experiences
are really just something physical happening in our brains.

Aisha: What? Now just hold on a minute. You're getting a bit carried
away!

Kobir looked surprised. Why was Aisha suddenly disagreeing
with what he was saying?

Kobir: What's the problem?

Aisha: Look. I know it's true that when I have this experience, something also happens in my brain.

Kobir: Yes, that's right.

Aisha: But then you said that my experience *is* something physical
happening in my brain, didn't you?

Kobir: Of course.

Aisha: Well, I don't believe *that*! Science may have shown that when we
have experiences, something also happens in our brains. In fact, it
seems clear that our minds and our brains interact. But that doesn't
prove that our experiences just *are* something happening in our
brains, does it?

161

Why Aisha thinks her experience can't be in her brain

Aisha is surely right to say that while science may have shown that whenever something happens in our minds something also happens in our brains, it doesn't follow that what happens in our minds just *is* what happens in our brains.

Still, is there any reason to suppose that Aisha's experience isn't something happening in her brain? Aisha thought there was.

Aisha: Actually, I think it is pretty obvious that my experience *can't* be anything happening in my brain.
Kobir: Why not?
Aisha: OK. Smell your coffee.

Aisha and Kobir both took a big sniff.

Aisha: Now, what's your experience *like*?
Kobir: What do you mean, what is it like?
Aisha: Focus your attention on the experience. There's something it is like to have that experience, isn't there? Something it's like *for you,* from *inside your mind.* So, tell me, *what* is it like?

Kobir took another sniff.

Kobir: Mmmm. It's difficult to describe. It's very pleasant. Sort of *sharp and tangy.*
Aisha: Yes, that's what mine's like, too.

Kobir: So what's your point?

Aisha: Well, if you were to look inside my brain right now while I'm having this experience you wouldn't find anything *sharp and tangy*, would you?

If you were to get inside my brain and examine it, you would just find lots of sludgy grey brain stuff. No matter how closely you observed what's going on in my brain, nothing sharp and tangy would show up, would it?

Kobir: I guess not.

Aisha: So, if my experience is sharp and tangy, but nothing in my brain is sharp and tangy, then my experience can't be anything in my brain, can it?

What do you think of Aisha's argument? Has Aisha shown that her experience isn't physical?

Do we have souls?

Kobir certainly wasn't convinced by Aisha's argument. In fact, he wasn't sure he understood what Aisha was suggesting.

Kobir: I don't follow. So what *is* your experience, then, if it isn't physical? Surely it *must* be physical. There is only the physical universe, after all.

But Aisha thought there had to be more than just the physical universe.

Aisha: I disagree. There's no way anything physical could have *this*, the sharp and tangy experience I'm having right now. There's no way it could actually *be conscious.* So, as I *do* have such experiences, as I *am* conscious, I can't be some physical thing, can I? I must be some other sort of thing.

Kobir: What sort of thing?

Aisha: I must be a *soul.*

Now Kobir was really confused. He asked Aisha what she meant by a 'soul'?

Aisha: A soul isn't part of the natural, physical universe that you scientists deal with. I'm not talking about a *physical* object, an object made out of *physical* matter, like a mountain, a lake, a peanut or a bowl of trifle. I'm talking about *some other sort of stuff entirely.* I'm talking about *non-physical* stuff. *Supernatural* stuff. *Soul* stuff!

Kobir: So you believe that you are not part of the physical universe? You – the thing that has conscious experiences, thoughts and feelings and so on – are a *soul?*

Aisha: Yes. That's right.

Kobir: And I have a soul too?

Aisha: Of course. We both have souls.

How does a soul experience smells?

Let's call Aisha's theory that each of us has a soul the *Soul Theory.*

According to Aisha, she has a physical body. But she herself is not something physical. She — the thing that has conscious experiences, the thing that thinks and feels — is a soul. This means that after her physical body has died and no longer exists Aisha can still carry on.

So how, according to the Soul Theory, does Aisha come to experience things in the physical world? How, for example, does Aisha come to experience the smell of the coffee in front of her?

Aisha agrees with Kobir that tiny particles from the coffee float up her nose. These particles then stimulate cells inside her nose — the cells that Kobir was talking about. The cells then send electrical impulses up to her brain.

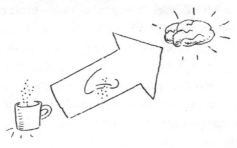

But, according to Aisha, Kobir is wrong to say that what happens in Aisha's brain is her experience. It's her soul that has the experience, not her brain.

So how does Aisha's brain cause her soul to have the experience? Well, according to Aisha, it's as if her brain had a little transmitter. This transmitter allows her brain to send a message on to her soul.

That's how Aisha's soul comes to experience the smell of the coffee.

Heaven and reincarnation

Many religious people believe in the Soul Theory, of course. Some even believe that after their physical bodies die their souls carry on. They go up to Heaven.

Others believe in *reincarnation*: they believe that when they die their souls pass on to a new physical

body (though it might be a non-human body: they could be reborn as a dog or a slug).

But though many people believe in the Soul Theory, it certainly is a lot to swallow. Even if you believe in the Soul Theory you have to admit: the claim that there's not just physical stuff, there's also some sort of supernatural, soul stuff as well certainly doesn't sound very *scientific*, does it?

A problem with the Soul Theory

Aisha got up and walked over to the cake counter. In front of her were two plates.

One plate had iced buns. The other had chocolate brownies. Aisha decided she wanted a chocolate brownie. So she put out her hand, put her fingers round one of the chocolate brownies and picked it up.

Then Aisha sat down next to Kobir again and started munching on her brownie.

Kobir: Honestly, Aisha. You talk such rubbish! There are no such things as souls. Souls are unscientific!

Aisha: Why?

Kobir: Look. Your body just moved. Your hand went out and picked up one of those chocolate brownies.

Aisha: Of course.

Kobir: Now, what *made* you hand move?

Aisha: Well, my hand was moved by the muscles in my arm. Those muscles were in turn moved by electrical impulses coming down from my brain.

Kobir: Yes. I agree. That is the scientific view. Your hand was made to move by *something that happened in your brain.*

Aisha: Yes.

Kobir: But I thought it was supposed to be your *soul* that made your hand move?

Aisha: It did. It made my hand move by making something happen in my brain. It's as if my brain had a little receiver that can receive messages sent from my soul.

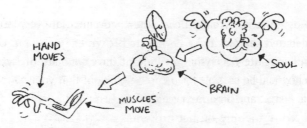

My soul made something happen in my brain. That made my muscles move. That made my hand grab the brownie.

Kobir: So what happened in your brain was made to happen by your *soul?*

Aisha: Yes. Of course.

Kobir: What happened in your brain wasn't made to happen by what's going on *physically?*

Aisha: No. Obviously not.

Kobir thought that he had now spotted a problem with Aisha's theory. He took a sip of coffee and started to explain the problem to Aisha.

Kobir: I think I've discovered a problem with your theory, Aisha. The brain is a part of the physical universe, isn't it?

Aisha: Of course.

Kobir: Well, it seems that what happens in the physical universe is always fixed in advance by how things are physically.

Aisha: How do you mean?

Kobir: Look. One minute before you picked up that brownie, you hadn't made any decision about whether to have a brownie or an iced bun, had you?

Aisha: No. I hadn't even noticed the brownies or the buns.

Kobir: Right. Yet it seems that if scientists knew absolutely everything there is to know about what was going on physically in this café one minute before you picked up that brownie . . .

Aisha: Absolutely everything? Down to the movement of every last atom in my brain?

Kobir: Yes, absolutely everything: if they did have *all* that information, then it would be possible for them to figure out that your hand would go out and pick up that brownie when it did.

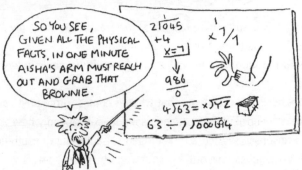

You see, what happens in your brain, the movement of your hand – *all* these physical events are fixed in advance by how things are *physically*. Here's another example: the fact that our two bodies walked into this café this morning was fixed in advance by how things were physically two hours ago, even before we decided to come to the café.

Aisha: And so . . . ?

Kobir: And so that means there's no possibility of something non-physical like a soul affecting what happens at the physical level. That means *your soul won't be able to have any influence on what your body does.*

Aisha scratched her head and looked puzzled.

Aisha: Why not?

Kobir: Look at it this way. Suppose that you had decided *not* to pick up a brownie. Suppose you had decided to pick up an iced bun instead. Your hand would have picked up that chocolate brownie *anyway*.

It would pick up the brownie because it would be *made* to by how things are physically.

Aisha: Ah. I see. You are saying that when it comes to the physical universe, everything that happens is made to happen by how things were previously. So there's no room left for anything non-physical to affect how things turn out. My soul won't be able to affect what my hand does.

Kobir: That's right. So, given you *can* make your hand do what you want it to do, it seems you can't be a soul. The Soul Theory must be wrong.

Aisha: Oh dear.

Kobir has just explained a very serious and very famous problem with the Soul Theory: if there were such things as souls, it seems they wouldn't be able to affect what our bodies do. Philosophers have tried a number of different ways of solving this problem. But I'm not sure any of their solutions really work. So perhaps, like Kobir, we should reject the Soul Theory.

A mystery

Someone who rejects the Soul Theory – who believes there's only *physical* stuff – is what's known as a *materialist*. According to materialists, there's just the natural, physical world. That means that I – the thing that has conscious experiences, that thinks, feels and so on – must somehow be *part* of the physical universe.

Still, there is a great mystery facing materialism. The mystery is this: just how could part of the physical universe come to have the spark of consciousness? How could a mere lump of physical matter feel sadness or pain? How could it have *this* – the experience I have when I smell the cup of coffee on the desk in front of me? How, simply by bringing atoms and molecules together in a particular way, can one make *one of these:* a mind? That is what materialists like Kobir have to explain.

Kobir's theory

Actually, Kobir didn't think there really was that much of a mystery to solve here. He now started to explain to Aisha his theory about the mind.

Kobir: I think that each different type of mental state is actually just a type of *brain state.*

Aisha: A brain state?

Kobir: Let me explain. The brain is a very complicated organ. It is made up of about a million million cells. These cells are called *neurones.* The neurones are woven together to form an incredibly complex web.

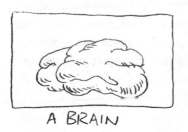

A BRAIN

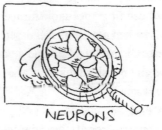

NEURONS

Aisha: But what have neurones got to do with consciousness? What have they to do with my experience of pain, for example?

Kobir: Well, when someone is in pain, their brain is in a certain *state.* Certain neurones are firing in their brain.

171

Aisha: I see.

Kobir: And it seems to me that for someone to be in pain *just is* for those neurones to be firing. Pain *just is* that particular brain state. The pain and the brain state are *one and the same thing.*

Aisha: I'm not sure I understand.

Kobir: Look, often we discover that what we thought were two different things are actually *one and the same thing,* don't we? For example, an explorer might discover that the mountain he can see from a particular jungle and the mountain he can see from a particular desert are actually *one and the same mountain.*

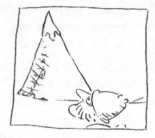 

The explorer hadn't realized up till that point that he had been looking at the very same mountain but from two different sides.

Aisha: Ah! I see. You are saying that just as the mountain the explorer had seen from the jungle turned out to be the very same mountain that he had seen from the desert, so pain may turn out to be a certain brain state. Pain and a brain state may also turn out to be one and the same thing.

Kobir: Exactly!

Aisha: And the same goes for all our other conscious experiences, too?

Kobir: Yes, that's right. The same goes for feeling happy, for experiencing the colour yellow, for experiencing a bitter taste, and so on. Each of these different experiences is actually just a brain state.

Aisha: So *this* – the experience I'm having right now as I smell this coffee – is just a brain state?

Kobir: Yes. That's right.

Let's call Kobir's theory that our experiences and so on are really just brain states the *Brain Theory*.

'But the pain is in my foot ...'

You might have the following worry about the Brain Theory. Surely, you might think, when I feel a pain in my foot, the pain is located in my foot. So it isn't in my brain, is it?

Is this a good objection to the Brain Theory? Perhaps not. Here's one way of defending the Brain Theory against this objection. Sometimes, when people have had their legs amputated, it seem to them that they can still feel their legs. In fact, they often report feeling pain in their feet. But of course, these people don't have feet any more. Their feet no longer exist.

In that case it can't be right to say that the pain these people feel is located in their feet. So where is their pain, then, if it isn't

in their feet? Well, these people wouldn't feel any pain if something wasn't happening in their brains, so an obvious suggestion to make is that their pain is in their brains. And if their pain is located in the brain, then presumably so is yours and mine.

Kobir's water example

Aisha now asked Kobir a question.

Aisha: OK. If pain is a brain state – if to be in pain is just for certain
neurones to be firing in the brain – then *which* brain state is it?

Kobir: I have to admit: I don't know. We scientists
haven't figured out which brain state pain is
just yet. But there is every reason to suppose
that we *will* find out one day. Take a look at
this glass of water.

Being a scientist I can tell you that water is H_2O.
The glass is filled with molecules, each of which is made up of two
atoms of hydrogen and one atom of oxygen, like this.

Kobir sketched out this diagram on the back of a menu:

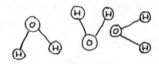

Kobir: Scientists have shown that H_2O is just what water is. They have
discovered that water and H_2O are *the very same thing.*

Aisha: What's this got to do with pain?

Kobir: Well, I believe that one day scientists will similarly discover which
state of the brain pain is. Perhaps they will do this by scanning the
brains of people who are in pain.

I'm saying that just as water turned out to be H_2O, so pain will turn out to be a certain brain state. Why not?

Kobir's Brain Theory certainly sounds very 'scientific', doesn't it? In fact, many scientists think it pretty obvious that something like the Brain Theory must be true.

The eyeless alien argument

Still, Aisha felt sure that the Brain Theory had to be wrong. It seemed obvious to her that her conscious experiences couldn't possibly turn out to be brain states. She now had one last attempt at explaining why.

Aisha: I'm afraid I still believe that your Brain Theory is false.

Kobir: Why?

Aisha: I've already explained why. Brain scientists can enter into my brain. But they can never enter my mind. The mind is a *private place*, quite separate from the physical world.

Kobir: I'm still not sure I understand your argument.

Aisha: OK. Let me give you another example. I shall *prove* to you that my experiences aren't anything physical.

Kobir: Prove it? I doubt that!

Aisha: I accept your challenge! Let me tell you a story: the story of the *eyeless aliens.*

Kobir: The eyeless aliens?

Aisha: Yes. Suppose that there are intelligent alien creatures who don't have eyes. They are completely blind.

Kobir: So how do they find their way about?

Aisha: Mainly by touch – they have long wavy, tentacle-like arms – and by sound – they have big sensitive ears, just like bats.

175

Now these aliens are also conscious, of course. They also have conscious experiences. But, not having eyes, they don't have any experience of colour. However, the aliens are very curious about us humans. In particular, they would like to know what it is like to be a human being, to experience the world as we do. They would *especially* like to know what it is like to experience colour: to see the colour red, for example. So what the aliens do is this. They abduct you.

They take you up in their flying saucer. They tie you up. Then they make you look at a number of different things they know we describe as red: a ketchup bottle, a strawberry and so on.

Kobir: Weird! Why do they do that?

Aisha: Well, when you look at these things, you have an experience of the colour red. Then, while you are having that experience, the aliens scan your body, using an incredibly advanced scanner.

This scanner tells the aliens *absolutely everything* there is to know about what is going on inside you *physically* when you have that experience of red, including what is going on in your brain.

Kobir: Absolutely everything? Down to the last atom?

Aisha: Yes. Absolutely everything. Now, here's the big question: will all this *physical* information about you tell the aliens *what it is actually like* to have an experience of red?

Kobir: Hmmm. No. I guess not. They are blind. So they still won't know what it's *like* to see colour.

Aisha: Exactly. It seems that, no matter how much information the aliens gather about what is going on inside you *physically* when you have the experience, including what is going on inside your brain, that still won't tell the aliens what the experience is *actually like* from the point of view of someone having it.

Kobir: I see.

Aisha: So, here's my proof that the Brain Theory is false. The aliens *don't* know that you are experiencing *this* – what you and I experience when we look at that ketchup bottle. Right?

Kobir: Right. I agree that they still don't know *that* fact.

Aisha: But their scanner does tell them all the *physical* facts about you, right?

Kobir: Right.

Aisha: So, it follows that the fact that you are having that experience is not a *physical* fact about you! The experience itself is *non-physical*!

Kobir: But that can't be right.

Aisha: It *is* right!

Kobir: No way! The experience *must* be something physical. There's just *got* to be something wrong with your argument!

Aisha: So what's wrong with it, then?

Kobir: Er. I don't know.

The mystery of the mind

Let's now take a step back to see where we have got to. We have been looking at the question: *what is the mind?* Is the mind somehow *part* of the physical universe? Or is the mind something extra: something that exists in *addition to* the physical? In trying to answer this question, we have found ourselves being pulled in two different directions at once.

Kobir has been pulling us in one direction.

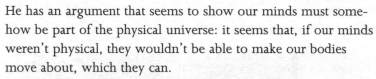

He has an argument that seems to show our minds must some-how be part of the physical universe: it seems that, if our minds weren't physical, they wouldn't be able to make our bodies move about, which they can.

So why not just accept that our minds are physical, then? Because Aisha has an argument that pulls us in the other direc-tion. Aisha's Eyeless Alien Argument seems to show that the facts about what goes on in our minds are hidden in a way that the physical facts about us are not. In that case it seems that the mind can't be physical.

So it seems that the mind has to be part of the physical world. Yet, on the other hand, it seems it can't be part of the physical world. So which is it? I have to admit: I'm not sure. And I'm not the only one. Today, at universities all over the world, philoso-phers and scientists continue to struggle with the question of how our minds and our physical bodies are related.

What do you think?

File 8

Does God exist?

The universe

I am sitting on top of a hill under a beautiful night sky.

The stars are twinkling brightly. To the east of me, the moon sits above the tree tops, almost full. To the west, I can see the spires of Oxford. Above the spires there is a faint purple glow where the sun set just a few minutes ago. Between the glow and the moon are suspended two bright points of light – the planets Venus and Jupiter.

As I sit here on this hill top, I am struck by how vast the universe is. Here we are, sitting on the cool outer crust of a huge ball of red-hot rock: planet Earth.

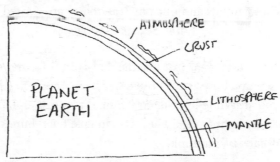

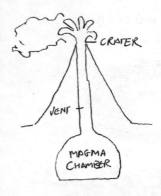

Every now and then a little molten rock – lava – spurts out to form a volcano.

The Earth turns on its axis once every twenty-four hours. That is what made the sun disappear from view a little while ago, of course: it was not the sun that moved, but the Earth that turned. The moon – another big ball of rock – goes round the Earth once a month.

And the Earth goes round the sun once a year.

Those two bright points of light over there – Venus and Jupiter – are also plan-ets. In fact, there are nine planets in our solar

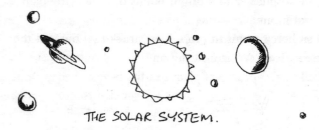

system, all of them rotating slowly around the sun.

THE SOLAR SYSTEM.

Our sun is a star just like the thousands of other stars that I can see up above me. Those other stars are much further away, of course. While light from the sun takes just eight minutes to reach us, light from other stars can take tens, hundreds or even thousands of years.

The stars I see spread out above me form part of a huge whirlpool of stars called a *galaxy*. Our galaxy is called the *Milky Way*,

the Milky Way being just one of the thousands of known galaxies in the universe.

Against this vast universe, planet Earth seems almost unimaginably tiny and insignificant.

Where did the universe come from?

When I look out across the universe, I often ask myself: How did all this rock and dust and space come to be here? Where did it all come from? What *made* it exist?

THE BIG BANG

Scientists have a theory about this. They say that the universe began with a huge explosion.

Scientists call this explosion the *Big Bang*.

The Big Bang happened a very long time ago: between ten and twenty thousand million years ago. The Big Bang was where all the matter in the universe came from. It was the beginning of space. In fact, it was the beginning of time itself.

But when scientists tell me this, it doesn't help me very much. It doesn't remove my feeling that something still needs explaining. Because I then want to know: *what made the Big Bang happen?* Why was there a bang, rather than no bang? That certainly is a great mystery, perhaps the greatest mystery of all.

The meaning of life
After a while, I stop looking up at the universe spread out above me. I look down at the grass.

I notice that, down in the shadows among the blades of grass, tiny insects are crawling about. Many of these insects are ants. They seem to be very busy. When I look even more closely, I see that the ants are pushing a leaf about.

It seems that ants are trying to push the leaf into a hole in the ground. That hole must be where the ants live. The leaf is a very tight fit. The ants struggle and struggle and still they can't get it into the hole. I wonder why the leaf is so important to them.

I could easily put my foot down and squash all the ants. I decide not to squash them. But I wonder what real difference it would make if I did. Look at their frantic activity, running around, trying to get that leaf into the hole. It all seems so pointless. So meaningless. What would it really matter if I did put my foot down and snuff them out?

Looked at from space, the Earth must seem a bit like a huge ants' nest.

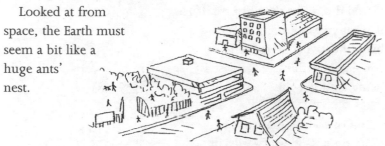

There we all are, rushing about, just like ants. We are born. We grow up. We go to the supermarket. We go to work. We watch TV. We have children. We die. Our children have children, who in turn have children. Generation after generation of ceaseless activity. On and on the cycle goes. But what is the meaning behind our brief journey through life? What is the point of our being momentarily alive and conscious on this tiny planet amid all this vastness? Is there any point?

God

As I sit here under the stars, I have been puzzling about the existence of the universe. Why is it here? What made the Big Bang happen? Why was there a bang, rather than no bang? I have also been wondering about the meaning of life. What is the point of our being here?

Many people would answer the question: what caused the universe to exist? by saying: God did. God created the universe. God made the Big Bang happen.

Many people also believe that it is God who gives meaning to our existence. They believe that there is a point to our being here. We do have a purpose: a divine purpose. That purpose involves loving and obeying God.

What is God like?

If God did create the universe, if He is what gives meaning to our lives, then what is He like? Some people think of God as being a bit like this:

But of course, this can't be quite right. God isn't really an old man with a big beard. He doesn't *really* sit on a cloud. If you were to fly about and examine all the clouds that there are, you wouldn't find an old man sitting on any of them. Rather, this is just an image that religious people use to help them think about God.

In fact, although I talk about God as being a He, many people nowadays don't even think of God as being male.

So what is God like, then, if He isn't an old man sitting on a cloud? According to Christians, Jews, Muslims and those of many other religious faiths, God has at least the following three characteristics.

First of all, God is *all powerful*. That means he can do absolutely anything. He created the universe. And he could destroy it again, if he so chose. God can bring the dead back to life, turn water into wind and send you to the moon in the blink of an eye.

Secondly, God is supposed to be *all knowing*. God knows

everything there is to know. He knows all that has happened, and all that will happen. He knows our thoughts. He knows our every secret. He even knows that it was me who sneaked downstairs last night and stole the last cream cake from the fridge.

Absolutely nothing is hidden from God.

Thirdly, God, is supposed to be *all good*. God loves us and would certainly never do anything bad.

Why believe in God?

Of course, many religious people have faith in the existence of God. They believe in God's existence without reason. They just believe.

But as philosophers we are interested in whether there is any *reason* to believe in the existence of God. Is there any evidence to suggest that God exists? Can we show by argument that God exists? Or is there perhaps some reason to suppose that God doesn't exist? These are the questions we are going to look at here.

Bob and Kobir arrive

I lie back in the grass and look up at the stars. After a while I hear two voices in the distance. They seem to be getting nearer. Eventually I recognize who it is. It's Bob and Kobir out for an evening stroll (you will remember Kobir, who is a science student, from the last chapter).

Bob is a footballer. He's staying with Kobir for the weekend. The two of them have been kicking a ball around in the park.

A couple of minutes later they arrive on top of the hill. We all say 'Hello,' and sit down on the grass.

I explain to Bob and Kobir that I have been thinking about God, the Big Bang and the meaning of life.

They are pretty impressed! Bob says that he believes in God. Kobir, on the other hand, says he doesn't.

Now, Bob and Kobir are good friends. But there's nothing they enjoy more than having a philosophical argument. So it isn't long before they are busy arguing about whether or not God exists. This is how the argument starts.

Bob: Look. You have to admit, many millions of people all over the Earth believe in God. If all those millions believe, then there's got to be *something* to it, surely?

Kobir: I'm afraid that's rubbish. Millions of people used to believe that the Earth is flat and that the sun goes round the Earth. They were quite wrong about *that*, weren't they?

Bob: Well OK. I admit they were wrong about that.

Kobir: So you see, most people *can* be wrong. Just because many or even most people believe in God doesn't show that He exists.

Bob: OK. I suppose it's true that most people *can* be wrong. But it's *likely* that they're right isn't it?

Kobir: No. Not if they don't have *reason* to believe. And of course, the explanation of why people believe things is not always that they have reason to believe. Sometimes there's another explanation.

Bob: Like what?

Kobir: Well, many of those who believe in God are simply *brought up* to have that belief. Indeed, belief in God is often drilled into people from a very young age.

That explains why they believe.

Bob: That doesn't explain why I believe in God. I was never sent to Sunday School. And neither of my parents believes in God.

Kobir: I would also say that many people believe in God not because they have any reason to believe that God exists, but just because they *want* to believe He exists. They believe in God simply because it is a nice, comforting thing to believe.

Bob: Why comforting?

Kobir: Well, it's a scary thought that we are all alone in the universe, that there is no ultimate meaning or point to our existence. It's quite frightening to think that when we die we are gone for ever. It is so much *nicer* to believe that there is a loving God who watches over us and who gives some point to our lives. It is so much *nicer* to believe that when we die we don't just cease to exist, but continue on. But just because this is a nice, comforting thing to believe doesn't give us the slightest reason to suppose that it's *true*, does it?

Is Kobir being entirely fair? Actually, in some ways believing in God can make life seem rather *less* comfortable. For example, some people who believe in God also believe in the Last Judgement and Heaven and Hell. They believe that after they die they will be judged by God and possibly sent to Hell as punishment for the bad things they have done.

That's hardly a very comforting thought, is it?

Still, it appears that most people who believe that God exists do also want it to be true that He exists. It seems they get quite a lot of comfort from their belief. So is Kobir right? Do most people believe in God simply because they want to believe or have been brought up to believe in God? Or is there also some *reason* to suppose that God exists? What do you think?

Bob's Big Bang Argument

The three of us lie silently on our backs for a few minutes. We listen to the sound the wind makes as it hisses through the trees down at the bottom of the hill.

Suddenly there is a whooshing sound followed by a deafening bang. It's a firework. It showers the sky to the north of us with thousands of silver flecks. We watch as they spiral downwards.

Bob: Look. I certainly *don't* believe God exists just because it's a *nice* thing to believe. After all, I'd like to believe that fairies exist, but I don't. For there's no *reason* to believe in them. There's no evidence that they exist. But there *is* evidence that God exists. That's why I believe in God.

Kobir: What do you mean? What evidence is there that God exists?

Bob: Well, Stephen mentioned the Big Bang a minute ago. Don't scientists believe that the universe we see spread out up there began with a huge explosion: the Big Bang?

Kobir: Yes.

Bob: Well then, my question is: what caused the Big Bang? Why was there a bang rather than no bang?

Kobir: I have no idea. That is a mystery.

Bob: Yes, it's a great mystery. After all, everything has a cause, doesn't it? Things don't *just happen*. Take that firework that exploded over there a few moments ago. That explosion didn't *just happen* , did it? It had to have a cause. Someone had to light the fuse, didn't they?

Kobir: I guess so.

Bob: But then the same applies to the Big Bang. The Big Bang must have had a cause too. Now if God exists, that would solve the mystery of what caused the Big Bang. That's why it's reasonable to suppose that God exists. God explains why the Big Bang happened. God lit the fuse!

Is Bob's Big Bang Argument any good?

I think that often, when it seems to people that God must exist, something like Bob's Big Bang Argument is at the back of their minds. Indeed, you can find much the same sort of argument in the writings of many philosophers and religious thinkers down through the centuries.

At first sight Bob's Big Bang Argument does *seem* quite convincing. But is it really any good? Does Bob's argument actually provide us with some reason to suppose that God exists?

Kobir certainly doesn't think so.

Bob: I'm afraid your argument is no good. You haven't given us any reason at all to suppose that God exists.

Kobir: Why not? Look, in a nutshell your argument is this: everything has a cause; therefore the universe has a cause; therefore God must exist as the cause of the universe. Right?

Bob: Yes. I suppose so.

Kobir: Well then, if *everything* has a cause, then what caused God? What made Him exist?

Bob: Good question. That's a mystery.

Kobir: So you have merely replaced one mystery with another, haven't you?

Bob: How do you mean?

Kobir: Well, we are still stuck with a mystery, aren't we? We started with the question: What caused the universe?

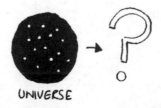

UNIVERSE

Scientists give us the answer: the Big Bang. But then we are left with a mystery, aren't we? For then there is the mystery of what caused the Big Bang.

Now you try to get rid of *this* mystery by saying that God caused the Big Bang. But then we face the mystery of what caused God.

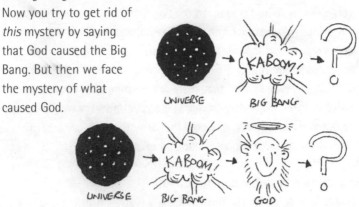

And so on. There's still a mystery left over.

Kobir is right. Bob suggested that it is reasonable to believe that God exists because that solves a mystery: the mystery of why the Big Bang happened. The trouble is, Bob has removed one mystery only by introducing another. Still, Bob doesn't give up that easily.

Bob: OK. Let's suppose God doesn't have a cause. Let's suppose God isn't the sort of thing that needs a cause. If God doesn't need a cause, then there's no mystery left over.

Kobir: But now you have contradicted yourself! You started your argument by assuming that *everything* has a cause. Now you are saying *not* everything has a cause: God doesn't.

Bob: But when I said everything has a cause I didn't mean *absolutely* everything. I meant everything except God, obviously.

Kobir: So you are saying there is one exception to the rule that everything has a cause: God.

Bob: Yes. God is the exception to that rule.

Kobir: But if there has to be an exception to the rule, why not just make the universe the exception to the rule instead? What reason have you given us to add God on to the beginning of the universe as an *extra* cause? You have given us no reason. But then you have given us no reason to suppose that God exists.

Bob: I guess you're right.

Kobir: You see, Bob, I admit that there *is* a mystery about where the universe came from. I admit that it is a great mystery why there is something rather than nothing. I just deny that this mystery gives us any reason at all to suppose that God exists.

Bob's Cosmic Watchmaker Argument

Bob sits up. He starts fiddling with his watch. Bob is clearly a bit upset that his Big Bang Argument doesn't work after all.

Eventually, after a few minutes, Bob has another go at convincing Kobir of the existence of God. He takes off his watch and tosses it on to the grass in front of Kobir.

Bob: OK, Kobir. Here's a better argument. Take a look at this watch. Suppose that you are walking along a deserted beach on a remote island somewhere. Suddenly you come across a watch just like this one. It's just lying there on the sand.

You ask yourself: how did the watch get here? Here are two suggestions. The first suggestion is: the watch was *designed*. It's a tool, made by an intelligent being – a watchmaker – for a specific purpose: to enable people to tell the time. The second suggestion is: the watch was made by the action of the waves, the wind and other natural forces. They formed the watch all by themselves, without the help of any sort of designer. Which of these two suggestions is more likely to be true, do you think?

Kobir: Well, obviously, the first suggestion is much more likely to be true.

Bob: You're right. A watch is not like a pebble, is it? Pebbles are formed without help from any intelligence. They really are formed by natural forces: the wind and the waves. But a watch is hardly likely to have been made in this way, is it?

Kobir: No.

Bob: In fact, the watch clearly has a purpose – to tell the time. So isn't it reasonable to suppose that there must be an intelligent being who designed it for that purpose? There must surely be a designer, a watchmaker, who made it.

Kobir: I agree.

Bob: Now take a look at my eye.

The eye is a very complicated object – far, far more complicated than a watch or indeed anything we human beings can make. Like the watch, the eye also has a purpose: to enable the creature attached to it to see. It does this job extremely well, doesn't it?

Kobir: Yes, it does. The eye is a marvellous piece of engineering.

Bob: Now ask yourself: how did the eye come to exist? What is more likely: that the eye came into existence by chance or that it was designed? Surely, given that the eye has a purpose, a purpose for which it is very well suited, it too must have a designer,. There has to be a designer – a sort of cosmic watchmaker – who designed the eye. That designer is God.

Is there a problem with Bob's Cosmic Watchmaker Argument?

What do you think of Bob's Cosmic Watchmaker Argument? Like the Big Bang Argument, different versions of it have been put forward down the centuries by philosophers and religious thinkers. But there are problems with it.

One problem with the Cosmic Watchmaker Argument is that nowadays we know all about *natural selection*. Natural selection can explain how eyes might come to exist without supposing they had any sort of a designer.

Natural selection

Here's how natural selection works. When someone is going to build something complex like a ship, aeroplane or building, they usually make a plan. This plan is called a *blueprint*. The blueprint shows exactly how the ship or whatever is to be put together.

Now, all living things also contain a sort of blueprint. They contain something called DNA.

DNA

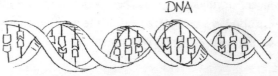

194

DNA is a long string of molecules. You will find one of these strings in every cell of a living thing's body. The string contains a blueprint for making a living thing of that sort. When plants or creatures reproduce, it is the string of DNA handed down from the parent plants or creatures that provides the blueprint for building it.

The DNA string in the new living thing is made by copying parts of the DNA string from the parent or parents. But in the process of copying, slight errors may creep in.

Because of these slight changes to the blueprint, the creature produced from it may be slightly different from its parent or parents. There will be slight changes to the creature. These changes are called mutations. They happen quite by chance.

Here's an example. A simple creature living in the sea may have, as a mutation, a single light-sensitive cell on its skin.

Now, this cell could be very useful to the creature. It may allow it to detect how deep it is in the sea (the deeper you go in the sea, the darker it gets). So in this environment the mutation would give the creature a slight advantage over other creatures of that sort.

Another one of these creatures may have as a mutation a brighter-coloured skin. This mutation may be a big disadvantage to the creature in that environment, making it more visible to other creatures that want to eat it.

Of course, the creature with the mutation that helps it to survive is more likely to be able to mate and reproduce itself than is a creature with a mutation that makes it less likely to survive. So the next generation of creatures is more likely to contain creatures with the light-sensitive cell and is less likely to contain creatures with the brightly coloured skin. Those mutations which help creatures survive and reproduce in that environment are likely to be passed on and those which make survival less probable are wiped out.

As further mutations are added over thousands and thousands of generations, the creatures slowly change. They gradually *evolve*. They adapt to their environments. The process is called *natural selection*.

You have probably come across fossils: pieces of rock that have taken on the form of living creatures that lived millions of years ago. When you look at fossils, you can see the kinds of change that I have been talking about taking place. For example, it seems that the first birds to exist actually evolved from certain sorts of dinosaur.

We have even traced parts of our own evolutionary tree. We now know that human beings share a common ancestor with apes. It is no accident that we look so similar to them.

So how did the *eye* appear? It didn't just appear from
nowhere. It evolved over millions and millions of years. It
evolved because it greatly helps creatures to survive and
reproduce. Perhaps the process began with a single light-
sensitive cell appearing in some simple organism living in the
sea. Gradually, over many generations, more light-sensitive cells
were added. In this way, the eye slowly began to evolve, until
finally you see the sorts of eye that are around today.

So one big problem with Bob's Cosmic Watchmaker
Argument is this. Before we knew about natural selection, it
seemed difficult to explain how eyes, and living creatures generally,
could come to exist on the Earth. We couldn't see how any
natural process could have produced complex living creatures.
For this reason, many people supposed that there must be a
supernatural being – God – who made the creatures. But now that
we know about evolution and natural selection, this particular
reason for believing in the existence of God has disappeared.

We don't know the *whole* story of how life on Earth developed,
of course. I am just guessing about how the eye might have
evolved. The point is that we can see that, in principle, the
existence of all the different sorts of life on Earth can be very
probably be explained in wholly natural terms without our
having to talk about God at all.

197

What is it reasonable to believe?

Kobir explains natural selection to Bob. After he's explained, Bob admits that the eye does not after all seem to provide much evidence for the existence of God.

I'm now feeling pretty hungry. Bob and Kobir say that they are hungry too, so we decide to go for a curry at my favourite Indian restaurant. We get up, dust ourselves down, and start off down the hill. There's a gravel path which crunches underfoot. The moon lights our way, casting long shadows out in front of us.

As we walk downhill, Kobir tells Bob that he doesn't think there are any good arguments for the existence of God. There's no proof of the existence of God. Indeed, there is little if any evidence to suggest that God exists.

Bob heads his football in the air a few times. Then he points out, quite correctly, that even if there is no good reason to suppose God does exist, that doesn't prove He *doesn't* exist. Kobir agrees that this is true.

Bob: But then shouldn't we remain *neutral* about whether or not God exists? I mean, if we can't show He does exist, but can't show He doesn't exist either, isn't remaining neutral the most reasonable view to take?

Kobir: Actually, I don't so. I think that, if there is no reason to suppose God exists, then the reasonable thing to believe is that He *doesn't* exist.

198

Another firework explodes above us. We stand and watch for a moment as it sends shimmering red sparks across the sky.

Bob: But why? Look, think about the question of whether or not there is life out there in other parts of the universe. It seems that at the moment we can't show that there definitely is life out there, but neither can we show that there isn't. In which case, surely the most reasonable position to take is to remain neutral.

Kobir: I agree. I think we should remain neutral on whether there is life out there. But the question of whether or not God exists is different.

Bob: Why?

Kobir: Because while there is little if any reason to suppose God exists, there *is* some good evidence that there must be alien life forms.

Bob: What evidence? We haven't discovered life on other planets.

Kobir: True. But we know that life evolved here on this planet, don't we? And we also know there are countless millions of other planets in the universe, many of which are very similar to our own. In which case it seems not improbable that life will have evolved on at least one of those other planets too. So there *is* pretty good evidence for the existence of life out there. It's just that we don't have *conclusive*

ALIEN LIFE FORMS

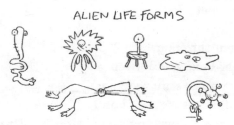

evidence. On the other hand, it seems to me that there is little if any evidence to suggest that God exists.

Bob shrugs his shoulders. He doesn't look convinced. So Kobir continues.

Kobir: Look. Compare believing in fairies. If there's little if any reason to suppose that fairies exist, then it is surely more reasonable to believe that they *don't* exist rather than to remain neutral. Don't you agree?

Bob: I suppose so. I certainly believe that fairies don't exist. It's silly to believe in fairies.

Kobir: Well, then. The same is true of God. If there is little or no reason to believe that God exists, then surely the reasonable thing to believe is that He doesn't exist. Isn't it as silly to believe in God as it is to believe in fairies?

Bob feels quite insulted by Kobir's comparing belief in God to belief in fairies. And perhaps Kobir is being a bit unfair. After all, plenty of very intelligent people believe in God. And surely, believing in God is certainly not silly in the sense that it is frivolous or trivial: believing in God can have huge, life-changing consequences.

Still, the question remains: is there any more *reason* to believe in God than there is to believe in fairies? If Kobir is right, there isn't. But then isn't it more reasonable to believe that God *doesn't* exist, rather than to remain neutral on whether or not He exists? What do you think?

The problem of suffering

As we near the bottom of the hill, a large shadowy shape starts to loom up in front of us. It's the local hospital. Many of the windows are lit. Through some of the windows we can see figures moving around. At one window quite near to us, we notice a woman. She looks sad, as if she has been crying.

As we walk past the hospital, Kobir starts to explain why he thinks that, actually, there is very good evidence to suggest that God doesn't exist.

Kobir: I think you should agree, Bob, that if there's no reason to suppose God does exist, then the reasonable view to take is that He doesn't. But in any case, we have all been overlooking something. You keep suggesting that there is no reason to suppose that God doesn't exist. But actually, there is.

Bob: What do you mean? What evidence is there that God *doesn't* exist?

Kobir stops and points at the hospital.

Kobir: There's my evidence. God is supposed to have at least three characteristics, isn't he? Isn't He supposed to be all powerful, all knowing and all good?

Bob: That's right.

Kobir: Well now, there is a great deal of pain and suffering in the world, isn't there? People get horrible diseases. Many of the people in that hospital right now are suffering from terrible, painful diseases. There are also wars. Famines. Earthquakes. You have to admit: in many ways, the world is not a very nice place to be. It seems it could definitely be nicer.

Bob: That's true. It could be nicer.

Kobir: The problem is, if God has these three characteristics – if He really is all powerful, all knowing and all good – then *why* is there pain and suffering in the world? *Why* isn't the world nicer?

Bob: I don't really see the problem.

Kobir: Well if God is all powerful – if He can do anything – then he can *stop* the pain and suffering, can't He?

Bob: Yes. I suppose He could.

Kobir: In fact, he could have made the world so that it contained no pain and suffering in the first place, couldn't He? He could have made it so that we couldn't feel the sensation of pain, for example. He could have made a world free of disease. He could have made a much more pleasant world for us. In fact, He could have made the Earth like Heaven is supposed to be. But he didn't. So *why* didn't he?

Bob: I don't know. Perhaps he didn't realize how things would turn out.

Kobir: But He *must* have realized. For God is all knowing. He knows everything, including how things will turn out. In which case it seems that God makes us suffer *on purpose*!

Bob: But God would never do that! God is good. He would never make us suffer on purpose.

Kobir: There's the problem. Either God isn't all powerful, or God isn't all knowing, or God isn't all good. But God, if He exists, has all three of these characteristics. Therefore God doesn't exist!

This is a very old, very famous and very serious problem facing those who believe in God. Religious thinkers have been struggling with the problem for a very long time. Let's call it the Problem of Suffering. Can the problem be solved?

The Free Will Answer

The three of us think about the Problem of Suffering as we walk. Some people who believe in God have tried to deal with the Problem of Suffering by arguing that responsibility for the pain and suffering in the world lies not with God, but with us. And in fact this is precisely what Bob now suggests.

Bob: You are forgetting something. God gave us *free will*.

Kobir: How do you mean?

Bob: God gave us the ability to *choose for ourselves* how we will act. Without free will, we would be just like machines or robots. We'd simply be caused to act in the way we do. We couldn't do otherwise. But we *can* choose to do otherwise. For example, we chose to walk up this hill this evening. But we could just as easily have chosen to go to the cinema instead.

Kobir: How does free will help you solve the problem about suffering?

Bob: Well, unfortunately we often choose to do things that result in pain and suffering. We start wars, for example. Now God cannot be held responsible for a war, can He? The suffering caused by our wars is *our* fault, not His.

Kobir: But wouldn't it have been better if God hadn't given us free will? Wouldn't it have been better if he had just *made us* so we always do the right thing? Then there wouldn't be any pain or suffering. There wouldn't be any wars.

Bob: No, because then we would be mere puppets, mere robots, wouldn't we? It is much better that we have free will, despite the fact that we do sometimes end up causing suffering.

A problem with the Free Will Answer

Let's call Bob's answer to the Problem of Suffering the *Free Will Answer*. The Free Will Answer is quite ingenious.

However, there are big problems with it. As Kobir points out, one of the most obvious problems with the Free Will Answer is that it seems much of the pain and suffering in the world isn't caused by us.

Kobir: The trouble with your argument is that not *all* of the suffering in the world is down to us. OK, we cause wars. But what about a horrible disease? What about a disease like cancer which kills millions of people every year in a very unpleasant way. How is that disease *our* fault? How did *we* cause it? Or take a flood.

A flood may drown many thousands of people. How can that be *our* fault? It seems it can't be. But then there can be no God.

Bob throws his football in the air a few times while he thinks for a moment.

Bob: Perhaps the disease and the flood *are* caused by us. It's just that we don't *realize* that we caused them.
Kobir: How do you mean?

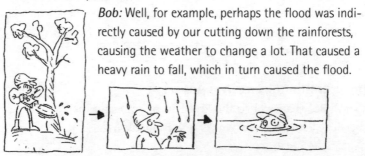

Bob: Well, for example, perhaps the flood was indirectly caused by our cutting down the rainforests, causing the weather to change a lot. That caused a heavy rain to fall, which in turn caused the flood.

Kobir: Maybe. But it's very hard to believe that *all* the pain and suffering in the world is somehow caused by us, isn't it? How do we make earthquakes happen, for example? It's certainly very hard to believe that, if only *we* were to act in certain ways, then there would never be *any* pain or suffering at all!

Bob: I guess you are right. I guess God, if He exists, must be responsible for at least *some* of our suffering.

Is suffering God's punishment?

Bob has one last stab at dealing with the Problem of Suffering.

Bob: Perhaps the suffering that God causes is intended as a *punishment.*

Kobir: A punishment for what?

Bob: For our sins. For the wrongs we have done. God is good. He loves us. But just as good and loving parents must sometimes punish their children when they do something wrong, so God must sometimes punish us.

Bob's suggestion makes Kobir rather angry.

Kobir: Honestly, that really is a terrible suggestion!

Bob: Why is it terrible?

Kobir: Look. Many of the disasters that occur happen to people who can't be blamed for anything at all. Very young babies, for example. Even if *we* have done something wrong, *they* haven't done anything wrong, have they?

Bob: I suppose not.

205

Kobir: So why is it fair to punish *them*? Suppose our law courts were to punish the babies of adults who had committed crimes?

That would hardly be fair, would it? In fact, that would be a pretty *horrible* thing to do, wouldn't it?

Bob: I guess so.

Kobir: Right. So why is it any less horrible if God punishes the babies of adults who have done wrong? Surely a good God would never do such a cruel and despicable thing.

Bob and Kobir have been talking about the Problem of Suffering. The problem is: God is all-good, all-knowing and all-powerful, then why is there so much suffering in the world? As you can see this is a very serious problem for those who believe in God. Bob hasn't really managed to solve the problem. Can you think of a better solution?

Faith
The three of us finally arrive at the restaurant and go inside.

I'm now very hungry indeed, so I order a huge plate of poppadoms for us to nibble on while we make up our minds about what curry to order. In between nibbling on his poppadom, Bob makes a very interesting point about believing in God.

Bob: OK. Suppose I accept that there's little if any evidence that God exists. Suppose I accept there's no good reason to suppose He exists.

Indeed, suppose I accept there's even some evidence to suggest that God *doesn't* exist. Still, this is all irrelevant when it comes to my belief in God.

Kobir: Why?

Bob: Because when it comes to believing in God, it's not a question of believing for a *reason*. *Reason* has nothing to do with it. Belief in God is a matter of *faith*. You must *just believe*. Many people have faith in the existence of God. And faith is a very positive thing to have, don't you agree?

Is Bob right? Is faith in God's existence a good thing to have?

It is worth remembering that faith can sometimes be a dangerous thing. For example, faith can be used to control people. Once people have let go of reason, once they just believe, then they are easily controlled. The unscrupulous leader of a religion can take advantage of a simple, trusting faith and use it to his or her own advantage.

Faith, taken to an extreme, also makes if difficult to communicate with people. One can no longer reason or argue with them. If people with an extreme faith get it into their heads that they should do some terrible thing (perhaps kill those with religious beliefs different from their own), it may be impossible to make them see that what they are doing is wrong. They won't listen to reason.

On the other hand, there is no doubt that faith in the existence

THE COMPLETE PHILOSOPHY FILES

of God can have a positive effect. It can and does help many people. If you trust in the existence of a good God, that may help you to deal with some of the bad things that happen to you in life.

BEFORE   AFTER

It is also true that faith in the existence of God has transformed some people's lives for the better. Rather than being selfish and cruel, they have become generous and noble.

Religious faith has even led people to lay down their lives to save others (though we should remember that it is not only those who believe in God that do such noble and unselfish things).

So there are good things about having faith in the existence of God.

What does it all mean?

For those who have religious faith, life does have meaning. We are here for a purpose: God's purpose. Many believe that that purpose is to love and obey God. But what if you don't have faith? What if you don't believe there is a God? What is one to say about the meaning of life then? If there is no God, then is life meaningless?

If there is no God, then perhaps it is up to us to give life its meaning. The purpose our lives have is the purpose that we give to them. If that is true, then we each have a big responsibility. You can choose to live a meaningless life, or a meaningful one. What sort of life you live is up to you.

File 9

Astrology, flying saucers and ESP

Mysterious World

Aisha is slumped in an armchair.
   She's idly flicking through
the pages of a magazine.
Suddenly, in rushes Tom, one of
her housemates. Tom has been
shopping and is rather excited
about a book he's just bought
from Big Al's Discount
Bookstore. The book is called
Mysterious World and has a large picture of a flying saucer on the
front cover.

Tom: I've got this fantastic book! Take a look. It has lots of great
   chapters on weird and spooky stuff: ghosts, alien abductions, the
   prophecies of Nostradamus, the Loch Ness monster, astrology,
   numerology and palm-reading.

Aisha takes the book and flicks through the pages. She looks unimpressed. In fact she's rather rude about *Mysterious World*.

Aisha: Ah yes. I've seen it. It's a load of rubbish.

Aisha passes *Mysterious World* back to Tom, who seems a little disappointed by her reaction.

Tom: Why do you say that? Shouldn't you be more open-minded?
Aisha: I *am* open-minded.
Tom: But there's plenty of evidence in this book to suggest that there *really is* a lot of weird, paranormal stuff going on in the world. You shouldn't be so dismissive.

Like Tom, many people firmly believe in the kind of things discussed in Tom's book. A great many suppose that by looking to the stars astrologers can predict what will happen and provide us with valuable advice on what we should do.

Some believe in palmistry: they suppose that how your life will go is written on the palm of your hand.

Lots of people claim to have seen ghosts. A surprising number think they have been abducted by aliens. And many people believe in *extra-sensory perception*, or ESP — the ability to 'see' what is happening, or even what will happen, without using our five normal senses of sight, touch, taste, smell and hearing.

For example, you occasionally hear tales of people who say they 'just knew' that someone close to them had suffered an accident even though that person was miles away at the time and there was no normal way in which they could have known. It seems it must have been some sort of weird, paranormal experience that let them know what happened.

OH NO! RANDY'S HAD A TERRIBLE ACCIDENT!

Many people believe in the paranormal. But, of course, there are also many who don't. Like Aisha, they dismiss claims about astrology, flying saucers and ESP. Sometimes they can be pretty rude. They accuse those who believe in such stuff of being gullible fools.

So what should we believe? Is belief in astrology, flying saucers, miracles and ESP a lot of silly superstitious nonsense? Or might there really be something to it?

How open-minded should we be?

Of course, we want to be open-minded. We shouldn't just assume that there's nothing to any of these claims and simply ignore the kind of evidence presented in Tom's book.

But, on the other hand, we don't want to be too open-minded. We don't want minds so open that any old rubbish can easily end up lodging there.

After all, there are so many ridiculous beliefs you might pick up: that the Moon is made out of concrete; that ice is poisonous; that humans have three legs, and so on. If you are too open-minded, your head will soon fill up with junk beliefs.

So let's be open-minded. But let's also try to filter out, as best we can, silly or unreasonable ideas. Let's think hard about the arguments and carefully weigh up the evidence before we allow new beliefs in. That way, there's at least a fair chance that many of our beliefs will be true.

Belief in weird stuff is popular

Let's get back to Tom and Aisha. Why is Tom so confident that there must be something to the claims made in *Mysterious World*?

He begins to flick through the book and comes to a stop at the chapter on astrology.

Tom: OK, what about astrology? It says here that astrology is thousands of years old, and that some of the world's greatest scientists – including even Isaac Newton — have believed in it. Millions of people all over the world use astrology and testify that it *does* work. Even a US President is reported to have consulted an astrologer. Yet *you* confidently dismiss astrology as a load of old rubbish. How can you be so sure?

Tom is right that millions are convinced that astrology can give them an insight into their future. Many claim that they really do 'fit' their astrological star sign. In fact astrology is now a huge industry. Billions of pounds are spent every year on astrologers. Isn't Aisha being far too quick to dismiss astrology as 'rubbish'?

She doesn't think so.

Aisha: Look, I admit that *very many* people, often very intelligent people, believe in astrology. But the fact that lots of people believe something doesn't necessarily give us much reason to believe it's true.

Tom: Doesn't it?

Aisha: No. After all, lots of people *don't* believe in astrology. So you see, *either way, lots of people must be wrong.*

Believing what we want to believe

But Tom's point is not just that a great many people believe in astrology. Tom thinks they have *good grounds* for believing in it.

Tom: But surely the reason so many people consult astrologers and have done for thousands of years is that there's plenty of *evidence* that astrology really can give us an insight into the future.

Aisha: So you say. But sometimes people believe something not because there's good evidence that it is true, but for other reasons.

Tom: Like what?

Aisha: Well, sometimes people believe things because they *like* to believe in them. The fact is that we desperately *want* to believe in the weird and wacky. It's exciting to suppose that there are ghosts and demons, that there are cosmic influences shaping our lives, and that we have supernatural powers.

Liars, fakes and charlatans

Tom admits that he would like to believe that the claims made in his book are true. But, as he points out, that doesn't show that they *aren't* true.

Tom: OK, we *want* to believe in the weird and supernatural. But *that doesn't mean there's nothing to it, does it?* And in fact there really is *lots and lots* of evidence of weird and paranormal stuff happening.

Aisha: Is there?

Tom: Certainly. Thousands claim to have witnessed supernatural stuff going on.

Aisha: But many of these people are simply lying!

As Tom points out, it is hardly likely that *all* these people are lying about what they have experienced.

Tom: Well, yes, *some* may be lying. But not all. Many people really do believe they have witnessed something miraculous happening.

Aisha: True. But perhaps they have been *deceived.* There have always been people willing to take advantage of our huge fascination with the weird and wacky. Throughout history there are well-documented cases of tricksters happy to con the gullible by telling them fantastic tales, offering to put them in contact with the dead, selling them 'magical' charms, and so on.

There's little doubt that, even today, a huge amount of fraud and fakery is going on.

It's easy to fake it

Aisha is correct that there are undoubtedly many fakes and charlatans about.

You have probably seen illusionists performing fantastic feats. The magician David Copperfield flies in front of an audience of thousands, apparently without the help of any harness or wires. Others catch bullets in their teeth and cause people to vanish.

Now, as I say, these people are illusionists. They are happy to admit that they engage in trickery and sleight-of-hand. Yet their tricks are at least as convincing as most supposedly 'genuine' cases of the paranormal.

In fact, it's easy to master highly convincing illusions in just a few hours. A friend of mine recently learnt how to bend spoons. He can even do it without touching them. I have no idea how he does it. Yet he tells me it's all a trick.

Given that it is so easy to master tricks that are just as convincing as the 'genuine' paranormal events, it's highly likely that at least some of these 'genuine' cases are faked too.

Pedlars of tales

As Aisha also points out, there's plenty of money to be made, not just from faking miraculous events, but from re-telling stories about them.

Aisha: Because we *like* to believe in this stuff, there's no shortage of books, magazines, newspapers and TV companies willing to feed our fascination.

Newspapers will always run astrology columns, whether there's anything to astrology or not, simply because they can sell more newspapers that way and so make more money. Television programmes on the weird and wacky can get huge audiences, particularly if they sensationalize reports of fantastic things happening and give little time to anyone who wants to look at the evidence more critically.

Twisting the tale

Aisha is right that people usually have an interest – sometimes a financial interest – in telling tales of the supernatural. That should lead us to treat their 'evidence' with caution.

Another reason he should handle such tales with care is that they often reach us third- or fourth-hand. People may think they are telling the story just as it was told to them. But it's still easy for the story to become embellished along the way. The story-teller is likely to focus on those aspects of their story that are most amazing, and to play down any features that would make it seem less fantastic. A report of a 'strange light in the sky' can quickly become a tale of alien abduction.

Aisha sums up her case:

Aisha: So it seems to me it's not at all surprising that there are these reports of the weird and supernatural in our newspapers and on television. In fact, given our gullibility, the ease with which we can be taken for a ride, the extent to which stories can evolve along the way, and the huge profits to be made from telling them, you would expect such reports *anyway,* whether or not there was any truth to them. *So the mere fact that there are so many reports gives us little if any reason to suppose they are true.*

Is Aisha right?

Tom's stars

Tom accepts that many of the reports concerning weird and supernatural goings-on probably are unreliable. But he remains convinced that it's still *perfectly reasonable* to believe in astrology, flying saucers and ESP.

Tom: Look, I admit that there are fakes and charlatans. I admit that there's lots of money to be made peddling dubious stories about astrology, ESP, ghosts and so on. But that doesn't explain away *all* the evidence we have for these things, does it?
Aisha: It doesn't?
Tom: No. We also have *good, solid* evidence.
Aisha: Give me an example of this good, solid evidence.
Tom: Well, my *own* experiences confirm that astrology really does work. So I don't need to rely on the testimony of others.

Tom starts to tell Aisha about his recent experience of an astrological prediction 'coming true'.

Tom: I'm a Sagittarian. Last Monday I read in the astrology column that I could expect a pay rise. And this week I got a pay rise. So you see, there's a piece of evidence that astrology works! And this bit of evidence doesn't come from a dubious source. It's based on what I have experienced *myself.*

Many who believe in the power of astrology can point to countless such examples of astrological predictions turning out to be correct. How are astrologers able to make all these correct predictions if astrology doesn't work?

Making vague predictions

Aisha scratches her head.

Aisha: Let's take a closer look at your evidence. You say this astrological prediction was in Monday's paper?

Aisha rummages in the pile of papers beside the sofa and pulls out Monday's. Then she starts to rifle through the pages.

Aisha: Ah, here we are. 'The Great Magica's predictions for the next week. Sagittarius. Next week brings good news and bad. A friend feels betrayed, and there may be some hostility. Honesty is the best policy. At work things are looking up. You will soon be rewarded for all your hard work.'

Tom: See? It says I'll soon be rewarded for all my hard work. And this week my boss gave me a rise. The Great Magica knew I would get a pay rise!

SAGITTARIUS
NEXT WEEK BRINGS
GOOD NEWS AND BAD.
A FRIEND FEELS
BETRAYED, AND THERE
MAY BE SOME HOSTILITY.
HONESTY IS THE BEST
POLICY. AT WORK
THINGS ARE LOOKING
UP. YOU WILL SOON BE
REWARDED FOR ALL
YOUR HARD WORK.

But *did* she? What do you think?

The Great Magica's predictions are pretty *vague*, aren't they? She doesn't actually say that every Sagittarian will get a pay rise. She says only that there will be a 'reward' for hard work. But she never specifically mentions money. This means that, even if Tom had received a box of chocolates or a day off from his boss, the Great Magica's prediction would still have come true.

It would also have come true if he had managed to sell more cars than usual. That too might count as a 'reward'.

In fact, the astrologer's prediction could be seen as 'true' if Tom had received a tip or even just praise from a grateful customer.

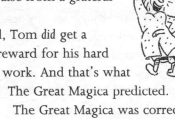

Still, Tom did get a reward for his hard work. And that's what The Great Magica predicted. The Great Magica was correct.

So did she really know what would happen?

THE COMPLETE PHILOSOPHY FILES

How astrology columns *really* work

No. She didn't. Newspaper astrology columns don't provide us
with any sort of insight into the future. Aisha explains how they
really work.

Aisha: Look, you read the astrology column every week. Every week
   Magica makes a number of rather vague predictions. Now because
   her predictions are vague – because there are so many different
   ways in which they could 'come true' – you should actually expect
   quite a few of them to 'come true' just by chance.

Aisha is right. But then the fact that one of the Great Magica's
vague predictions came true this week doesn't give us the
slightest reason to suppose that astrology gives her some strange
power to see into the future.

Aisha: Also, notice that the Great Magica made a *number* of predictions
   for Sagittarians. For example, she said "A friend feels betrayed, and
   there may be some hostility. Honesty is the best policy."
Tom: True, she did.
Aisha: But you have just ignored *this* prediction, haven't you?
Tom: Er, yes, I suppose I have.
Aisha: Why?
Tom: To be honest, I forgot about that one. It doesn't seem to have
   come true.
Aisha: Right, because you don't immediately see how it applies to you,
   you ignore it. In fact, some weeks you can't find *anything* in the
   Great Magica's predictions that rings true, can you?
Tom: Well, yes, *some* weeks I can't. But she usually gets *something*
   right!

Aisha is getting pretty exasperated.

Aisha: Of course she does! Because the Great Magica makes loads of vague predictions, she is bound to get a *few* right *just by chance.* Readers remember when a prediction comes true – that's not surprising, of course, because it's quite dramatic: it seems the astrologer 'knew' what would happen! Readers also tend to forget about the predictions that *don't* come true – again, that's not surprising as nothing happens later on to remind them about the prediction. So you see, by focusing only on the 'hits' and forgetting about the 'misses', gullible people like you can convince yourselves that the Great Magica has some sort of magical insight into the future!

An astrology experiment

Perhaps you aren't convinced by Aisha's explanation of how astrology columns work. Perhaps
you still think there's something to it.

If you do, then try this simple test. Cut
out the predictions for the twelve different
star signs from last week's newspaper.
Make a note of which prediction is for
which star sign, and then remove the star
signs so that only the predictions are left,
like this:

NEXT WEEK BRINGS GOOD NEWS AND BAD. A FRIEND FEELS BETRAYED, AND THERE MAY BESOME HOSTILITY. HONESTY IS THE BEST POLICY. AT WORK THINGS ARE LOOKING UP. YOU WILL SOON BE REWARDED FOR ALL YOUR HARD WORK

Now show your friends just the predictions
and ask them which prediction is for their star sign.

If the astrologer has *any* sort of insight into the future, then your friends should have a better than one-in-twelve chance of picking out the prediction that's for their sign. But in fact, your friends won't be able to figure out which predictions are theirs. Because the predictions are so vague, they will probably find that most of the predictions have 'come true' for them.

Try it and see.

Astrological charts

Of course, many astrologers admit that the kind of predictions that appear in newspapers and magazines are just 'a bit of fun'. Most astrologers would say that a *proper* astrological chart, based on specific information about a person's date and time of birth, is likely to be *much* more reliable.

But is this true?

In 1979, a researcher into astrology put an advert in a magazine offering free personal horoscopes. Each person who answered the advert received a real horoscope drawn up by a reputable astrologer. When someone received their free horoscope, they were also asked how accurate they and their friends found it to be.

Amazingly, of the first 150 people who responded, 94% said their horoscope was accurate, and 90% of their friends and family thought it accurate too.

Doesn't this show that personal horoscopes *really are* accurate?

No, it doesn't. True, in this experiment everyone received a real astrological chart drawn up by a real astrologer. But it was *the very same* horoscope each time. They all got a chart based on the birth details of the notorious mass murderer Dr Petiot, who was executed in 1947. Petiot admitted killing 63 people and dissolving their bodies in a tub of quicklime!

Yet 94% of the people given Petiot's chart were convinced that the chart accurately described them!

AND NOW LET'S SEE WHAT'S GOING ON INSIDE YOU! HA HA HA!

DR. PETIOT

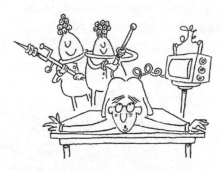

'YOU ENJOY MEETING NEW PEOPLE AND ARE ALWAYS CURIOUS ABOUT WHAT'S GOING ON INSIDE THEM.' HMMM, THAT SOUNDS JUST LIKE ME!

What this case again shows is that most of us are easily duped into thinking that astrologers know things about us that they couldn't possibly know if astrology didn't work. The fact is it's incredibly easy for us to convince ourselves that astrologers are accurate no matter what they might happen to say.

Flying saucers

Tom still thinks that Aisha is being far too quick to rubbish *everything* in *Mysterious World*.

Tom: OK. So you don't believe in astrology. But surely you're wrong to be sceptical about *all* the things discussed in this book. What about flying saucers and alien abductions, for example? Just two years ago, an accountant was taken up into a flying saucer.

He reports having been subjected to strange internal examinations.

Then the aliens dropped him off in some woods in the middle of the night.

Aisha: Hmm.
Tom: Thousands of people have witnessed such things. *Thousands* have seen flying saucers in the sky. They can't *all* be deluded, can they?

Tom thinks it's totally unreasonable to dismiss *all* this evidence. Yet Aisha is *still* sceptical.

Aisha: I don't think there's enough evidence to make it sensible to believe that people are abducted by flying saucers.
Tom: But there's lots of hard evidence too. What about the *films* and *photographs* of flying saucers?
Aisha: Many have been exposed as fakes. One of the most famous turned out to be a car hubcap. And why is it that the pictures are *always* fuzzy and difficult to make out? Out of all the thousands and thousands of photographs that have been taken of UFOs, why isn't there even *one* nice, clear picture of a flying saucer?

THAT'S RIGHT SON, FLING IT IN THE AIR!

Tom: Well, it's often dark. People are excited. It's not surprising if the camera shakes a bit. But look, even if the pictures *aren't* that great, the people who took them know what they saw.

Aisha: Do they? Let me tell you about the very first flying saucer.

The very first flying saucer

Aisha: It was way back in 1947. Kenneth Arnold, an American pilot, was flying his plane in broad daylight. It was a routine flight. Visibility was good. There was nothing out of the ordinary. Then, suddenly, Arnold spotted nine strange flying objects. On returning to the airfield, Arnold described what he had seen. It wasn't long before his report of 'flying saucers' had been transmitted across the country. The press went wild!

Soon, others started to see saucers, and of course the rest is history. We've been seeing these strange, saucer-shaped craft in the sky ever since. Flying saucers have since been immortalized in countless stories and films, including *Close Encounters of the Third Kind, Men in Black* and *The Day the Earth Stood Still.*

Tom: But if there have been many thousands of reports of flying saucers, many from highly qualified pilots, why don't you believe they exist?

Aisha smiles wryly.

Aisha: Because I know that *Arnold didn't see flying saucers.*
Tom: He didn't?
Aisha: No. He never said he saw saucers. Arnold said that the craft he saw looked like *boomerangs.*

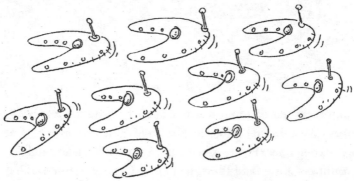

Tom: Boomerangs?

Aisha: That's right. He merely said that they *flew* like saucers would if skipped across a lake. They sort of bounced along.

Tom: Oh.

Aisha: But in the excitement that followed the sighting, that particular detail was lost. Arnold was reported as having seen saucers.

Now think about it: why have there been thousands of reports of flying *saucers* since 1947, if what Arnold saw did not look like saucers but boomerangs?

Tom: Hmm. That's a good question.

Aisha: What's more likely? That some of the reports of saucers made since 1947 have been reliable, it's just that back in 1947 the aliens coincidentally happened to change the shape of the spacecraft from boomerang to saucer?

Or that the reports of saucers since 1947 are actually a result of the *power of suggestion*.

Tom: Power of suggestion?

Aisha: Yes. People saw a distant plane or a cloud or a meteor or a bright star or some other vague light in the sky, or merely

hallucinated, and, because they *expected* an alien craft to be saucer-
shaped, they subconsciously turned what they saw into a saucer.
Tom: Well, I guess that *is* the more likely explanation.

Tom is right. Our tendency to 'see' whatever we strongly want
or expect to see has been studied extensively by scientists. The
only even *half*-plausible explanation for the thousands of flying
saucer reports made since 1947 is that they are down to the
power of suggestion.

Of course, the fact that the accountant who claimed to have
been abducted by aliens said he was kidnapped by a *flying saucer*
also tends to undermine his credibility. What is more likely, that
the accountant really was taken up by a flying saucer, or that he
had a vivid dream, hallucinated or made the whole thing up?

Surely it's much more plausible that he is either deluded or
else is deliberately deceiving us.

'Seeing' things
Of course, you will already be familiar
with the power of the mind to
'see' things that aren't
there.

Have you ever
lain on your
back and
watched the
clouds scud by?
It's possible to
'see' all sorts of
things in them:
faces, animals,
cars, countries...

...or perhaps you have sat in bed and watched as your dressing-gown transformed itself into a hideous creature.

The more you stare, the more real the creature seems, until you can almost convince yourself it is real.

I have 'heard' faint voices in the hiss of my TV set.

I have also become absolutely convinced I could smell a gas leak, when in fact there wasn't any gas at all.

The Mars face

In fact, our ability to 'see' things that aren't there partly explains one recent mystery: the Mars face. In 1976, the space probe Viking Orbiter 1 was taking pictures of the Cydonia region of Mars. On 25th July it photographed what appeared to be a huge alien face carved into the surface of the planet.

Many people believe that the face is a sculpture created by an alien race in their own image.

Certainly, the face does look a bit reptilian.

But the truth is that the face is actually a rather lumpy hill that, when lit from a certain angle, happens to cast shadows that resemble a face.

There are many thousands of hills, craters and other features on the surface of Mars. You would *expect* to find, just by chance, one or two that resemble familiar things. And because it is *particularly* easy for us to 'see' randomly arranged blobs and shadows as faces (faces are one of the easiest things to 'see' in clouds and campfires, for example) it isn't terribly surprising that a 'face' was discovered on the surface of Mars.

So the Mars face is really a result of two things: our ability to 'see' things as faces combined with the probability that a face-like combination of blobs and shadows would show up somewhere or other on the surface of a nearby planet.

I'm afraid the Mars face provides little evidence of an alien race. We can similarly explain why, every now and then, someone cuts open a piece of fruit that appears to contain a piece of writing or an image of someone.

Cut open enough pieces of fruit and eventually you are going to find a face-like combination of pips just by chance.

Miracles

Let's get back to Tom and Aisha. Tom has moved on to the chapter of *Mysterious World* that focuses on miracles.

Tom: OK. What about miracles?
Aisha: Miracles?
Tom: Yes. It says here that every day, fantastic things happen. Statues start to weep. People are suddenly cured of fatal diseases.

Tom pointed to the page in front of him.

Tom: Here's a particularly good example. A couple of years ago, in South America, a train went out of control. It was just about to crash into a station full of people, killing hundreds.

But at the last moment the points in front of the train failed, sending it harmlessly off on to another track.

Now how do you explain *that*? The points failed at the precise moment the runaway train came along! Obviously, that wasn't just a coincidence. Someone or something must have acted from 'beyond' to divert the train. It was a *miracle*!

Aisha: You mean God, or some other sort of supernatural being, lent a helping hand?

Tom: Exactly!

The power of coincidence

In fact, Aisha is happy to admit that a sort of 'miracle' happened.

Aisha: I agree. There *was* a 'miracle'. But only in the sense that there was a very happy *coincidence*. I don't see that there's much reason to suppose that some sort of supernatural being intervened.

Tom: Why not? You can't *seriously* maintain this was just a coincidence, can you?

Aisha: Yes I can. It almost certainly was just a coincidence. Look, there are *billions* of people all over the Earth, each one of whom has many thousands of experiences each day.

Tom: True.

Aisha: Now with *that* many people around experiencing that many things, some are bound to experience some pretty fantastic coincidences. Millions of people will be *very, very* lucky during their lifetime. Thousands will be stupendously lucky, perhaps having their life saved by a truly amazing coincidence. Hundreds will be so lucky as to be almost beyond belief. One or two will have good luck of such mind-wrenchingly, gob-smackingly awesome proportions that most of us simply won't be able to believe or comprehend just how lucky they have been.

Tom: Hmm. I *guess* that's true.

Aisha: Yet now you point to one case of fantastic good luck and say 'See, that shows there must be some sort of supernatural intervention involved!' Well, you're wrong. It doesn't. I'm afraid you have simply underestimated just how much amazing good fortune we should *expect* to find in the world.

I think Aisha is right. In fact, it would be truly peculiar if some people *didn't* get stupendously lucky every now and then. That really *would* be evidence for some sort of supernatural intervention.

Extra-Sensory Perception

Tom flips forward a few pages and comes to the chapter on psychics.

Tom: Ah. Then what about psychics? There's a great deal of evidence that they really do have some sort of weird, paranormal power. Even my auntie is convinced.

Aisha: She is?

Tom: Yes. A few weeks ago, her psychic told her that she had an uncle called 'Harold' who had a slipped disc and died of a heart attack. Yet my Auntie had *never even mentioned* Harold before. How could Auntie's psychic have known these details if she didn't have the gift of extra- sensory perception?

Tom is right that this sort of testimony about the powers of psychics is very common. Doesn't it provide us with pretty good evidence that extra-sensory perception (or ESP) really exists?

Perhaps. But before we make up our minds, let's look a little more closely at what *really* happened when Tom's auntie visited her psychic.

Auntie's visit to the psychic

Auntie enters a dimly lit room. The psychic is sitting at a table with a crystal ball.

Psychic: Hello, dearie. Do sit down.
Auntie: Thank you.
Psychic: Now... I'm getting a name.

The room goes deathly quiet.

Psychic: Henry... or Harold...?
Auntie: Uncle Harold?
Psychic: Yes, that's right! Hmm... I'm sensing some back trouble.
Auntie: Amazing! He slipped a disc just before he died.

The psychic waves towards the middle of her chest.

Psychic: Am I right in thinking it was trouble *here* that killed him?
Auntie: How did you know? It was a heart attack!
Psychic: Yes, yes. That's right. He just told me it was his ticker that got
   him in the end.

Auntie thinks that her psychic knew she had an uncle called
'Harold' who had a slipped disc and died of a heart attack.

Certainly, you can see why Auntie believes her psychic has
genuine psychic powers. But let's look a little more closely at
what the psychic *actually* says.

How the psychic fooled Auntie

The psychic begins with a name: Henry. Then she leaves a
pause. She gets no response from Auntie, so she tries another
name: Harold. This time it's a name Auntie recognizes.

But notice that most people of Auntie's age are likely to know
people with one or other of these two names (try asking anyone
over the age of 60 whether they know, or knew, anyone with
either name – I bet they do). So the fact that Auntie recognizes
one of the two names is hardly surprising.

Also notice that the psychic doesn't say that Auntie's *uncle* was
called 'Harold'. Actually, it is Auntie who gives the psychic that
piece of information. The psychic merely asks if either name
means anything to Auntie.

So far, *the psychic hasn't told Auntie anything at all.*

235

What happens next? The psychic says she senses 'back trouble'. But notice how very vague this statement is. The psychic doesn't say whom this back trouble is supposed to afflict. It could be Auntie's back that she's talking about. Or Harold's. Or some other person known to Auntie. Or it could be a *prediction* of back trouble to come. As almost everyone suffers from back pain at some point or another, it's not particularly surprising that Uncle Harold had back trouble himself.

Also notice that the psychic doesn't say *what sort* of back trouble she has in mind. Again, it is Auntie who tells the psychic about Harold's slipped disc, not the other way round.

So the psychic still hasn't given Auntie any information. In fact it *is Auntie who's providing all the information.*

Then the psychic asks if Harold died from trouble somewhere in the chest area. Notice that she doesn't *claim* that he did. She merely *asks* if he did. And remember that Auntie has already told the psychic that Harold is dead. Notice that, if Harold didn't die from trouble in the chest area, the psychic can still stress that she was merely *asking*, and hasn't yet made a mistake. But as almost *everyone* does die from trouble in the chest area in the end (even diseases of the head and limbs usually kill by travelling to organs in the torso), it was hardly surprising that poor old Harold went the same way.

Notice that when Auntie tells the psychic that Harold died of a heart attack, the psychic claims this was *something she knew already.* But what evidence is there that she did?

So far, *none at all.*

I have based Auntie's conversation with her psychic on some real conversations with psychics. This example illustrates just one or two of the very many techniques that psychics can use to convince people that they have genuinely psychic powers.

Though Auntie believes her psychic knew various details about her uncle Harold, it turns out that it was Auntie who supplied all the information. By making vague claims, asking questions and fishing for information the psychic cleverly managed the conversation to make it seem as if she was actually communicating with Auntie's dead uncle.

Of course, I am not suggesting that all psychics *deliberately* trick their customers. Most psychics really believe they have psychic powers. They don't just manage to convince other people of their paranormal gifts. They end up convincing themselves too.

Perhaps some psychics really do have genuinely psychic powers. But the fact that thousands of people are taken in by this sort of conversation on a regular basis doesn't really provide much evidence that they do.

The strange case of Clever Hans

Psychics may not just be using trickery to create the illusion that they have paranormal powers. They may also be reading very subtle clues in their customers' behaviour.

Let me tell you the true story of the horse Clever Hans.

Back in 1888, Hans's owner decided that he would try to teach Hans maths. After a great deal of careful training, Hans was eventually able to tap out with his hoof the answer to mathematical questions. For example, ask Hans 'What is twelve divided by four?' and Hans would tap his hoof three times.

Hans could perform even without his trainer present. There was no deliberate trickery involved: Hans's owner believed his horse really could do maths.

Clever Hans soon become world-famous, his abilities baffling both scientists and public audiences alike.

So could Hans *really* do maths?

No. He couldn't. Eventually, a young psychologist tested whether Hans could still perform if asked the questions by someone who didn't know the answers. It turned out he couldn't.

Somehow, Hans was reading tiny changes in the behaviour of his questioners, tapping his foot until some unconscious cue — such as a slight tensing of the questioner's body — told him when to stop. Someone who didn't know the answers was unable to supply Hans with these cues, which is why Hans then lost his mathematical powers.

What moral should we draw from this tale? Well, if a horse can learn to read such subtle, unconsciously-given signals, then no doubt a psychic can too. It may be that many psychics have learnt — perhaps without realizing that this is what they are doing — to read the same sorts of cues in their customers' behaviour. While impressive, there would be nothing spooky and supernatural about such an ability.

So it turns out that there are all sorts of perfectly normal ways in which psychics might convince their customers that they have supernatural powers.

A less than mysterious conclusion

Tom puts *Mysterious World* down on the coffee table. It lands with a thump.

Tom is feeling rather frustrated. Despite coming up with what seem to him to be perfectly good reasons for believing in astrology, flying saucers and ESP, Aisha remains entirely unconvinced.

Tom: Look, you can't *prove* that there are no flying saucers. You can't *prove* that there's nothing to astrology.

Aisha: Well, if you mean there's *some* room for doubt, then, yes, I admit I can't prove we aren't visited by flying saucers. My point is that there just isn't anything like the evidence needed to make it *reasonable* to believe in such things.

Tom: But shouldn't you be open-minded?

Aisha: I am open-minded in the sense that I am perfectly willing to look at any new evidence that might come along. But the fact remains that there's *very little reason* to suppose that we are visited by flying saucers, and so on. The evidence for saucers is extremely suspect. Mostly it takes the form of *testimony*: people tell about seeing saucers, meeting aliens, being abducted. But there's plenty of reason to distrust this testimony, isn't there? In fact, given our fascination with flying saucers, the ease with which we can be fooled, the power of suggestion, the way in which tales can become embellished, and the money to be made from peddling such tales, we really should *expect* a great deal of testimony *anyway*, whether or not there's anything to it.

Tom: But you admit there *might* be something to it?

Aisha: Yes. It *might* be true

239

that we are visited by flying saucers. It *might* be true that some people have psychic powers. But then it *might* be true that the moon is made of concrete...

... that French people are really from Pluto...

... and that George W. Bush is Elvis Presley with plastic surgery.

It *might* be true. That's not to deny that the evidence really doesn't support *any* of these claims. So it's downright irrational of you to believe them. *All* of them.

Is Aisha being fair?

In this chapter I have given you plenty of reasons for being *careful* about accepting evidence of weird, supernatural things happening. But it's up to you to figure out whether there is, after all, enough good evidence to make it reasonable to believe such things happen. Perhaps there is.

What do you think?

File 10

Killing people

It's wrong to kill

We all know that killing is wrong. In fact we think of killing as one of the very worst things a person can do. But is it *always* wrong to kill? Are there any exceptions to the rule?

Obviously, we think it's fine to kill bacteria and viruses. And we are happy about killing plants, especially if we are going to eat them.

Generally speaking, we think there is nothing wrong with killing these sorts of living thing.

Many also believe it's OK to kill *animals* (though of course not everyone agrees about that). Where I live, the majority think it's morally acceptable to kill and eat pigs, cows and chickens for food. Most people are also willing to annihilate insects, slugs and snails, particularly if they are eating our cabbages.

So when we say 'It's wrong to kill', it's clear we don't mean it to apply to *all* living things. In fact it seems we really only mean it to apply to *other people*.

In this chapter, I am going to look at the question of whether there are any exceptions to the rule that we shouldn't kill other people. Is it always wrong to take another person's life? Or are there some situations in which it *is* morally acceptable?

Capital punishment

Let's start with the death penalty, otherwise known as capital
punishment.

While almost
everyone believes it is wrong to kill other people, many make
an exception for murderers. They think that the death penalty is
an acceptable punishment for those guilty of deliberately killing
another person.

A number of countries have the death penalty, including
Saudi Arabia and the United States. Murderers and other
criminals have been put to death by hanging, beheading,
electrocution, shooting, lethal injection, or gas.

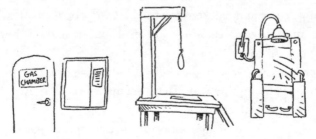

But is it *really* morally acceptable for us to kill murderers? Should
we consider them an exception to the rule?

As you are about to discover, Carol certainly thinks so.

Stringing up Dick Rotten

Carol and Aisha are watching the news on TV.

The newsreader has just reported that in the US the murderer Dick Rotten has finally been executed after spending six years on death row.

Carol is delighted.

Carol: Hooray! And about time too.

Aisha is a little surprised at Carol.

Aisha: Why are you so happy? Someone's just been *killed*! It's wrong to take another person's life.
Carol: Always?
Aisha: Yes. There's *never* an excuse. There was no *need* to kill Dick Rotten. They could have put him in jail instead.

Getting your own back

Carol admits that they didn't *need* to kill Dick Rotten.

Carol: True, they didn't have to kill him. But Rotten killed somebody else, didn't he? He murdered an innocent woman. So *justice has been done*! He's been killed in return.

There's no doubt that this is the way many people think about the death penalty. It's right to execute murderers: they're simply getting what's coming to them.

But Aisha thinks this is a very childish attitude to take.

Aisha: That's a brutal way of looking at life, isn't it? It's the morality of the school playground. Someone does something to you, so you do it to them! Remember when we were at school and Mary poked me in the eye?

I poked *her* right back.

Now I got told off for behaving like that, didn't I?

Carol: Yes, you did. Miss Tick was very cross. She said that two wrongs don't make a right.

Aisha: So why is it OK for *adults* to take revenge? Why is it right for them to kill the killer? I don't think it is.

The Bible

Carol suggests that perhaps the Bible can be used to justify the death penalty.

Carol: But what about 'an eye for an eye'? That's what it says in the Old Testament, isn't it? Surely we are *entitled* to get our own back.

Aisha: But why not quote from the New Testament, where Saint Paul very clearly says that we should not return evil for evil, but 'leave vengeance for God'?

And remember that one of the Ten Commandments is simply 'Do not kill'. It doesn't say 'Do not kill, *except for murderers*', does it?

Aisha is correct: the Bible doesn't appear to support the death penalty.

Aisha: It just seems to me that taking a life is wrong, *no matter what.* Killing is wrong, *full stop.*

Two arguments for the death penalty

We have seen that Aisha believes there are absolutely no exceptions to the rule that we shouldn't kill other people. So she thinks it is wrong to kill murderers.

Still, perhaps there are good reasons why at least some murderers should be executed. Can you think of any?

Carol thinks hard. After a minute or so, she comes up with a couple of arguments which she thinks do justify capital punishment. In fact, they are probably the two most popular arguments for the death penalty.

Let's look at the arguments one at a time and try to figure out whether they are any good.

Here's the first.

Argument one: deterrence
Carol begins by arguing that, by executing some murderers, we will *deter* others from committing the same crime.

Carol: What about *deterrence*?

Aisha: You mean, people will think twice before murdering someone if they believe they may face a death sentence?

Carol: Exactly.

Aisha: But isn't prison a deterrent too? People will also be afraid of committing murder if they think they're likely to be locked up for years and years.

Carol: But the deterrent effect of the death penalty is *stronger*. So, if we have the death penalty for murder, *innocent lives will be saved.*

At first sight, the deterrence argument looks pretty plausible. If capital punishment saves innocent lives, isn't that a *very* good reason for having it?

Is the death penalty a stronger deterrent than prison?
Aisha is not convinced.

Aisha: Trouble is, I'm not sure the death penalty *is* a stronger deterrent than jail. If it was, then you would expect countries with the death penalty to have lower murder rates, right?

Aisha: But actually, countries with the death penalty *don't* usually have lower murder rates. Compare the United States and Western Europe. Many states in the US have the death penalty. No Western European country does. Yet the murder rate is actually much higher in the US than it is in Western Europe.

Carol: Oh.

Aisha: And when we look inside America, we find that those states that have the death penalty tend not to have the lowest murder rate, but the highest! Like Texas.

Carol looks irritated.

Carol: But hang on a minute. Maybe the reason Texas has the death penalty is *because* of its higher murder rate, rather than the other way round.

Aisha: What do you mean?

Carol: Well, perhaps, because it has a problem with murder, Texas thinks it needs to introduce the death penalty. In fact, I bet the murder rate would be *even higher* if Texas didn't have capital punishment!

Aisha's eyes narrow.

Aisha: But again, that's not what the evidence suggests. Studies have repeatedly failed to show any deterrent effect. When states introduce the death penalty, as often as not the murder rate *goes up*. And when they *stop* executing, as often as not, the murder rate *falls*.

What Aisha says is true: it's not at all clear that execution does act as a stronger deterrent than a heavy prison sentence.

For example, when California carried out an execution every other month (between 1952 and 1967), murder rates increased

10% annually, on average.
Between 1967 and 1991, when
there were no executions in
California, the murder rate
increased by only 4.8% annually.

Of course, figures like these
should always be treated with
caution. With a little careful selection
it's easy to make the evidence show
whatever you want it to show. But perhaps it's worth mentioning
that a survey of experts – from the American Society of
Criminology, the Law and Society Association and the Academy
of Criminal Justice Sciences – showed the overwhelming majority did not believe the death penalty to be 'a proven deterrent to
murder'. These people will have looked very closely at the
evidence and will be in a particularly good position to judge.

The 'common sense' justification

Still, you might think it pretty obvious that the death penalty must
be a stronger deterrent than jail.

Why is that? Well, ask most people what they would prefer,
death or a long stretch in jail, and I'm sure they would choose
jail. Jail would be considered less awful (though still pretty

awful, of course).

So isn't it just *common sense* that the death penalty is a stronger deterrent?

Maybe not. To begin with, the death penalty will only act as a significantly stronger deterrent than a prison sentence if the murderer thinks they are likely to be caught. What about those calculating murderers who carefully weigh up the consequences before committing their crime? Presumably, these people only commit murder because they think it highly unlikely they'll be convicted. But then the death penalty isn't going to put them off much more than a long jail term. Neither is much of a deterrent if you're pretty confident you're going to get away with it.

What, then, about the rest: those who commit murder without considering the consequences? Some murders are committed in a frenzy of panic or hatred. The murderer lashes out in a blind fury without thinking at all. But if these people don't bother to weigh up the consequences, then the death penalty is hardly likely to put them off killing either.

So while the death penalty may deter *some* people, it probably won't be very many. And where the death penalty does deter more than jail, it probably won't be by very much. And, as we have seen, when we look at the statistics, that is exactly what they appear to bear out.

So, despite its popularity, the deterrence argument for the death penalty turns out, on closer inspection, to be a rather bad argument.

Argument two: the murderer cannot kill again

Carol decides to give up on the deterrence argument. She moves on to her second argument.

Carol: OK, here's another reason why we should have the death penalty for murder. By killing the murderer, *you prevent them killing again.*

Carol is, of course, perfectly correct: you can hardly go out and murder more people if you're dead.

Carol: You must have read that newspaper report about the murderer
Evil Bert. He was recently released.
And he immediately went out and
killed ten more people!
Aisha: I know. It was a shocking case.
Carol: So you see? If Evil Bert had been
executed, innocent lives would have been
saved! What's more important, the life of a
murdering monster like Evil Bert, or the lives of his future victims?

Carol is correct: a number of released murderers have killed again. Isn't this a good reason to execute them instead?
  Aisha doesn't think so.

Ashia: You haven't succeeded in justifying the death penalty, I'm afraid.
For of course the *other* option was to lock Evil Bert up and throw
away the key. If we lock someone up for life, then they can't kill
again, can they?
Carol: Well, I suppose not.
Aisha: Maybe it's true that certain murderers should *never* be released.
Obviously to release Evil Bert was a mistake. It doesn't follow that
it's best if murderers are executed, does it?

Carol has to admit that it doesn't follow. We could just keep them permanently locked up. In fact, in the US courts already have this option.

Justifying exceptions to the rule

We have been looking at what are probably the two most popular arguments for capital punishment. The first argument is that the death penalty saves innocent lives by deterring would-be murderers. The second is that if we kill murderers we will save innocent lives by preventing them from killing again. We have seen that, when examined more closely, neither argument is particularly convincing.

Now my own view – and of course you may not agree with me: you should think this through for yourself and make up your own mind – is that unless we can come up with some pretty good reason why we should execute murderers, then we shouldn't execute them.

Why do I think that? Well, we all admit that, *generally speaking*, it's wrong to take another person's life. We all sign up to that general rule, don't we – even those of us who favour the death penalty?

But if we all accept it's generally wrong to kill another human being, then it is up to those who favour the death penalty to explain why killing murderers *is* an exception to the rule. It's not up to opponents of the death penalty to explain why it isn't.

The bottom line is this: we all accept that it's wrong to kill anyone unless there is very good reason to do so. So we shouldn't kill murderers unless we can come up with a very good reason to do so.

So far, we haven't seen any particularly good reasons why we should execute murderers. So, unless Carol can come up with a better reason for executing them (and perhaps she can), I think she should accept that we shouldn't execute them.

An argument against the death penalty

Let's now take a look at one of the most popular arguments *against* capital punishment.

In the United Kingdom capital punishment was abolished back in 1965. One popular argument against reintroducing the death penalty is that innocent people would almost certainly end up being executed. Since capital punishment was abolished there have been a number of famous cases in which innocent people were convicted of murder. The mistake was discovered and these innocent people are now free.

But if the UK still had the death penalty for murder, these innocent people would all be dead. The injustice done to them could never be rectified.

So it is clear that, *because the UK doesn't have the death penalty, a number of innocent lives have been saved.*

There's also little doubt that in the US *innocent people continue to be executed.* Since 1973, 102 prisoners have been released from death row in the USA after evidence of their innocence emerged. Some came very close to execution after spending many years under sentence of death. This suggests that, in all probability, a number of people have been executed who were innocent.

Of course, some might say that this shows, not that murderers shouldn't be executed, but that the US legal system needs to be improved so that fewer innocent people are convicted of murder.

Still, there's little doubt that, if we have the death penalty, some innocent people are inevitably going to be executed no matter how careful we are. Is that a price worth paying for having the death penalty? What do you think?

Making up your own mind

As I say, I am not in favour of the death penalty. It seems to me that when we look at the arguments carefully they turn out clearly to support the abolition of capital punishment.

But of course, I make mistakes. Perhaps you disagree with me. Maybe you can come up with better arguments for the death penalty. You might even be able to find a fatal flaw in the popular argument against the death penalty.

We all have a duty to think for ourselves and make up our own minds about whether or not it's right to execute murderers. Don't just uncritically accept what I happen to think.

Executions are fun!

But do be careful that you don't simply give in to the desire for vengeance.

Let me admit something. There are bad people in the world who, frankly, I would really rather *enjoy* seeing executed. Yes, that's right: even though I have argued against the death penalty, a part of me still says, 'Let's string Dick Rotten up! Let's strap Evil Bert to the electric chair!'

Action movies often appeal to such feelings. We love to watch the villain get his come-uppance in the final scene, dying

in some particularly gruesome way.
It's highly satisfying to watch the evil
fiend get impaled on a huge metal
spike.

We all have these feel-
ings. They're perfectly
natural. We shouldn't be *too*
ashamed of them.

But you should be wary of automatically giving in to them, of
assuming that if you *feel good* about what is happening, then it *is
good*.

While the death penalty has many supporters, it seems to me
that, for some, the real motivation is that they feel angry and
want vengeance. They enjoy the idea of the murderer being
killed. They want to see him writhe and squirm in agony, just
as his victim did.

But I'm afraid these feelings don't justify capital punishment. The fact that we rather enjoy killing murderers doesn't make it morally acceptable.

Killing the guilty in defence of the innocent

We have seen that Aisha thinks it's *always* wrong to take another person's life no matter what. She thinks there are absolutely no exceptions to this rule.

I agree with Aisha that we shouldn't execute murderers. But I am not so sure that there are *no* exceptions.

Carol now comes up with an interesting case.

Carol: OK, perhaps it's true that we shouldn't kill murderers. But it's not *always* wrong to kill.

Aisha: Why not?

Carol: Suppose that Evil Bert runs into your home carrying a gun. It's clear he's going to murder you and your family.

AND NOW I'M GOING TO KILL YOU ALL... HA HA HA!

Now suppose you have a gun, and that you know the only way to stop Evil Bert is by shooting him dead. What should you do?

PAH! YOU'll NEVER SHOOT! AND NOW YOU DIE!!!

THE COMPLETE PHILOSOPHY FILES

Aisha: Shoot Bert dead, I guess.

Carol: Right. But then you think that it *is* OK to kill another human being in this sort of case.

Aisha: Hmm. I guess so. Killing someone who's about to murder innocent people is morally acceptable if that's the only way to stop them. But that's the only exception to the rule that we should not kill.

Almost everyone agrees that this really is a legitimate exception to the rule: do not kill. Surely it would be wrong to stand back and let Evil Bert slaughter an innocent family, even if the only way to stop him is by killing him.

So it seems Aisha is wrong. Sometimes it *is* right to kill. But is this the only sort of exception?

Notice that Carol's case involves killing a bad person so that innocent lives might be saved. But what about killing an innocent person to save innocent lives? Is *that* ever morally the right thing to do?

That's the question that we are going to examine in the rest of this chapter. Let's look at some different puzzle cases to see if we can figure out the answer.

The Grand Vizier's conundrum

The Grand Vizier was a humane and civilized advisor to the ruler of Moldania. One day, he was faced with a terrible decision. His country was invaded by the Warls, an awful, vicious race. They executed the ruler of Moldania and took the Grand Vizier to the City Square where they had lined up one hundred Moldanian children against a wall.

The Grand Vizier was presented with the following dilemma. He could shoot just one of the hundred children himself, and the others would then be set free. Or, if he refused, all one hundred children would be shot.

There were no other choices available to the Grand Vizier. For example, there was no possibility of the children being rescued. What should the Grand Vizier do?

On the one hand, the Grand Vizier could kill an innocent child. That would save the lives of 99 other children. The Grand Vizier knew that the Warls would be true to their word and release the 99 other children because he knew that this was something they always did on invading a country, and they had always been true to their word before.

On the other hand, the Grand Vizier could keep his hands clean and refuse to shoot an innocent child. But he knew the child would immediately be shot anyway, and so too would 99 others.

This is an awful decision for anyone to face.

Personally, I think I would kill one child in order to save the rest. I think that, on balance, that would be the best thing to do.

But if this is the correct decision, then it follows that killing an innocent person is sometimes the right thing to do.

What would you do, and why?

The submarine case
Here's another case. You are the head of a powerful country that possesses several nuclear-armed submarines. You know that

one of these submarines has developed a mechanical fault that will shortly result in it launching all its nuclear missiles, killing millions of innocent people as a result.

You cannot contact the submarine's crew to prevent the launch. The only way to stop the catastrophe from happening is to destroy the sub, killing everyone on board.

What should you do?

It seems pretty clear to me that the right thing to do is to destroy the submarine, even though that would involve killing its entirely innocent and blameless crew. The alternative is just too awful to contemplate.

So it seems to me that sometimes the right thing to do is to kill innocent people if the result will be many more innocent lives saved.

The astronaut case

Here's a third example for you to think about.

The Spaceship Goliath has suffered a terrible accident, leaving only two crew members alive. The two astronauts, Sarah and Sade, are trapped in two different sections of the blasted hull. Sharon and Sade are rapidly running out of air. You have been despatched by Space Command to rescue the two astronauts and you arrive only minutes before Sarah and Sade will run out of air and suffocate.

Then you make a tragic discovery. You find that you can rescue only one of the two astronauts. For in order to rescue one of the astronauts, you will have to shut off the air supply to the other. You discover, in other words, that you can save one of the women only by killing the other.

What should you do?

Again, it seems pretty clear to me that the right thing to do in this case is to save one of the two lives, even though you can only do so by killing an innocent person. Surely it would be morally wrong to sit back and watch both women suffocate when one of them could be saved.

Calculating innocent lives saved

We have just looked at three cases in which it seems that the right thing to do is to kill an innocent person. That seems particularly clear in the last two cases. So it seems that sometimes it is OK to kill the innocent if the result will be innocent lives saved.

So, when faced with such decisions, is the right thing to do just to calculate what action will result in the most innocent lives saved, and then do that?

That sort of calculation would appear to give the right verdict in our first three cases. But what about the next case? Consider the Great Glugh's dilemma.

The Great Glugh's dilemma

The Great Glugh, ruler of Blastonia, was faced with a tough call. The chief of the Blastonian rescue services told the Great Glugh that a group of cavers was trapped after one of them, Ned, had became stuck in the exit hole. It wasn't Ned's fault: a rock had tumbled down and wedged him in.

The cave below Ned was flooding fast. Ned couldn't be safely removed without special equipment that was several hours away. But unless Ned was removed within the next half hour or so, the 20 other cavers trapped underneath Ned would all drown – though Ned himself would survive.

The chief of rescue services asked the Great Glugh what should be done. The 20 cavers could be saved, but only if the Great Glugh gave permission to kill Ned and cut his body out of the exit hole.

What should the Great Glugh's decision be?

In the first three cases, it seemed the right thing to do was to take an innocent life in order that other lives might be saved. If the right thing to do when presented with this sort of dilemma is simply to calculate which course of action will result in the greatest number of innocent lives saved, then obviously the right thing for the Great Glugh to do in this case is to kill Ned and save the other cavers.

But is that the right thing to do? I am not so sure.

What do you think?

The transplant case

Here's a case in which it seems pretty clear to me that it would be quite wrong to kill an innocent person in order to save an innocent life.

We are the doctors in charge of two patients. Tim, one of the patients, has brain disease. He will be dead within a week or so.

The other patient, Jim, has heart failure. He will certainly die within a few hours unless he receives a heart transplant.

Unfortunately, no transplant donor has been found.
But then we happen to notice that Tim has exactly the same tissue type as Jim. So Tim's heart could be safely transplanted into Jim and Jim would almost certainly survive.

What is the right thing to do? If we wait for Tim to die before we take his heart it will be too late. Both men will die. The only way to save Jim is by killing Tim.

But Tim isn't happy about being killed before his time is up. He wants to spend his last week with his family.

What should we do?

Of course, we could kill Tim anyway. We could do it secretly and painlessly. We could do it at night while Tim is sleeping. Neither Tim nor his family need be any the wiser. His family would just think Tim had died from brain disease a little earlier than expected. It's clear that if, when faced with these life-and-death situations, the right thing to do is always to do whatever will save the most innocent lives, then obviously the right thing to do in this case is to save Jim by killing Tim.

But is that the right thing to do?

Pretty obviously not! Almost everyone agrees that it would be morally very wrong indeed to kill Tim, even if the result would be that Jim survives.

Tim's 'right to life'

But why would it be wrong to kill Tim?

Some people would say: because human beings have rights. In particular, they have a right to life, a right not to be killed. True, a life might be saved by killing Tim. But it's wrong deliberately to infringe someone's rights, especially their right to life.

That's why Tim shouldn't be killed.

> TIM HAS A RIGHT TO LIFE. IT IS MORALLY WRONG TO INFRINGE IT, NO MATTER HOW GOOD OUR INTENTIONS.

A tricky puzzle

But hang on a minute. If we should never under any circumstances infringe an innocent person's right to life, then it follows that it's also wrong to destroy the submarine in the submarine case. Blowing up the submarine would certainly involve infringing the crew members' rights to life. Yet it seems pretty clear that in the submarine case we should kill the crew.

The same is true of the astronaut case. In fact the astronaut case is a lot like the transplant case. In both, we can save one of two people only by killing the other. If we do nothing, both will die. Yet in one situation – the astronaut case – it seems that we should kill, while in the other – the transplant case – it seems we shouldn't.

So what's the essential difference between the transplant and astronaut cases, the difference that explains why it is OK to kill in one case but not the other?

I guess that, like me, you feel it *wouldn't* be wrong to kill one of the two astronauts in order to save the other. And I also guess that, like me, you feel pretty sure it *would* be wrong to kill the brain-diseased patient to save the heart patient. But that puts us both in a very awkward position. If we feel it's OK to kill in one case but not the other, then it's up to us to justify treating the two cases differently. I'm not so sure I can do that. Can you?

The case of the conjoined twins

As I say, it seems to me that sometimes it is morally acceptable to take an innocent life and sometimes it isn't. But, as we have seen, it's very hard to explain why it is OK to kill the innocent in some cases but not others. You may have an explanation of your own.

Here's a final case for you to think about. This time, it's not a case that I have made up. It's a *real* life-and-death case. I shall leave you to decide what should be done, and why.

A couple of years ago two girls were born joined together at the chest. They were conjoined, like this:
One twin was called Mary, the other Jodie.
Jodie was bright and alert, but Mary had only a rudimentary brain and depended for her blood supply on Jodie's heart.

The parents and doctors faced a terrible decision. Leave the two girls connected and both would die within a matter of months. Separate them, and Jodie would probably survive, though Mary would certainly die.

The doctors involved believed that they should operate to separate the two girls. That way, at least one girl might be saved. But the parents, devout Catholics, objected on religious grounds. They believed that the operation to separate the two girls shouldn't go ahead, for it would involve killing one of the two girls. And that, they felt, would be wrong. Of course, they knew that the result of not killing Mary would be that *both* children would shortly die.

The doctors went to court and obtained permission to operate against the parents' wishes. Mary was killed. But Jodie survived.

But *was* that the right thing to do? Is this like the astronaut case, in which we thought it right to kill one innocent person in order to save the other? Or is it more like the transplant case, where we agreed that it would be wrong to kill one patient in order to save the other?

What do you think, and why?

File 11

Does Murderous Mick deserve to be punished?

Here's Murderous Mick. He's just been captured trying to rob a bank. Mick shot a bank guard in the back, just for fun.

Obviously we think very badly of people like Murderous Mick. We hold them responsible for their dishonest, selfish and cruel behaviour. We believe that they deserve punishment. Mick will end up locked up in jail for years.

I guess you think, 'And quite right too. That's what Mick deserves.'

A 'common sense' view

That people who rob and murder deserve to be punished for what they do is, of course, the 'common sense' view. But is 'common sense' correct about this?

THAT'S RIGHT. I'M BLAMELESS!

As we will soon discover, there's a famous philosophical argument that *seems* to show that we are mistaken: Murderous Mick doesn't deserve punishment. In fact he's entirely blameless!

But before we get to that famous argument, let's quickly look at an obvious exception to the rule that people deserve to be punished for the harm they cause.

Mr Black gets shoved out of the window

We don't always hold people
responsible for what they do.
Suppose Mr Black gets pushed
backwards out of a window.
He lands on top of Mr Brown.

Mr Black's OK.
But unfortunately, by
landing on Mr Brown,
Mr Black breaks Mr
Brown's arm.

Is what happened Mr Black's fault? Does he deserve to be punished?

Surely not. Murderous Mick might deserve punishment, but not Mr Black. Why is this? After all, like Murderous Mick, Mr Black caused a serious injury.

The answer, it seems, is that Mr Black had *no control* over what happened. He was quite unable to stop himself being pushed out of the window or falling on Mr Brown.

How can it be Mr Black's fault that Mr Brown ended up with a broken arm? Surely we can only hold someone responsible for doing something they actually had some control over.

But, as I say, we *do* suppose that Murderous Mick deserves punishment. We suppose that, unlike Mr Black, Mick didn't have to do what he did. Instead of going in for bank robbing, murder and mayhem, Mick could have chosen to do good things with his life. Mick deserves punishment because, unlike Mr Black, he was *free to do otherwise*.

That, at least, is the 'common sense' view.

An extraordinary argument

Let's now turn to the famous philosophical argument I mentioned earlier. The argument is extraordinary because it seems to show that no one can ever be held responsible for what they've done.

Not even Murderous Mick!

Your first reaction to this is probably to say, 'Are you nuts? Of course Mick deserves punishment!' But don't make up your mind just yet. Let's take a closer look at the argument first. I call it, for obvious reasons, the *we-never-deserve-punishment argument*. I'll break the argument down into three parts.

The we-never-deserve-punishment argument. Part one: laws of nature

The argument begins with a scientific discovery. The universe, it seems, is everywhere ruled by *laws*. These laws of nature, as they are known, govern everything that happens physically. You might think of the laws of nature as a list of instructions that everything in the universe is compelled to obey, down to the very last atom.

For example, there's a law that governs how bodies attract each other gravitationally. Take the two planets Earth and Venus. These two objects exert a gravitational pull on each other. And there is a law of nature that says exactly how much pull these objects will exert on each other. The amount of pull depends on how massive the objects are and how close they are together. Big objects close together exert a strong pull.

Little objects far apart exert a weak pull.

Every pair of physical objects in the entire universe, from the tiniest pebble on the beach to a whole galaxy, must obey this law. There are no exceptions.

There are many other laws of nature, of course. In fact *everything that physically happens in the universe is governed by such laws*. This means that, if you know exactly how the universe is set up at any particular moment in time, down to the movement of the very last atom, and if you know all the laws of nature, then it is possible in principle for you to work out what will happen next, down to the movement of the very last atom.

It's as if the universe is a train and the laws of nature are its rails. If you know how fast the train is moving, and you know how the rails are laid, then you can predict exactly where the train will be at any point in the future. The train has no choice

about where it will end up. It's compelled to travel in a particular direction by the rails. The same is true of the physical universe. Every piece of physical matter is in the vice-like grip of the same rigid laws. It's impossible for anything to happen other than what actually happens. Earthquakes, volcanoes, rockfalls, the tides, ice ages: everything that goes on physically is made to happen, and could in principle have been predicted long beforehand.

Philosophers have a name for the view that everything that physically happens in the universe is determined by laws. It's called *determinism*.

The we-never-deserve-punishment argument. Part two: we're nature's puppets

Which brings me to part two of the we-never-deserve-punishment argument. We are physical beings ourselves. We have physical bodies. But then it follows that our bodies are in the grip of the same physical laws as everything else.

What does this mean? Well, if we are also in the grip of these laws, then it seems *we are not free to do anything other than what we actually do*. For example, I just scratched the top of my head. But if determinism is true, I was no more able not to scratch my head than a pebble is free to float in mid-air or water is able to flow up hill unaided. Everything I do is physically determined, and could in principle have been predicted long before I decided to do it.

So *I am not free*. As physical beings, we are nature's puppets, dancing on her strings.

'But there are no laws of human nature...'

Before we get to part three of the we-never-deserve-punishment argument, let's quickly deal with a worry you might have about part two.

'Surely,' you may say, 'there are no laws governing *human behaviour*, are there? For example, there's no law that says that when someone is hungry and they know that there's food in the fridge, they will go to the fridge.'

Suppose Mary is hungry and she knows the only food is in the refrigerator.

270

Now, knowing human behaviour as I do, I can say that it's pretty likely that Mary will go to the fridge fairly soon. But there's no guarantee that she will. Perhaps Mary's on a diet. Or perhaps she's saving the food in the fridge for a party she's planning to have that evening.

The most I can say is that Mary will probably go to the fridge. There's no law compelling her to go to the fridge. She's free either to go or not to go.

Is this a good objection to the claim that we aren't free?

I don't think so.

True, there are no laws of human behaviour. But even if there are no laws of human behaviour, does it follow that Mary is free?

No, it doesn't follow. I admit there's no law that says that a hungry person who knows there is food in the fridge will go to the fridge. But a human being is a storm of tiny particles.

A HUMAN BEING IS A STORM OF TINY PARTICLES.

Mary is made out of molecules that are made out of atoms that are made out of electrons, protons and neutrons which are made out of still tinier particles all whizzing around. Each and every one of these particles is in the grip of the laws of nature. They cannot do anything other than what they do in fact do. Now it's *the laws governing these particles* that determine how Mary will behave. It is these laws that compel her to do whatever she does in fact do.

So Mary is not free. There may not be laws of human behaviour. It doesn't follow that what we do isn't determined by laws.

We human beings think we're free. But we're not really free. Our freedom is an illusion. We're nature's puppets.

The we-never-deserve-punishment argument. Part three: we're not to blame

Now we reach the final part of the we-never-deserve-punishment argument. If none of us is ever free − if we are unable to do anything other than what we in fact do − then how can we ever be held responsible for what we do? How can we ever deserve punishment?

After all, we said about Mr Black that he didn't deserve to be punished for landing on Mr Brown. That was because he had no control over what happened. He was compelled to land on top of poor Mr Brown.

But if determinism is true, the same is true of what Murderous Mick did. Murderous Mick was no more able not to shoot that poor bank clerk than Mr Black was able not to land on top of Mr Brown. Neither was free to do anything other than what they did do. But then neither deserves blame or punishment, surely?

True, the 'common sense' view is that someone like Murderous Mick deserves both blame and punishment. But it seems that 'common sense' is just wrong about this.

SEE? I TOLD YOU I'M BLAMELESS!

Philosophy v. 'common sense'

This is a fantastic conclusion, of course. In fact, like me, you probably can't make yourself believe the conclusion is true.

Still, is it rational to carry on believing that we are free and that we do sometimes deserve punishment? Am I justified in believing these things?

It seems I'm not. The we-never-deserve-punishment argument does appear to show that no one is free, and that no one ever deserves to be punished.

In philosophy you often come across arguments that contradict 'common sense'. One of the most fascinating, and sometimes infuriating, things about philosophy is the way it can challenge what we normally just take for granted.

Common sense has been wrong before, of course. It was once the 'common sense' view that the Earth is stationary. Almost everyone thought it 'just obvious' that the sun went round the Earth, not the other way round. But of course, all these people were mistaken. Science showed 'common sense' to be wrong.

Perhaps, by showing that everything that happens physically is determined, science has also shown that 'common sense' is wrong about us being free.

Sometimes, when 'common sense' views are challenged, people get very cross. That happened when scientists first showed that the Earth moves. They would shout 'That's just ridiculous! Of *course* the Earth doesn't move. You're just being *stupid!*' And they would stomp off in a huff.

I suppose that reaction is understandable. No one much likes having their most basic and fundamental beliefs challenged. It can be very uncomfortable to have someone come along and pick holes in what you have always taken for granted.

Still, the fact is that the really 'stupid' people were those who blindly stuck with 'common sense' even after they had been presented with overwhelming evidence that the Earth does move.

The same is true of someone who simply dismisses as stupid the conclusion that we're not free just because it's contrary to 'common sense'.

Where do we go from here?

So we have a puzzle – a very famous puzzle – that many philosophers have struggled with down the years.

On the one hand, we all believe that we are free. For example, I think I am free, right now, to do something different: to make a cup of tea, jump up and down on the spot, or shout 'Bananas!' out of the window.

But, on the other hand, we have seen an argument that appears to show that we're all completely mistaken about being free! I am no more able to do something different than water is free to flow uphill. We are, in truth, Nature's puppets, dangling helplessly on strings!

But if we aren't free, it seems, shockingly, that no one ever deserves punishment. Not even Murderous Mick!

All over the world, philosophers are struggling with this difficult puzzle. Are we free? Or aren't we? What's the answer? What do you think?

Faced with such an apparently devastating philosophical argument, defenders of the 'common sense' view that we are free have only one option. They must show that there is something wrong with the argument.

But if there is something wrong with the we-never-deserve-punishment argument, then what is wrong with it?

What do you think?

Meet the Fates

Before we try to figure out what, if anything, is wrong with the we-never-deserve-punishment argument, let's have a quick look at another, slightly different version of the view that we aren't free.

THE FATES

The Ancient Greeks believed in the Fates.

The Fates are beings who lay out the course of your life, giving you no option about how things turn out. For example,  if the Fates say you will be injured by a car next Wednesday, then you will. Try to avoid being injured if you want. But it will do no good. You can even stay in bed all day.

Somehow or other, the Fates will get you.

Those who believe in this sort of fate are called *fatalists*. Fatalists believe that there is no point in trying to prevent things from happening. For example, a fatalist might say, 'There's no point wearing a seatbelt: if I'm going to die in a car crash then I am going to die in a car crash – there's nothing I can do about it. What will be will be.'

Now the reason I mention fatalism is that it's very important not to muddle it up with determinism. Fatalism says that *our actions can have no effect*. Do what you like: things will still turn out the same way. Determinism, on the other hand, doesn't deny that our actions can make a difference to how things turn out. It just denies that we can act other than how we do.

There's no reason to suppose that fatalism is true. The Ancient Greeks might have believed in fate, but there's no evidence that our actions will have no effect on how things turn out. Quite the contrary, in fact. Wearing a seatbelt really can save your life.

But it *does* seem as if determinism is true. Science has revealed that the physical universe is governed by laws. And, being part of the physical universe, these laws apply to us as well. So we cannot do other than what we do.

Having clarified the difference between determinism and fatalism, let's take a closer look at the we-never-deserve-punishment argument.

Tom's 'proof' that he is free

Tom and Carol are sitting in The Magic Café here in Oxford. They often discuss philosophical puzzles over lunch and today they are talking about free will.

Carol has just explained the we-never- deserve-punishment argument to Tom. But Tom is totally unconvinced. He points to Carol's plate of vegetarian lasagne.

Tom: So you think that, even if I were to take your lunch, place it on the floor, and jump up and down on it, I would be entirely innocent and blameless? You think I would deserve not even one ounce of condemnation?

Carol looks up from her plate a little nervously.

Carol: Er, yes. You're not going to, are you?

Tom: No. But what if I did? I can't *really* believe you would think me blameless.

Carol: Well, I would probably feel very cross. I admit that. But then I feel cross when my computer crashes or when my car won't start. That doesn't mean that I think my computer and car deserve blame and punishment for not working, does it? That doesn't show that I believe they have free will.

Tom: No, I guess not. But still, it's obvious to me that I *am* free. I can *prove* it.

Carol: OK, go ahead and prove it.

Tom: Very well. Right now, I am free either to raise my arm or not raise my arm.

Tom sits motionless for a moment, and then suddenly raises his arm.

Tom: There, I raised my arm. But I was free not to raise it. I could have done either. So you see I *am* free. I am *not* nature's puppet.

Has Tom really proved that he is free? No, as Carol now explains.

Carol's water argument

Carol: You may *feel* free. But that doesn't guarantee that you *are* free. True, you may not *know* about the laws that compel you to behave as you do. But just because you don't know about them doesn't mean that they aren't there. They *are* there. That's precisely what science has shown.

Tom: But look, sometimes I raise my arm and other times I don't. So you see: I'm free to do either.

Carol: But the fact that you sometimes raise your arm and sometimes don't doesn't show that you are free.

Carol points to the water in her glass.

Carol: Look, sometimes water lies still like this. But sometimes it runs quickly in streams.

Sometimes it falls as rain or hangs in the air as a cloud. Does the fact that water behaves in these different ways on different occasions show that water is not governed by natural laws?

Tom: No. I guess not.

Carol: Right. So there you are, then. The fact that *you* behave in lots of different ways doesn't show that *you* aren't in the grip of the same laws.

Tom scratches the back of his neck. It still seems to him that, unlike the water in the glass, he is free to do his own thing.

Tom: But water behaves differently only because the circumstances in which you find it are different. Liquid water sometimes flows and sometimes doesn't, but that's because sometimes it's on a slope and sometimes not. Water will always behave exactly the same way if the circumstances are exactly the same.

Carol: That's true.

Tom: But I *don't* always behave in the same way, even when the circumstances *are* exactly the same. Yesterday we came into the Magic Café and I ordered soup. Today I ordered salad. Yet the circumstances today are just the same as they were yesterday. So you see – I am free in a way that the water in that glass is not.

Carol: No, you aren't. There are subtle differences between how you are today and how you were yesterday. Your internal make-up is different today. Your brain chemistry is subtly different, for example. Different patterns of neurons are firing. There are *all sorts* of differences. It's these differences that explain why you behave differently today, that explain why you made a different choice. If the situation today really were *absolutely* identical to the situation yesterday, right down to the very last atom, then you *would* have chosen soup today as well.

It seems Carol is right. It might seem obvious to you that you're free. But on closer examination it's not so obvious after all. In fact we still haven't spotted anything wrong with the argument that we're all nature's puppets.

The freedom of the soul

But Tom doesn't give up easily.

Tom: I still believe I'm free. It seems to me that you have a much too narrow, scientific view of the universe. Yes, science is powerful. But there is more to we humans than science can ever explain.

Carol: What do you mean?

Tom: I mean that each of us has a soul.

Carol: A soul?

Tom: Yes. Your soul is your *conscious mind*, that part of you that makes choices and decisions.

Carol: I see.

Tom: It is something outside the natural order. It's not part of the physical universe at all.

Carol: It's a non-physical thing?

Tom: That's right. It's even capable of existing on its own, without *any* physical body.

Many religious people believe in the existence of souls, of course. They believe that the death of the physical body does not mean the end of the person. What's essential to the person – their soul – can carry on. It is the soul that many Christians believe goes up to heaven after we die.

On Carol's view, people are physical things. They are not separate from their bodies.

But according to Tom, a person has a soul. The soul is something separate, something non-physical.

But what have souls to do with free will? Tom explains.

Tom: Being non-physical, the soul is not controlled by physical laws. Being apart from the physical world means it can do its own thing. So it *is* free.

This is an ingenious suggestion. Has Tom explained how we can be free after all?

A problem with the soul theory

Carol: But you haven't given me any reason to suppose that souls exist, have you?

Tom: Well, I suppose not. Not yet.

Carol: And in any case, even if souls *do* exist, they s*till wouldn't allow us to act freely.*

Tom: Why not?

Carol: Because our bodies *are* physical. So they *are* in the grip of the laws of nature. What *they* do is determined in advance by how things are physically. But that means our bodies *still* can't do anything other than what they do, in fact, do.

Tom raises an eyebrow.

Tom: I'm not sure I follow.

Carol: Well, let's suppose you are right and I am a non-physical soul. According to you, I'm free to decide either to take a bite of that cake or to take a sip of that water.
I decide to take a sip of water. But if determinism is true, what happens to my body is already fixed by the laws of nature. If the laws of nature say that my arm will reach out and grab the cake, then it will, whatever *I* might happen to decide.

So you see, even if we do have
souls and they *are* free, that *still*
wouldn't give us any control over
what our bodies did.

Tom: Oh. I see.

Carol: In fact, if we had souls, they
would be disconnected from our
bodies, unable to have *any* effect
on what they did. So, as we clearly
can affect what our bodies do, it
follows that *we don't have souls.*

This is an interesting line of argument. If
determinism is true, it really would seem to
follow that we don't have souls.

Is the brain an exception to the laws of nature?
But Tom is unpersuaded by Carol's argument.

Tom: You're simply assuming that what your body does is fixed by the
laws of nature plus how things are physically. But *that's not true.*
Your soul can come in and affect what's going on physically.

Carol: How does it do that?

Tom: It's as if the soul and the brain are equipped with little transmitters and receivers.

When I decide I want to raise my arm, my soul transmits a signal to my brain. That causes something to happen in my brain, which in turn causes electrical signals to be sent to my arm. That raises my arm.

Carol: But that's *ridiculous!* That would mean that something happening in your brain has no *physical* cause. Being caused by the signal sent from something non-physical – your soul – it would not be physically determined.

Tom: Exactly.

Carol: But *every* physical event has a physical cause. That's a law of nature.

Tom: Yes, generally speaking, physical events have physical causes. But there's an exception to the rule: the human brain. Some things happen in the brain that *don't* have a physical cause. Some of what goes on in the brain is caused by *the soul* – something *non-physical.*

Carol: So the laws of nature apply throughout the entire universe, with one exception: the human brain?

Tom: Yes.

Carol: What a load of unscientific tosh!

Tom's explanation of how the soul and the body interact is certainly a lot to swallow. The suggestion that the laws of nature apply throughout the entire universe *except for one place*, the human brain, is pretty implausible. Why suppose that the laws of nature make an exception of the human brain?

Why it may still be right to punish Mick

Up to now, we haven't spotted anything wrong with the we-never-deserve-to-be-punished argument.

So let's suppose, for the sake of argument, that it's true that we can't act freely and so never deserve punishment. Does it

I'M BLAMELESS! SO YES, YOU SHOULD RELEASE ME!

then follow that it is a mistake to punish murderous Mick for what he did? Should we release him?

Actually, it doesn't follow. Even if Murderous Mick doesn't deserve punishment, there are still good reasons why we should send him to prison. Here are three:

First, punishment may have a *deterrent* effect. Even if we can't act freely – even if we are physically determined – our behaviour can still be altered. And it might be altered by the threat of punishment. People may be *caused* to act differently if they think they will go to prison. If we punish people for committing crimes, then people may be less likely to commit those crimes. If so, then here is a good reason for punishing criminals anyway, whether or not they deserve it.

Second, by sending a criminal to prison we may be able to help them. Some prisons aim to *rehabilitate* prisoners, so that they are less likely to offend again. Again, even if we are not free, rehabilitation may *cause* us to act differently.

Third, by locking murderers like Mick up, we can *prevent* them from murdering again.

SEE – THERE ARE STILL GOOD REASONS WHY WE SHOULD LOCK YOU UP.

OH DEAR.

So there are still good reasons why we should lock Murderous Mick up: deterrence, rehabilitation and prevention. Of course, none of this is to say that Mick deserves to be locked up. It's just that it seems to be a good idea to lock him up anyway, whether or not he deserves it.

The puzzle

In this chapter, we have looked at a famous philosophical puzzle: the puzzle is raised by the we-never-deserve-to-be-punished argument. Philosophers call it the *puzzle of free will*.

Philosophers have been struggling with the puzzle for hundreds of years. Even today, at universities across the world, philosophers and scientists are still trying to solve it.

The puzzle is this: it seems that, if determinism is true, then we can't act freely. But then it appears that none of us ever deserves punishment for what we do.

Yet this is *absurd*, isn't it? *Of course* we can act freely. *Of course* we sometimes deserve to be punished for what we have done. Don't we?

What do you think?

File 12

Where did the universe come from?

The Big Bang

Sometime between eight and twenty billion years ago
something utterly astonishing happened. The universe began.

It started with the Big Bang: a colossal explosion in which
matter, space and even time itself came into being.

THE BIG BANG.

When you look up at the night sky, what you see is the
debris left by this extraordinary event. The countless stars,
planets and galaxies are the smoky entrails of that huge,
unimaginably violent moment of creation.

We know that the Big Bang happened. But why did it
happen? Why does the universe exist?

Or, to put it another way, why is there something rather than nothing?

This is a question with which mankind has been struggling for thousands of years. It is, perhaps, the greatest mystery of all.

God

One of the most popular answers to the question about the origin of the universe is that it was created by God. That is the answer we looked at in File 8. In this File, we look at two more arguments for the existence of God.

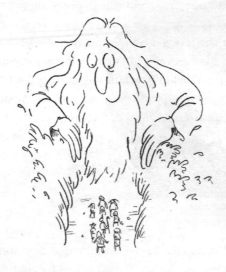

Is belief in God justified?

Very many people believe in God. For
some, belief in God is a matter of faith.
They insist you should just believe. It
doesn't matter whether or not there
are good grounds for believing.
But as philosophers, we want to
know what it's reasonable to believe.
We want to know if there is good
evidence of His existence. Is there a
sound argument for the existence of God?

FORGET REASON!
YOU MUST SIMPLY
BELIEVE!

We are going to look at two important arguments for
God's existence. Our job will be to think like detectives.
We're going to take a cool, careful look at the arguments and
the evidence and try to figure out, as best we can, what is most
likely to be true.

Let's start with our first argument.

Argument one: the levers-of-the-universe argument

Aisha has spent the weekend in France with her friend Tom, and now they are travelling back to England on the ferry. They are out on deck, lying on their sun-loungers and sipping tea as the ferry glides peacefully through the night.

It's cold, and the stars are twinkling brightly. Over to the right, a few streaks of cloud are bathed by the last pink glow of sun. To the left, a full moon is beginning to peek over the horizon. Ahead of them, to the south, they can just make out some lights on the French coast.

Tom takes another mouthful of tea and places his cup carefully on the table between them.

Suddenly, there's a faint whoosh, followed by an explosion of light over to the south. A ship has launched a flare.

Tom watches as the flare drifts slowly downwards, bathing the horizon with its eerie green light. Then Tom picks up his cup and starts to speak.

Tom: You know, the more I think about it, the more certain I become that there just must be a God.

Aisha: What makes you so certain?

Tom: We inhabit a universe governed by *laws*, don't we?

Aisha: You mean, the *laws of nature*?

Tom: Exactly. The laws that govern gravity and motion and so on. The laws that scientists investigate.

Aisha: I see.

Tom: Now, the universe could have been governed by quite *different* laws, couldn't it?

Aisha: In what way?

Tom: Well, take gravity for example. Gravity is a sort of pulling force that all physical objects exert on each other.

Tom pours some more tea into his cup.

Tom: Big objects like the Earth have a lot of gravity. Which is why we stick to it rather than float off into space. It's gravity that keeps us glued to the deck right now, and that's pulling the tea out of this teapot and into this cup.

Aisha: I know.

Tom: Now the laws governing gravity could have been different, couldn't they? Gravity *could* have been much stronger. Or much weaker.

Aisha: I suppose it could.

Tom: In fact, we can think of the universe as having levers that fix what the laws of nature are. The gravity lever is set at a particular position.

But it could have been set much higher...

... or much lower...

... couldn't it? In fact it could have been set so that there is no gravity at all.

Aisha: I guess so.

Tom: But scientists tell us that if the various laws of nature had been only a *little* bit different, life could never have evolved.

Aisha: Really?

Tom: Yes. For example, if gravity had been just a *bit* stronger, the universe would have lasted only a moment or two after the Big Bang before collapsing in on itself in a Big Pop. Or, if gravity had been just a *bit* weaker, stars and planets capable of supporting life would never have formed.

Aisha: I see.

Tom: Either way, *we would not be here.*

Tom appears to be right. Many scientists now believe that if the laws of nature had been only slightly different, then conscious beings such as ourselves could never have evolved.

Tom: Now, if the levers of the universe were set at *random*, the chances of hitting on a combination of positions that would produce conscious beings like us would be incredibly small.

Aisha: So you say.

Tom: Yet the levers were set that way, weren't they?

Aisha: Yes.

Tom: It's just too much of a coincidence that the levers are set like that. It's far more plausible that someone *deliberately* set the universe up this way. Someone must have *fine-tuned* the universe to produce us!

Aisha: And this someone was God?

Tom: It's the only plausible explanation!

Let's call Tom's new argument the *levers-of-the-universe argument.* Is it a good argument?

I must say, this is one of the best-looking arguments for the existence of God that I have come across. At first sight, the argument does look very persuasive indeed.

Are you convinced?

The lottery fallacy

Not everyone is persuaded by the levers-of-the-universe argument. One common criticism is that it involves the lottery fallacy. Aisha starts to explain the problem.

Aisha: That's an ingenious argument. But *still* no good, I'm afraid.
Tom: Why not?
Aisha: Look, suppose I enter a lottery. One million tickets are sold, of
  which I buy just one.
  But then mine turns out to be the winning ticket. Now the chances
  of my winning were very small, correct?
Tom: Yes. A million to one against.
Aisha: Yet I did win. So here's my big question: *Is it likely that someone
  rigged the lottery in my favour?*

Tom thinks hard for a moment.

Tom: I don't think so.

Aisha: Why not?

Tom: Well, one of the million tickets had to win. And *whichever* ticket won would have had only a one-in-a-million chance of winning.

Aisha: Right. So the fact that my ticket had only a one-in-a-million chance of winning gives me no reason to suppose the lottery was rigged in my favour.

Tom: I agree.

Aisha smiles.

Aisha: But your levers-of-the-universe argument involves *exactly the same sort of mistake!*

Tom: Why?

Aisha: Well, the levers of the universe had to be set some way or other, didn't they? And each of the different ways the levers might have been set was equally likely, correct?

Tom: Yes.

Aisha: So the mere fact that it's very unlikely that they should just happen to be set *this* way, to produce us, gives us no grounds for supposing we have been anything other than lucky. There's no reason to suppose someone must have *deliberately* positioned the levers this way.

Tom scratches his head. He has to admit: Aisha does appear to be right. If it's a mistake to suppose someone deliberately rigged the lottery in the winner's favour, then surely it's a mistake to suppose that someone deliberately rigged the universe in our favour.

Tom: Hmm. *Maybe* you are right. *Perhaps* my argument does involve the same mistake.

Does Tom's levers-of-the-universe argument involve the lottery fallacy? I'll leave you to make up your own mind about that.

Argument two: the simplicity argument

Tom now comes up with his second argument for the existence of God. I call it the *simplicity argument*.

It takes Tom a couple of minutes to explain the argument. He starts by talking about *electrons*.

Tom: OK. Whether or not my levers-of-the-universe argument works, I think I *still* have another really good argument left.

Aisha: What is it?

Tom: Let's start by thinking about electrons.

Aisha: Electrons?

Tom: Yes. An electron is one of the tiny, whizzy particles scientists think atoms are made out of.

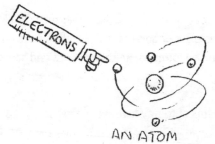

AN ATOM

Aisha: I know.

Tom: Now, *no one has ever seen an electron*, have they? Not even down a microscope. They are far smaller than anything we might observe.

Aisha: Of course.

Tom: But if no one has ever observed an electron, why do scientists suppose they exist?

Aisha furrows her brow and thinks hard for a moment or two.

Aisha: Well, there are things that we *can* observe that electrons explain. For example, they explain why lightning storms happen. And they explain why various chemical reactions occur.

This is all perfectly true. Electrons explain these and many other things too.

The gremlins theory

Tom continues with the next part of the simplicity argument.

Tom: But look, the mere fact that electrons, if they exist, would *explain* these things doesn't *by itself* give us much reason to suppose they exist.

Aisha: It doesn't?

Tom: No. After all, there are *all* sorts of invisible things that might explain why lightning storms, chemical reactions and so on happen, aren't there?

Aisha: Such as?

Tom: Well, we *could* appeal to tiny invisible *gremlins*, couldn't we?

We could say that these gremlins like big flashes and bangs, so they go up into the sky to make storms.

A GREMLIN

And they dislike chaos and irregularity, which
is why they always make chemicals behave the
same way in test tubes.

Aisha: You're right. We *could* appeal to gremlins
instead of electrons. But that would be a
ridiculous explanation.

Tom: Why?

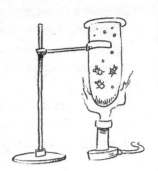

Aisha is correct. The gremlin theory is a
downright silly theory. But why?

Aisha thinks she has the answer.

Aisha: Because the gremlin theory is terrifically *complicated*: it involves
lots and lots of little beings with their own complex little minds, all
running around making things happen.

Tom: I agree. In fact, with their complex minds filled with their likes and
dislikes, *these gremlins are at least as complicated as what they're
supposed to explain.*

Aisha: Exactly.

Tom: The electron hypothesis, on the other hand, is *simple and elegant.*
It involves just a single sort of entity with a few very simple
properties. So while we're not justified in supposing gremlins exist,
we *are* justified in supposing electrons exist.

Tom and Aisha are right. It can be reasonable to suppose that
certain unobservable things exist if they provide the neatest,
simplest explanation for the complex order we find around us.

'If it's reasonable to believe in electrons, then it's reasonable to believe in God'

Tom sinks back in his lounger. He is about to reach the
punchline of the simplicity argument.

Tom: But if it's reasonable to believe in electrons, then it's reasonable to believe in God!

Aisha can't see what Tom is getting at.

Aisha: Why do you say that?

Tom takes another sip of tea, and starts to explain.

Tom: It's simple. The universe isn't just a random, chaotic mess, is it? It is full of order. It is full of rich patterns and regularities. It's governed by laws.
Aisha: True.
Tom: Now we can explain all this order and complexity by supposing that there is something invisible behind the scenes that accounts for the order we see around us. Something *very simple*.
Aisha: And what would this simple thing be?
Tom: God, of course. For *God is a very simple being*.
Aisha: He is?
Tom: Yes. He is a single entity with three simple properties: infinite power, infinite knowledge and infinite goodness. And yet, by supposing this single, simple entity exists, we can account for the complex order we see around us. It can all be explained as a result of God's grand design. God made the universe this way *for us*, so that we could evolve and develop and finally come to understand the universe and the God who created it for us.

So you see – I can give exactly the same justification for believing in God as you gave for believing in electrons! If you believe in electrons, then you should believe in God, too.

Is Tom correct? Can we justify belief in God in the same way we justify belief in electrons?

Aisha's criticism of the simplicity argument

Aisha doesn't think God can be quite as simple as Tom makes out.

Aisha: You claim that the theory that God created the universe gives a very simple explanation for the complex order we see around us?
Tom: I do.
Aisha: And God *designed* the universe?
Tom: That's right. Down to the very last detail.
Aisha: But if God designed the universe, then *all the order and complexity of the universe was present in God's mind before it was created.*
Tom: True.
Aisha: But that makes God at least as complex as what you are using Him to explain!

I think Aisha is right. True, the theory that God created the universe does *appear* simple and elegant. But only while we think of God as being just infinitely powerful, knowledgeable and good.

IT'S TRUE. I DESIGNED THE UNIVERSE. SO EVERY LAST DETAIL OF THE UNIVERSE EXISTED IN MY MIND BEFORE I CREATED IT.

When we look more closely at the theory, it turns out that God must actually be highly complex. If every last feature of the universe was planned by God, then *all* its complexity existed in God's mind before He created it.

301

But then *God is at least as complex as His creation.*

So it looks as if the theory that God created the universe suffers from the same problem as the gremlins theory: God is no less complex than what He's supposed to explain. It seems we are left with no more reason to believe in God than we have to believe in gremlins.

An argument *against* the existence of God

So far, we have looked at three arguments for the existence of God. Aisha hasn't been persuaded by any of them.

Of course, even if it's true that there aren't any good arguments for the existence of God, that doesn't show that there's no God. Just because we can't show that something is true doesn't mean it isn't true.

Faith

If belief in God is unreasonable, does that matter? After all, many of those who believe in God insist that reason has little to do with their belief. They insist we must *just believe*, irrespective of what the arguments or the evidence might suggest. Belief in God is ultimately a matter of faith, not reason.

Let's finish by taking a closer look at this sort of religious faith.

Placing our faith in others

Some argue that, just as it's a good thing to place our faith in those around us, so it's also a good thing to place our faith in God. In fact, that's just what Tom thinks.

Tom: Look, even if there's little reason to suppose God exists, it is still a good thing to believe. Faith is life-enhancing!

Aisha: In what way?

Tom: Well, you agree, don't you, that it's good to place our faith in others? Take the captain of this ship, for example. We place our faith in him when we get on board. We trust he will act responsibly.

Aisha: True.

Tom: In fact we *have* to have faith in other people, in their trustworthiness and kindness, don't we? I trust my bank manager to look after my money. I trust my shopkeeper not to sell me rotten or poisoned food. I trust my friends to stand by me when I am in trouble. Without this sort of trust life would be difficult, if not impossible, wouldn't it?

Aisha: That's true, too. In a sense, *faith makes the world go round.*

Tom: So you see, placing our faith in others is a positive, life-enhancing thing to do. Indeed, we generally consider it an *admirable* thing, don't we?

Aisha: Generally speaking, yes we do.

Tom: But then *it must also be a positive, life-enhancing thing to place our faith in God.* Don't you agree?

Faith in Santa Claus: a bad side to faith?

Aisha shakes her head.

Aisha: I'm afraid I don't agree. Look, when we talk about 'placing our faith in others', we mean trusting in their good character, trusting that they will act kindly and responsibly. Right?

Tom: Yes.

Aisha: But *that* sort of faith simply takes for granted that the people in whom we place our trust *actually exist.* It's only admirable to place your trust in someone if you already have *pretty good reason* to suppose the person in question is really there. Otherwise it's downright silly.

Tom: Is it?

Aisha: Yes. Look, think about this case. Two children are looking forward to Christmas Day. But their parents are penniless. They can afford neither Christmas dinner nor gifts. But they don't want to disappoint their children. So what do they do?

Despite the fact that they have little reason to believe that Santa Claus exists, and plenty of reason to suppose he doesn't, these parents *place their faith in Santa* to deliver presents on Christmas Day! Not only that, they encourage their children to  believe in Santa too. 'Don't worry, kids', they say. 'Have faith in Santa. He's a good person. I am sure he will bring us presents on Christmas Day!' What would you think of such parents?

Tom: They are very foolish!

Aisha: Of course.

Tom: Worse than that, they have misled their poor children. These children are bound to be terribly upset and disappointed come Christmas Day when no presents turn up.

Aisha: I agree.

Tom: The parents' behaviour is *downright irresponsible*!

Aisha: Absolutely. But if I am right that there are no decent arguments for the existence of God and an extremely good argument against, *isn't it just as silly and irresponsible for religious people to encourage others to place their faith in God?*

Is Aisha right? If she is correct about the arguments (and that is a very big 'if', of course) is it as foolish to encourage others to believe in God as it is to encourage them to believe in Santa?

Certainly, there can be a bad side to faith: a person who has given up on reason and who 'just believes' is easily controlled by his or her religious masters. Such people can easily be persuaded to do bad things, including killing those who don't agree with them.

The 'faith' of such a religious fanatic is clearly not a very good thing.

A good side to faith

But there's no doubt that religious faith can also be a force for good. Faith in God has helped some people deal with the terrible things they have experienced.

And it has inspired many generous and noble acts (though of course it's not just those with faith who behave generously and nobly). Across the globe, people of faith are busy helping others.

Indeed, religious faith has utterly changed some people's lives for the better.

BEFORE   AFTER

Is it reasonable to believe in God?

But while religious faith can be a force for good, the question remains whether belief in God is reasonable.

Tom looks out over the black waters.

Tom: So you really don't believe in God?

Aisha: I'm afraid not. I can no more make myself believe in God than I can make myself believe in Santa Claus. There's no reason to suppose the universe had a creator. And, even if it did, it's perfectly clear its creator isn't the being you call God.

Tom: I disagree. God exists! It is a reasonable thing to believe. Give me a little while, and I'll think of a better argument...

Can you think of a better argument?

File 13

Is time travel possible?

Brad Baddely's rescue

The clouds part and the time machine splutters to a halt, gyrating wildly in the air. Captain Brad Baddely of the time commandos struggles manfully with the joystick as it bucks violently in his hands.

MUST... GAIN... CONTROL... NNGH!

Finally, he gains control and settles his dying machine clumsily on the muddy ground.

Baddely peers through the cockpit window. It's difficult to make out the terrain through the rivulets of rain. He opens the hatch and steps out into a bleak and storm-ravaged landscape.

'So this is planet Vargy,' he whispers to himself. Baddely knows he will soon be dead. There is no way he can repair the failed doobriemat on his time machine. And in just a few minutes' time Planet Vargy will be hit by a huge comet, annihilating everything on its surface.

The time commando scans the horizon. No signs of life. Baddely lets his mind drift wistfully back to Earth, to the family he will never see again.

Suddenly there's a noise: the shriek of another time machine zooming in overhead. The gleaming teardrop glides down and lands gently in the mud beside him.

The hatch springs open.

'Hey! Get in!' The voice from inside sounds oddly familiar. A head peers round the door. Baddely is astonished to find himself looking into a face exactly like his own.

'Who are you?' asks Baddely.

'I've come to rescue you! Quick, hop in and let's get out of here!'

Within a few seconds both time commandos are safely aboard, the time machine sweeping gracefully into the air before accelerating into outer space.

Baddely stares at Planet Vargy in the rear monitor. The comet strikes the surface of the planet, creating a wall of fire that consumes all in its wake.

'Phew! That was a close one. So tell me, who are you?'

'I'm you.'

'Me?'

'Yes. I'm the future you. I've travelled back in time from your future to rescue you. Thank goodness I succeeded!'

'But that's in direct contravention of the time commandos' Prime Directive: No time commando must ever arrange to meet him or herself!'

'Yes. I know. But on this occasion there was no choice. I couldn't let my best buddy – me – get cooked on Planet Vargy, could I? So I travelled back in time to save you. I mean, me.'

Baddely furrows his brow. So he had contravened the Prime Directive, had he? Shouldn't he arrest himself?

Then a faint smile plays across Baddely's lips.

'Well, I won't tell if you won't.'

'It's a deal. But just remember that in a week's time you must travel back to Planet Vargy as it was ten minutes ago to save yourself.'

'What if I forget?'

'You won't. After all, I'm here, aren't I?'

Baddely dropped himself off at the nearest time commando space station.

'Good luck in saving yourself!' shouts Baddely's rescuer as he pilots the time machine back into the air.

'Good luck?' mutters the rescued Baddely to himself. 'Don't need it! I already know that I'll succeed!'

Baddely watches the time machine manoeuvre through the airlock before it streaks back to the future.

'Goodbye, amigo!'

Is time travel illogical?

Kobir and Carol are watching Kobir's favourite show — *The Time Commandos* — on TV.

Kobir: Wow! Great episode!
Carol: It's drivel! It doesn't even make sense.
Kobir: It made sense to me.
Carol: Time travel is illogical. It involves all sorts of logical *contradictions.*

Carol believes that the very idea of time travel is simply confused. She thinks it's *illogical*, which is just to say that it involves *logical contradictions*.

What's a logical contradiction? It's a claim that contradicts itself. Here's an example. If I say: "I am two metres tall and I am not two metres tall," then I have contradicted myself. I am claiming that something is true — that I am two metres tall — but I'm also claiming that it's not true. And it's impossible for a claim to be both true and not true.

Here's another example. Suppose someone claims that there might be round squares somewhere in the world. They go off to look for them.

Of course, we *know in advance* that they won't find any, don't we? But why?

Because the very idea of a round square is illogical. A circle, by definition, does *not* have straight sides. A square, by definition, does. So a round square would have to both have straight sides and not have straight sides. And that's a contradiction.

Notice that when a claim is illogical, we don't have to go and observe the world to check whether or not it's true. We can know *just by thinking about it* that it's not true.

Now Carol, like a number of philosophers, thinks the same is true of time travel. She thinks that the *very idea* of people travelling through time – as they do on *The Time Commandos* – involves contradictions. So we can know *just by thinking about it* that time travel is impossible.

But there are other philosophers who, like Kobir, believe that time travel *is* perfectly logical. Perhaps the universe won't allow time travel. That's something that *science* will have to investigate. But, according to these philosophers, there's certainly no *contradiction* involved in supposing that people might travel through time.

So who is correct, Kobir or Carol? In this chapter we're going to get to grips with some important arguments – arguments that some of the world's leading philosophers and scientists are grappling with right now.

Baddely has and has not been rescued

Let's begin by finding out why Carol thinks time travel is illogical. She starts to explain.

Carol: Look, Baddely is supposed to travel back in time to save himself. But that means at the moment when both Baddelys are standing there on planet Vargy, it's both true that Baddely has already been rescued and not true that he has already been rescued. Right?

Kobir: Hmm. I guess it is.

Carol: After all, it's true that if we asked the just-crashed Baddely whether he has already been rescued from planet Vargy yet, he will say no. The rescue has yet to take place. But if we ask the other Baddely whether he has been rescued yet, he will say yes, he remembers it well. After all, if the rescue hadn't already happened to him, then he wouldn't have been able to travel back to the present.

Carol is correct: it does seem as if it's both true and not true that the rescue has already happened.

Kobir: That's correct, I guess.

Carol: Well, then, *there is a contradiction, isn't there?*

Kobir: It does *seem* like a contradiction, yes.

313

Carol does appear to have discovered a contradiction in the story about Baddely. And if there's a contradiction, then the story is illogical. It's no more possible for this episode of *The Time Commandos* to be true than it is for a round square to exist.

But *is* there a contradiction?

Two sorts of time

But Kobir is not convinced there's really a problem.

Kobir: I see what you are getting at. But actually, now I think about it, I don't think there is a contradiction.
Carol: Why not?
Kobir: We just need to distinguish between *two sorts of time.*
Carol: Two sorts of time?
Kobir: Yes. Some philosophers distinguish between *personal time* and *external time.*
Carol: What's personal time?
Kobir: Personal time is what gets measured by, say, *Baddely's own wristwatch.* For the Baddely that does the rescuing, his rescue took place in the past in his personal time. It's part of his personal history.
Carol: So what's *external* time?
Kobir: External time is the time that gets measured by, say, a *clock ticking away in orbit around Planet Vargy.* Baddely uses his time machine to travel backwards in external time, the time measured by that ticking clock. But even as he travels backwards in external time he is still travelling forward in his personal time.
Carol: I see. So why is there no contradiction?
Kobir: Well, you said that, as the two Baddelys stand there on the surface of Planet Vargy, it's both true and not true that the rescue has already happened. Right?
Carol: Yes. For one the rescue has happened. For the other it has yet to happen. And that's a contradiction.

Kobir: But that's *not* a contradiction. For as the two Baddelys stand there at the *same point* in *external* time, they are at *different points* within their *personal* time. Their wristwatches tell quite different times, don't they?

Carol: Of course.

Kobir: So what lies in one Baddeley's future lies in the other's past.

Carol: Correct.

Kobir: But there's nothing contra-dictory about *that*, is there? It can be true that something *hasn't* happened at one point in a person's history, and also true that it *has* happened at another, later point in his or her history. That occurs all the time, doesn't it? What's in a person's future ends up in his or her past. Right?

Carol: I guess so.

Kobir: So you see, there's no contradiction!

What is it like to travel in time?

Carol sees that perhaps Kobir has explained away the appearance of a contradiction. But she thinks she's spotted another problem with The Time Commandos. She's not sure if they *really* travel in time at all.

Carol: OK, maybe you're right. Maybe there's no contradiction involved in supposing that, as the two Baddelys stand there on the surface of Planet Vargy, it's true that the rescue has taken place, and also true that it hasn't.

Kobir: I *am* right!

Carol: But there's *another* problem with the claim that Baddely travels in time.

Kobir: What problem?

Carol: OK, think about this question: what happens when Baddely travels forward in time? How does it *seem* to him?

Kobir: You mean, what does he see going on around him?

Carol: Yes.

Kobir: Well, in episode one of *The Time Commandos*, when Baddely first uses the time machine, it's parked in a huge hangar. The gleaming time machine is in the centre, surrounded by technicians and lots of complicated-looking machinery. Baddely climbs aboard and shuts the hatch. He sits in the pilot's chair. Then he pushes the time joystick forward very slightly to see what will happen.

Carol: And what *does* happen?

Kobir: The machine stays where it is. But it starts to accelerate forward in time.

Carol: So what does Baddely *see*?

Kobir: When Baddely looks out of the window he sees the technicians buzzing around like flies. The sun starts to shoot rapidly across the sky. Clouds scud past the open hangar door like birds. Everything *speeds up*. Like when you fast-forward a video.

Carol: And when he pushes the stick *further* forward?

Kobir: When he pushes the stick forward some more, things go faster still. Night and day flash past in seconds. The technicians move so fast they become a blur, and then invisible. It's only when Baddely pulls the joystick back to the centre position that things return to normal speed.

Baddely gets really, really slow

Carol now asks Kobir what it's like for the technicians watching Baddely's time machine.

Carol: Fantastic! But now what do the technicians watching the time machine see when Baddely first pushes the joystick forward?

Kobir: I guess Baddely and his machine disappear with a 'Pop!' as he sets off on his journey into the future.

Carol: But *that* can't be right, can it? If Baddely can see what's going on outside his machine as he travels forward in time, then that is because he is *still in the hangar*. Right?

Kobir: I guess so.

Carol: But if he is *still in the hangar*, then he *doesn't* disappear with a 'Pop!' does he? If he can still see the technicians around him, then he's still there to be seen by them.

Kobir: Weird. I guess that's true.
Carol: Only, from their point of view, Baddely will seem to be moving
    very, very slowly!
Kobir: Bizarre!

Surely Carol is right. If Baddely is there to see the other
technicians, then they must also be able to see him. And if
they are moving very quickly relative to Baddely, then Baddely
is moving very slowly relative to them.

Carol thinks this shows that Baddely doesn't *really* travel in
time at all. She explains by telling Kobir about another strange
device...

Stepping into the slow box

Carol: It's as if Baddely has
    stepped into the *slow box*.
Kobir: The slow box?
Carol: Yes. I saw a science fiction
    film the other night called
    *The Slow World of Doctor
    Calculus*. In the story, a
    scientist — Doctor Calculus —
    discovers how to make a
    device which, when you step
    inside it, slows down all the
    physical processes going on
    in your body. Step into the
    box and you grind almost to
    a halt. Your heart beats only
    once a minute. The electrical
    activity in your brain slows
    to a snail's pace.

To everyone around you, you seem like a statue. Try to talk to them and they will hear only a very low-pitched hum coming from your open mouth.

Kobir: How did it seem to Doctor Calculus when he stepped into the box?

Carol: Well, from *his* point of view, everything seemed to *speed up*. People would buzz about like flies. Their voices became high-pitched squeaks. The sun would shoot across the sky.

The world was a blur of frantic activity for as long as Doctor Calculus stayed in the box.

Kobir: Strange. But what has the slow box got to do with Baddely's adventure?

Carol proceeds to explain.

Carol: It seems to me that Baddely's time machine is really *just another slow box*. It's just as if he has stepped inside Calculus's device.
Kobir: Why?
Carol: Because Baddely never leaves the hangar. He stays right there. He just starts to function *very, very slowly* compared to those around him. From the technicians' point of view, when Baddely touches the joystick, he freezes like a statue. All that's happened is that he's now moving very, very slowly. And when Baddely slowly pushes the joystick forward some more, he starts moving even more slowly. Eventually, after several weeks of hanging around waiting, the technicians watch as Baddely finally gets the joystick back to its centre position and starts to move at normal speed again.
Kobir: I guess that's right.
Carol: But if all that's happened is that Baddely has been slowed down a lot, then *he hasn't really travelled through time at all, has he?*
Kobir: Hmm. Perhaps not.

Carol appears to be right. Certainly, Baddely and the other time commandos aren't supposed just to slow down when they go off on their time-travelling adventures. Yet it seems that this is all Baddely's time machine *really* succeeds in doing. It turns out it's just another slow box.

Carol: So you see, *The Time Commandos* is a very confused television programme! It pretends that people are travelling in time when actually they aren't!

Time hopping

Kobir scratches his chin. He's inclined to agree that there's more to time travel than just slowing down.

Kobir: You may be right about the slow box. It isn't *really* a form of time travel, is it? Certainly, a slow box won't allow you to travel *backwards* in time, as Baddely's time machine is supposed to.

Carol: True.

Kobir: But, even if there *is* a problem with the story in *The Time Commandos,* perhaps time travel is still possible. Perhaps what would *really* happen if you started to travel forwards in time is that you would *instantly* find yourself at a different point in time. Dial in 2:45 pm on 1 March 2090 and press the 'travel' button and 'Pop!' there you are, immediately transported to that moment in the future. I don't see that there's anything confused about the suggestion that someone might 'travel in time' in *this* sense.

Carol: Maybe not.

Kobir: In the slow box, Calculus continues to exist at all the points in time in between when he steps in and when he steps out. People outside the box can *still see him in there.* But I guess the machines in *The Time Commandos* don't work like that. They move from one point in time to another *without having to exist at all the moments in time in between.* They simply disappear with a 'Pop!' and reappear with another 'Pop!' in the distant future or past. It's as if they *hop* or *leap* from one point in time to another. You could call it 'time hopping'.

Kobir's suggestion that time machines might work by 'time hopping' does avoid the problem that Carol has been discussing: that Baddely's machine seems otherwise not to be a time machine, but merely a slow box.

Kobir: I admit that the episode where Brad Baddely saw the people around him buzzing about like flies as he travelled forwards in time was a bit confused. But it was only confused in supposing that that's how time travel would *look* from Baddely's point of view. It *wasn't* confused in supposing that time travel makes sense.

Changing the past: the strange case of Queen Victoria's pogo stick

Carol is flummoxed. She remains convinced that time travel is illogical. But so far she has struggled to show why. She now has another idea.

Carol: We have overlooked the most famous problem with time travel. A time machine would allow people to *change the past.* And that *really* is illogical.
Kobir: Why?

Carol comes up with an example.

Carol: It's false that Queen Victoria rode a pogo stick during her long reign. Correct?
Kobir: Of course it is. Pogo sticks hadn't even been invented back in Victoria's day.
Carol: But if we had a time machine, we could take a pogo stick back to 1840 and present it to Queen Victoria. She could ride the pogo stick. And so the course of history would be changed.
  When we travel back to the present day, we would find that it is now *true* that Queen Victoria rode a pogo stick. We might even discover pictures of her riding the stick.

QUEEN VICTORIA
ON HER POGO STICK.

Kobir: True.

Carol: The past would have *changed.* But it makes no sense to suppose that the past might be altered in that way.

Kobir: Why?

Carol: Well, there's a contradiction, isn't there? It's false that Queen Victoria rode a pogo stick. But also true. That's a contradiction.

Kobir: It *was* false that she rode one. But we have *changed* the past, so it's now true. I still don't see why that's illogical.

Carol: You don't?

Kobir: No. In fact in *The Time Commandos,* Captain Baddely goes back and changes the past *all the time.* In episode one millions of people are wiped out by a virus that a terrorist put in the water supply. Baddely and the other time commandos travel back in time and prevent the terrorist attack from happening.

Come to think of it, changing the past is *exactly* the reason the time commandos were created in the first place. The future Earth Government wanted a unit trained to travel back in time and prevent that terrorist disaster from occuring.

Shooting grandad

As Kobir still can't see what's illogical about changing the past, Carol comes up with another example.

Carol: OK, if Baddely can *change* the past, then he could go back in time and *prevent himself from existing,* couldn't he?

Kobir: You mean, by, say, going back in time and shooting his grandparents prior to the birth of his parents?

Carol: Exactly. If Baddely can change the past, then he could travel back to a time before his grandfather even met his grandmother, hide in the bushes outside his grandfather's house, and then shoot him dead.

Now if Baddely succeeds in preventing his grandparents from ever meeting, then one of his parents will never be born. And if one of his parents won't be born, then Baddely cannot be born either. So by travelling back in time *it would be possible for Baddely to prevent his own birth.*

Kobir: And that's illogical?

Carol: Certainly. In order to go back and prevent his birth, Baddely would need to have been born. But if he succeeds in preventing his birth, then he won't be born.

BADDELY SHOOTING HIS GRANDAD.

Kobir: I see the problem. If Baddely is born then he isn't. But if he isn't then he is. Either way, there's a contradiction. Either way, he's both born and not born.

Carol: Precisely. So you see, *time travel is illogical.* It generates contradictions!

Preventing the terrorist attack

Kobir can see what Carol is getting at.

Kobir: Actually, now you mention it, I think there may be a similar problem with episode one of *The Time Commandos*: the episode where Baddely and the other time commandos travel back in time to prevent that terrorist attack. Baddely travels back and succeeds in stopping the terrorist. The only problem is, as the time commandos were only created because the terrorist attack happened, by preventing the attack, Baddely must prevent the time commandos from being created! But if they aren't created, then the attack *will* go ahead.

Carol: You're right. That's illogical. If the terrorist attack happens, then it doesn't happen. But if it doesn't happen, then it does. Either way, it happens and it doesn't happen. So, either way, there's a contradiction!

Parallel futures

Has Carol really shown that time travel is illogical? Some philosophers and scientists have suggested that this sort of contradiction can be avoided if we suppose that there are *parallel futures*. Here's how the parallel universe suggestion works.

When Baddely goes back in time and prevents the terrorist attack, he actually creates a *new* future *in addition* to the one from which he travelled. So there is no longer a single future in which the terrorist attack both does happen and doesn't happen. That would be a contradiction.

Rather, there are now two futures. In one future, the terrorist attack happens, leading to the time commandos going back in time. But when they prevent the attack, they create a second, parallel future in which the attack never happens. It's this future to which Baddely and the other commandos return.

Now because the two futures are separate, there's no contradiction. There's no future in which the attack both happens and doesn't happen.

Compare this case: it *can* be true both that it's raining and that it isn't raining if we are talking about *two different places*, can't it? The contradiction disappears once we explain that we mean it's raining in one place but not in another.

Similarly it *can* be true both that the terrorist attack happens and that it doesn't happen if we are talking about *two different futures*.

A problem with parallel futures

While some philosophers and scientists think that parallel futures are possible, it turns out these parallel futures would rather undermine the whole point of the future Earth Government creating the time commando team.

Think about it: the future Earth Government creates the time commandos to prevent a terrorist attack that has killed millions of people. The commandos travel back in time and prevent the attack. But they only prevent it from happening *in a parallel future*. In the future from which the time commandos come – the future in which the Earth Government creates them – *the attack still happens*.

So from the point of view of the Earth Government that sent them, the mission is a failure. Millions still die!

Time travel without changing the past

The time commando stories do seem confused. But even if it isn't possible to change the past, maybe it's still possible to travel back in time and make things happen.

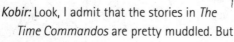

Kobir: Look, I admit that the stories in *The Time Commandos* are pretty muddled. But I'm not sure that you have really shown that time travel is illogical.

Carol: Why not?

Kobir: Well, perhaps we can't go back and *change* the past. Maybe the past is set in stone and cannot be altered. But still, we might go back and have an effect on how the past was originally set. We could go back and make something happen that *did in fact happen*.

Carol: For example?

Kobir thinks for a moment.

Kobir: OK, take the death of Elvis. We think that Elvis died in 1977, don't we? Now suppose that we get in a time machine and travel back to 1973.

Then we shoot Elvis dead.

Carol: But then we *would* have
changed the past. Elvis died on 16
August 1977.

Kobir: But *did* he? Maybe people just
think he did. But perhaps he was
actually shot dead in 1973, and
his record company, not wanting
to lose millions, employed a
lookalike – an imposter – to take
his place for those last few years.

Carol: Oh. I see. So we don't *change*
the past. We simply make
something happen *that did in fact
happen.*

Kobir: Yes! It's *already* true that Elvis
died in 1973. We're not changing
anything. There's no problem
about doing *that*, is there?

Carol: I guess not.

Trying very hard to shoot Grandad

Carol sees that there's no contradiction involved in Kobir's Elvis
time travel story. But she still thinks that time machines must be
impossible. She thinks that whether or not we *do* use them to
change the past, and so create contradictions, we *could* do. That
rules them out on logical grounds.

Carol: OK, I admit there's no contradiction involved in your story about shooting Elvis. Your story doesn't involve us *changing* the past. But the fact is, time machines *would* also allow us to *change* the past, and in a way that *would* create logical contradictions.

Kobir: Would they?

Carol: Yes, they would. For example, whether or not you *do* decide to go back and kill your granddad, you *could* go back and kill him, couldn't you? And that *would* create a contradiction, wouldn't it?

But Kobir doesn't see why such time machines would *have* to allow us to create contradictions.

Kobir: I don't see why time machines *must* give us the ability to generate contradictions. Suppose I do try to use a time machine to go back in time and shoot Grandad prior to his meeting Grandma. Suppose I actually try my *very hardest* to generate a contradiction!

RIGHT, I AM DEFINITELY GOING TO SHOOT GRANDAD!

What we know is that, *no matter how hard I try, I must fail!* Instead of transporting me, the time machine may blow up.

330

Or my gun may jam at the last minute.

Or I may succeed only in injuring my grandad.

Or I may accidentally shoot the wrong person.

We know that, *somehow* or other, I won't manage to kill Grandad.

Is Carol right? Does the impossibility of our changing the past show that time travel is impossible? Or has Kobir shown that time travel might still be possible after all?

I have to admit, I'm just not sure.

Time machines

Carol and Kobir have taken a long, hard look at time travel. So far, I don't think Carol has managed to come up with a good argument to support her claim that time travel is illogical.

True, certain *stories* about time travel don't make much sense. But I'm not at all sure that time travel *itself* is illogical.

Might we one day build machines that allow us to travel into the future or the past? Might you go back and watch dinosaurs feeding?

Might you travel forward billions of years and watch the destruction of the Earth from space?

Many science fiction stories are based on the assumption that such machines might eventually be built.

But is time travel *really* possible? Does the idea even make sense?

What do you think?

Chapter 14

Could a machine think?

Thinking

This is me.

And this is a table lamp.

One important difference between me and the table lamp is, of course, that I can think.

What do I mean by 'think'?

Well, for a start, I can do simple sums.

12 TIMES 12 IS... ERM... 144!

And I can figure out the answers to puzzles.

I can also understand language. When I hear other people speaking, I don't just hear noises coming out of their mouths.

ICK, WIBBY FLUB WOB.

I can grasp the meaning of what they are saying.

And of course, understanding language as I do, I can answer them right back.

Unlike a table lamp, I also enjoy experiences. I'm eating an apple while I type this. I can taste its rather bitter flesh, smell its slightly sweet aroma, and feel its waxy surface pressed against my finger tips.

I also feel emotions. Sometimes I'm happy and exhilarated. Other times I feel angry.

These are the sorts of things I am talking about when I say I can think. I have a rich inner mental life full of all sorts of thoughts and feelings.

A table lamp, on the other hand, can't think. In fact it hasn't got a mind at all. Could a machine think? We know that flesh and blood humans like ourselves can think. And we know table lamps can't. A table lamp is just a simple piece of machinery. By a *machine*, I mean a man-made device. Toasters, irons, cars and watches are all machines.

But what about *other* sorts of machine? Might they be able to think?

Do pocket calculators think?

Take pocket calculators, for example. They can do *one* of the
things I can do with my mind. They can perform mathematical
calculations. So do they think?

Actually, it doesn't sound right to
me to say that a pocket calculator
thinks. Surely a bit more is required for
thinking. Surely, in order to think,
you need a mind. And it seems to me
that in order to have a mind you need
to be able to do a bit more than just do
sums. There's far too much that pocket
calculators *can't* do. For example, they can't
enjoy experiences or have hopes and desires. All they
can do is add up the figures that we punch into them. That's
not enough for a mind.

Could a supercomputer think?

So I don't believe that pocket calculators can think.
But what about other, more complex
machines? What about
powerful super-
computers? Can they
think?

Many people would
say: no. A supercomputer
is really just a very sophisticated calculator: a sort of
big pocket calculator. And I
have already admitted that the ability to calculate is not, *by itself*,
enough for thinking. So not even a supercomputer thinks.

But is that true?

Could a robot think?

Even if supercomputers can't think, perhaps other machines might. What about *robots*, for example?

Suppose that one day robots are built that can walk and talk much as we do. They are built to behave just like humans. They seem to understand what we say to them. They even seem to have emotions, hopes, desires and so on. They talk about what they want to do.

They appear to be happy.

Sometimes they even seem angry.

337

Would *these* machines think? Would *they* have minds?

That's the question we are going to look at in this chapter.

Tim's new robo-friend arrives

Meet Tim.

It's the year 2500, and Tim has just received
a large box through the post. His friend Ed
wonders what it could be.

Tim: Ah. It's here at last!
Ed: What is it? It looks huge.
Tim: It's my new friend, Robo-Freddie.
Ed: Robo-Freddie?

Tim tears off the brown paper to reveal what appears to be a
young man sleeping inside a large cellophane-fronted box. On
the front of the box it says 'Robo-Freddie –
your mechanical pal! Indistinguishable
from the real thing'.

Tim: He's my new robot buddy. Wow! He
looks so real. I can't wait to wake him up.

Ed is shocked.

Ed: You've ordered a *robot friend*?
Tim: Yes. Remember you said you couldn't
come snowboarding with me next
week? Well, I didn't want to go all by
myself, so I ordered Robo-Freddie to keep me company. Next week
I'll be whizzing down the snow slopes with Freddie here. He'll be my
new pal.

Tim opens the front of the box and picks up Robo-Fr[e]
remote control.

Tim: All I have to do is press the start button here, and off he'll go!

X-generation sims
Ed walks up to the box and peers closely at the robot inside.
Robo-Freddie certainly does look real.

Ed: But this is just a piece of *machinery*. And a piece of machinery can't
really be your friend, can it? Or, if it can, then why not take the
vacuum cleaner instead – it would be much cheaper!

Tim isn't amused.

Tim: Obviously I can't be friends with a vacuum cleaner. After all, a
vacuum cleaner can't even talk, can it? But Robo-Freddie can. Robo-
Freddie is built to walk, talk and generally behave just like a human
being.
Ed: Just like a human being?
Tim: Yes. *Just* like a human being. Robo-Freddie is one of the new
X-generation sims, the first human simulators that are *absolutely
indistinguishable* from the real thing. So I will be able to
have conversations with Robo-Freddie, and go snowboarding with him. He even has a mechanical
digestive system, so we can go out for lunch
together!
Ed: So from the outside it's quite impossible to tell
Robo-Freddie from a real human?
Tim: That's right. So you see, while Robo-Freddie
may be mechanical, he can still enjoy a day's
snowboarding. Just like me.

.obo–Freddie's 'memories'

Ed still isn't convinced that Robo-Freddie will behave exactly like a normal human being.

Ed: Surely Robo-Freddie can't replicate *everything* a human being can do? After all, he has no past, does he? Real human beings have histories that they remember. But Robo-Freddie has no history.

Tim: No, he doesn't.

Ed: Until we turn him on, he won't have experienced anything, so there'll be *nothing for him to remember*. Ask him about his life up to now and he'll have nothing to say. So you see, Robo-Freddie *won't* behave just like a real human.

Tim looks a little smug.

Tim: You're wrong, I'm afraid. Robo-Freddie has no history. But he *does* have memories. Of a sort. X-generation sims like Robo-Freddie come with a choice of pre-programmed memories. Robo-Freddie will think that he's a real human with a real past. He'll remember having a mother and father. He'll remember going to school as a child. He'll remember his fifth birthday, when he got a new red bicycle.

Ed: He will?

Tim points to the manual lying open in Ed's hands.

Tim: Yes. It says so right there in his user's manual. So Robo-Freddie *will* be able to tell us all about his child-hood, where he grew up, where he went to school and what he did last week. Just like a real human.

Ed: But Robo-Freddie's memories won't be real memories, will they?

Tim: Well, no. His past is a work of fiction. None of it really happened. He never had a fifth birthday. He never got that bike. But Robo-Freddie *won't know that*! So you see? He *will* act just like a normal human being. In fact, there's no way you can tell he isn't human.

Ed: So no one will be able to tell he's a robot? Not even *him*?

Tim: Exactly. If you were to tell Robo-Freddie that he's a robot, he'd laugh at you and tell you not to be so silly.

Does Robo-Freddie have a mind?

Ed feels slightly upset that Tim is replacing him with a machine. But he also feels that, by going on holiday with a piece of plastic-and-alloy machinery rather than a flesh and blood human being, Tim is missing out on something vitally important.

Ed: Well, even if Robo-Freddie is outwardly just like a real human, the fact is that he can't be your friend.

Tim: Why not?

Ed: Because he's missing something crucial. On the outside, he is just like a real human being. But he doesn't have a *mind*.

Tim: A mind?

Ed: Yes. When *you* ski down the slopes, you'll be touched by the beauty of the mountains around you. You'll experience the icy blast of air on your cheeks and the crunchy feel of the snow under your board.

You'll feel exhilarated and glad to be alive. When strangers come up to speak to you on the slopes, you will understand what they're saying and be amused by their jokes. You'll have hopes and desires, anxieties and fears.

The problem is, when Robo-Freddie goes snowboarding with you, he won't have *any* of this rich inner life.

Tim: He won't?

Ed: No. He's *outwardly* just like a human being, I admit. But he's an empty shell. He merely *mimics* thought, feeling and understanding. He merely *mimics* some-one with hopes and desires, anxieties and fears.

Ed points through the cellophane window at Robo-Freddie's head.

Ed: There's no *mind* in there.

Tim: There isn't?

Ed: No. And, most importantly, he won't *really* feel any warmth towards you. His emotions are all fake. *That's* why he can't *really* be your friend.

Brains vs computers

Is Ed correct? Many would agree that while Robo-Freddie might *seem* on the outside as if he has a mind, his 'mind' is really nothing more than an elaborate, computer-generated illusion. Yet Tim is convinced Robo-Freddie's mind is as real as his own.

Tim: Look, I admit that Robo-Freddie isn't a real human being. For human beings are animals, not machines, and Robo-Freddie is most certainly a machine.

Ed: True.

Tim: But Robo-Freddie *does* have a mind. A *real* mind. Sure, Robo-Freddie may be made out of a different sort of *physical stuff* from me. Inside Robo-Freddie's head there are lots of plastic and metal components. Inside my head there's a brain made out of flesh and blood. But *so what?* If a flesh and blood brain like mine can produce this rich inner mental life, then why can't a plastic and alloy machine? *What does it matter* how we are physically put together inside?

How computers work

But Ed thinks it *does* matter how Robo-Freddie is put together. In particular, Ed thinks it matters that inside Robo-Freddie's head there's a computer.

343

Ed: Look, like any complex machine nowadays, Robo-Freddie is run by a
   computer.

Ed jabs a finger towards Robo-Freddie's head.

Ed: There's a computer right there in his head.
   Now let's get clear about how computers work. A computer is, in
   effect, a device for *shuffling symbols*, isn't it?
Tim: What do you mean?
Ed: Well, take the computer that sits in the middle of an automated
   railway system, making the trains run on time. The computer
   receives lots of *input* from the trains and tracks, indicating the
   position, speed and destination of the trains and how the points
   are set. This input takes the form of lots of sequences of *symbols:*
   strings of ones and zeros.

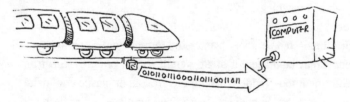

The symbols represent the trains, their position, and so on. The
computer then sends out other sequences of ones and zeros – its
output – that go off down cables to control the trains and points.

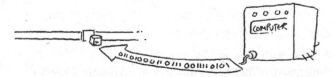

These symbols control the trains and points, making all the trains
arrive safely and in good time at their destinations.

Tim: Yes, I know all that.

Ed: Now, the computer running this railway system doesn't *understand* that this is what it's doing, does it? It doesn't understand that a certain sequence of ones and zeros represents a *train*. It doesn't understand that another sequence represents a *set of points*.

Tim: It doesn't?

Ed: No. All the computer does is follow its program, which makes it send out different strings of symbols depending on those it receives. It doesn't know where the symbols it receives come from. And it doesn't know what the symbols it sends out go on to do.

From the computer's point of view, it could be flying a plane or predicting the weather or translating Hebrew into English. It's all the same to the computer, isn't it?

Tim: Hmm. I *guess* so.

Ed looks triumphant.

Ed: Now this is true of *all* computers. Sequences of symbols get fed in. Then, depending on how the computer is programmed, it sends out other sequences of symbols in response. Ultimately, that's all *any* computer does, no matter how sophisticated it is.

Tim: Are you sure?

Ed: Yes. A computer doesn't *understand* anything at all. It just mindlessly, mechanically shuffles symbols according to its program.

Why Ed thinks Robo-Freddie doesn't understand

Tim can see where this is all leading.

Tim: And I guess you're going to say the same about the computer
   inside Robo-Freddie's head. It also understands nothing.
Ed: Yes. That's *exactly* my point.

Ed points at Robo-Freddie.

Robo-Freddie is, in effect, just another symbol-shuffling computer
housed inside a robot body. A computer designed to mimic understanding. But computers really understand *nothing at all.* So
Robo-Freddie understands *nothing at all.*

Shank's computer

Is Ed right? Does Robo-Freddie understand nothing? Tim still
isn't persuaded that Robo-Freddie lacks understanding, so Ed
decides to tell him about a very famous philosophical argument.
I call it the *Chinese room argument.*

Ed: I see you're still not convinced. So let me tell you about the Chinese
   room. It's a famous argument that was devised by the American
   philosopher John Searle way back in the 1980s.

Back in the 1980s, a computer engineer called Shank developed a computer that could answer simple questions about a story it had been told. For example, if the computer was given a story in which a boy called John climbed a mountain, and it was then asked, 'Who climbed the mountain?', the computer would give the correct reply: 'John'.

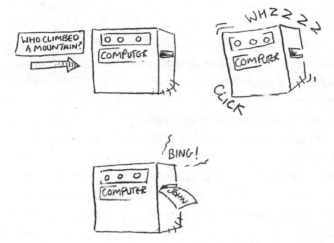

Now some people were very excited by Shank's machine. They claimed it actually *understood* the story it had been told, the questions it received and the answers it gave back.

But Searle disagreed. He thought that, while Shank's computer might *simulate* understanding, it didn't *really* understand anything at all. Searle devised a little story to explain why.

The story of the Chinese room
Ed proceeds to tell Tim all about the Chinese room.

Ed: Suppose a girl, Lucy, is locked in a room. She's given a list of
instructions and a sequence of cards with funny squiggly shapes
drawn on them. Then Lucy sits by a little hatch through which she's
handed more sequences of cards with
squiggles on.

Tim: What happens then?

Ed: Lucy's instructions explain how she
should shuffle the symbols she has
been given. She follows her instructions, and pushes the resulting string
of cards back through the hatch.

Tim: I see.

Ed: Now, what Lucy *doesn't* know is that the
squiggles drawn on the cards she's given are actually Chinese
letters. In fact, the first sequence of cards tells a story in Chinese.
The second sequence asks a question about the story. Her instructions
allow her to shuffle the two sequences together in such a way that
she can give back the right answer to that question.

Tim: Ingenious.

Ed: Now suppose the people *outside* the room feeding in symbols are
Chinese. And they don't know what's inside the room. They are likely
to think that there must be someone inside the room who understands
Chinese, right?

Tim: I guess so. After all, they feed a story and questions, both in Chinese, into the room, and they get correct answers back, also in Chinese. So it must seem to them as if there's someone inside the room who understands Chinese.

Ed: Exactly. Except Lucy *doesn't* understand Chinese, does she?

Tim: No, she doesn't.

Ed: Right. The Chinese room merely *mimics* the behaviour of someone who understands Chinese. Lucy herself is completely unaware that the shapes she is shuffling have any significance. She thinks they're just meaningless squiggles.

Tim: I suppose that's true.

Ed: You see, from Lucy's point of view, whatever *meaning* the symbols have is irrelevant. She's just shuffling them mechanically according to their *shape*.

Tim: And I guess Searle said the same about the computer programmed to answer questions about a story it had been told? Shank's computer didn't *understand* the story or questions. In fact it was unaware that there *was* a story. All it did was to shuffle symbols mechanically according to its program.

Ed: Exactly! It merely *mimicked* understanding. And of course, the same is true of *any* computer.

Ed now points to Robo-Freddie's head.

So the *same is true of Robo-Freddie*. He's just a computer housed in a robot body. A computer programmed to *mimic* the behaviour of a person with a mind. But of course there's no *real* understanding going on in there, as there is in *our* heads. There's just a complex symbol-shuffling device designed to *replicate* understanding.

The right stuff

I have to admit, Searle's Chinese room argument does *seem* very convincing. It does appear to show that no programmed computer could ever understand.

But then what more does Searle think is required for *real* understanding? What's the crucial difference between Robo-Freddie and a real human so far as understanding is concerned?

Ed explains.

Ed: In Searle's view, the reason why machines like Shank's computer and Robo-Freddie don't understand is because they're made out of the *wrong sort of stuff*.

Tim: Stuff?

Ed: Yes. Searle doesn't deny that machines can understand. After all, we are a kind of machine, in a way. We are *biological* machines. And we biological machines *can* understand. One day we may even be able to make such biological machines in the laboratory.

These man-made machines *would* be able to understand.

Tim: I see.

Ed: The trouble with Robo-Freddie is that he isn't made out of *biological* stuff. Metal and plastic is not the sort of material to use if you want to make a machine that *genuinely* understands. Flesh and blood machines can understand. Metal and plastic machines can't, no matter how complicated they might happen to be.

Is Searle right? Is it true that in order to make a machine that really understands, it needs to be made out of flesh and blood, or perhaps some other sort of biological material, like us?

Robo-Freddie's robo-brain

Tim doesn't believe a word of it.

Tim: Searle is mistaken. His argument *doesn't* show that in order to have a mind, you have to be made out of a certain sort of material.

Ed: Why not?

Tim: Look, suppose I agree, for the sake of argument, that no programmed symbol-shuffling computer can understand. That doesn't mean that Robo-Freddie here can't understand.

Ed: Why not?

Tim: Well, for a start *Robo-Freddie doesn't contain a symbol-shuffling computer.*

This comes as a bit of a surprise to Ed.

Ed: He doesn't?

Tim: No. Take a closer look at the user manual you hold in your hands. Robo-Freddie is one of the new generation human-simulators. According to his user's manual, Robo-Freddie is run, not by a programmed computer, but by one of the new *Robo-Brains.*

Ed: Robo-brains? What are they?

Tim: Well, you know that a human brain is made out of millions of cells called *neurons?*

Ed: Of course.

Tim: These neurons are woven together to form an incredibly complex web. And this web is buzzing with electrical activity.

Neurons are 'firing' all the time, passing on tiny electrical charges from one to another. Patterns of electrical stimulation come down nerves from our senses – our eyes, nose, tongue, ears and skin - and go *into* the web. That's what allows us to perceive the world around us.

Other patterns of electrical impulse are *sent out* by the web to control our arms, legs and so on, making us walk and talk.

Ed: Yes, yes. I already know all about that.

Tim is right. A brain is an incredibly complex network of neurons all spliced together. This network receives electrical stimulation from our senses. And it transmits electrical stimulation out to control our bodies.

Tim points to Robo-Freddie's user manual.

Tim: Now it says in that manual that *Robo-Freddie's robo-brain works in the same way.* Where we have neurons woven together to form a web, Robo-Freddie has robo-neurons woven together to form a web.

Ed: Robo-neurons?

Tim: Yes. Robo-neurons are tiny electrical devices that behave in the exact same way as real neurons.

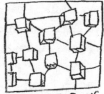

REAL NEURONS   ROBO-NEURONS

A robo-neuron does the exact same job a real neuron does. It sends out the exact same patterns of electrical stimulation.

Ed: So a robo-brain made out of robo-neurons will behave just like a real brain?

Tim: That's right. The exact same sort of electrical activity takes place inside it.

Ed rubs his chin gently. He looks a little bemused.

Ed: I see. So there's no s*ymbol-shuffling computer* in Freddie's head?

Tim: No. Forget about symbol-shuffling. We are talking about a machine that is structured *exactly like a human brain*. It's just made out of different sort of stuff.

Ed: I see.

Tim: That's why Searle's Chinese room argument isn't relevant here. Even if Searle's argument *does* show that no symbol-shuffling computer can understand, it doesn't show that Robo-Freddie here can't understand. For *Robo-Freddie doesn't contain a symbol-shuffling computer*. His artificial brain works in quite a different way. It works the same way a *real* brain does.

It seems Tim is correct. If Robo-Freddie has a robo-brain, then there's no symbol-shuffling going on in his head. No more than there is in an ordinary flesh and blood brain.

Meat vs metal and plastic

But Ed won't give up. He still thinks that Robo-Freddie can at best only *simulate* feeling, thought and understanding.

Ed: I'm sorry, but the fact is that Robo-Freddie here is an empty shell. He merely outwardly *replicates* a being with a mind.

Tim: I know that's what you *believe*. But what's your *justification* for claiming that Robo-Freddie has no mind? What's your *argument* for supposing he has no thoughts or feelings?

Ed remains convinced that Robo-Freddie is just an empty shell.

Ed: I just can't for the life of me see how you could produce what I have – a mind filled with understanding, thoughts, feelings and emotions – simply by gluing some bits of plastic and metal together.

Actually, Ed is right: it really is difficult to grasp how, simply by putting some bits of plastic and metal together in a particular way, you could create thoughts and experiences. How, just by fitting some mechanical components together, could you possibly create a mind? How do you make an *emotion* out of silicon chips? How do you build a *feeling* out of metal and plastic?

But while it may be difficult to understand how a lump of metal and plastic might have a mind, it is, of course, no less difficult to understand how a lump of meat might have a mind. For, after all, that's just what a brain is: a lump of meat.

Tim: Hmm. I agree. It *is* difficult to understand how that's possible. But then it's no less difficult to see how you could build a conscious mind by weaving *strands of meat* together, is it? As we know that a lump of flesh and blood *can* have a mind, why suppose that lumps of plastic and metal are any different?

Tim's point is a good one. Really, Ed's worry is about how *any* physical thing might come to have a mind, be it a plastic and metal thing or a flesh and blood thing. But then Ed's worry can hardly be used to justify the conclusion that while flesh and blood machines can have minds, metal and plastic machines can't.

Tim's neuron-swap argument

Ed has yet to come up with a good argument to support his claim that Robo-Freddie has no mind. And in fact, as Tim now explains, there's a pretty good argument to support Tim's belief that Robo-Freddie *does* have a mind. I call it the *neuron-swap argument*.

Here's how it goes.

Tim: Look, you think you are inwardly aware of *something* – thoughts, feelings, understanding and so on – something that Robo-Freddie, with his plastic and metal neurons, lacks. Correct?
Ed: Yes. He merely *simulates* thought, feeling and understanding.
Tim: But now suppose that, over the course of a year, surgeons were gradually to replace your organic neurons with robo-neurons like

Robo-Freddie's. Suppose that each week, about two per cent of your neurons are replaced, so that, after one year, you have a robo-brain just like Robo-Freddie's. What do you think would happen to your mind?

Ed thinks for a moment.

Ed: Well, as more and more of my fleshy neurons were replaced with plastic and metal ones, I would gradually cease to have a mind. Thought and feeling would slowly melt away. I would eventually end up a mindless shell, just like Robo-Freddie.

Tim: But your thoughts and feelings are something you are inwardly aware of, right? They are something you *know* about.

Ed: Of course they are.

Tim: So if your inner, mental life were to dwindle away like that, you would *notice* it, wouldn't you?

Ed: Of course I would!

Tim: In fact, you would probably say something like, 'Oh no! Over the past few months my mind has gradually been melting away! What's happening to me?!'

Ed: I'm sure I would say that. Yes.

OH NO!. MY MIND IS MELTING AWAY!

Tim smiles.

Tim: Except you *wouldn't* say anything like that, would you?

Ed: Why not?

Tim: Well, your new robo-neurons do *exactly* the same job as your originals. So, even as your fleshy neurons were replaced by robo-neurons, your brain would continue to operate just as it always has. Right?

Ed: Er, I guess so.

Tim: But as your outward behaviour – including what you say – is controlled by what's going on in your brain, your outward behaviour would remain unaltered too!

Ed: Oh. I see.

Tim: But then you *wouldn't* mention that your mind was melting away, would you?

Ed: Er, I suppose not. No.

Tim: So you see, you *think* you have a mysterious 'something extra' - some sort of inner, mental life – that Robo-Freddie, being a mere machine, lacks. But it turns out that this mysterious 'something extra' doesn't exist! *There's nothing you are inwardly aware of that you would lose if your brain were replaced by a robo-brain!*

This is a very interesting argument. It does seem to show that, while Ed might think that he has something that Robo-Freddie, being made out of plastic and metal, lacks, this mysterious something is an illusion.

Out of the closet

Ed looks confused. He still feels sure that Robo-Freddie's thoughts, feelings and understanding are all a sham. But is he right?

Tim: Look, I see you are *still* not convinced. So I shall tell you something I shouldn't.

Ed: Tell me what?

Tim: Take a deep breath.

Ed is getting irritated.

Ed: What?

Tim: I have something important to tell you.
Ed: What is it?
Tim: Go and take a look in the cupboard over there.

Ed walks over to the cupboard and slowly opens the door. Inside, he sees a large, cellophane-fronted box.

Tim: Turn on the light.

Ed reaches over and flips the switch in the closet. Suddenly, the cupboard is flooded with light. Ed staggers back in horror.

Tim: That's right. It's your packaging.

Across the front of the box is written, 'Robo-Eddie – your mechanical pal! New X-generation sim with robo-brain!'

Ed: It can't be true!
Tim: It is true, Robo-Eddie.
Ed: Don't be ridiculous! I'm a human!
Tim: No. You're a robot. I bought you to take with me on last year's

winter holiday. Only this winter you decided not to come. So I'm replacing you with this year's model.

Ed can't believe what he's hearing.

Ed: I ... I don't understand.
Tim: I think you do. *Still* think that robots can't have minds?

Ed slumps in a chair. His mind is reeling.
Or is it? Does Robo-Eddie have a mind to reel?
What do you think?

File 15

But is it science?

The rise of science

Just a few hundred years ago we had no electricity and no gas-fired central heating. For my ancestors, day-to-day life was usually hard, in large part spent just keeping warm, watered and fed.

People were ignorant, too. They had little knowledge of what was going on in the world. They thought the Earth was stationary and that the entire universe was just a few thousand years old. Plagues and epidemics were thought to have a supernatural origin. People believed that witches and demons roamed the land, causing illness and misfortune.

There were no vaccinations, no anaesthetics and very little effective medicine. Without disinfectants, antibiotics or even an understanding of the importance of hygiene, wounds easily turned septic. Infected limbs were sawn off without anaesthetic. One of the leading forms of medicine involved 'bleeding' people.

Now take a look around your house. Turn a tap and clean fresh water – as much as you want – pours out. Pick up the phone and you can immediately talk to somebody in Australia. A dark room is made bright at the flip of a switch. Your fridge keeps a wide variety of foods from around the world fresh for days on end.

There's a TV, radio and music system to entertain you and tell you about what's going on across the globe. You will live decades longer than your ancestors, thanks to vaccinations, antibiotics, surgery and the development of new genetic techniques. We regularly fly to different countries and continents in just a

few hours, just for the fun of it. Men have walked on the moon.
Our lives have been utterly transformed. But why?
Because of *the rise of science*.

THE RISE OF SCIENCE!

Science only really took off about 400 years ago. That's only
ten times as long as I have lived! Yet in this short period of time
science has changed our lives almost beyond recognition.

Pseudo-science

We have been looking at the short but impressive rise of
science. 'All very interesting,' I hear you say, 'but what is
science exactly?'

A good question. After all, if science is so wonderful, then it
would be very useful if we could say what it actually is. It
would also be helpful if we could say what makes for a *good*
scientific theory.

But in fact, despite the enormous importance of science
to our lives, it's astonishingly difficult to pin down exactly
what science is. Even scientists can struggle to explain what
distinguishes a good scientific theory from a bad one.

In fact, much that *looks* like science isn't science. Sometimes it's *pseudo-science*.

As you will soon discover, it can be extremely difficult to spot the difference between pseudo-science and the real thing. An *awful* lot of people are regularly duped into believing pseudo-scientific claptrap.

In this chapter we are going to look at one very famous example of pseudo-science. By the end of the chapter, you'll be much better able to spot pseudo-science when you see it.

But before we take a look at pseudo-science, it's worth reminding ourselves of two important facts about science. The first is that there are important limits to science. The second is that the rise of science has involved quite a struggle.

The limits of science

Of course, not *every* scientific discovery has improved our lives. We shouldn't forget that science has also given us pollution and weapons of mass destruction. And let's remember that there are *important questions science can't answer*. For example, science can't answer *moral* questions. It can't tell us how we *ought* to live our lives.

Here's a concrete example. Science will soon allow us to 'design' babies genetically. For example, you might choose to have a baby that is immune to certain diseases, or that is especially intelligent, or has particularly blue eyes.

> I'D LIKE MY DAUGHTER TO HAVE THOSE EYES, THOSE LIPS AND THAT NOSE.

These are things we will be able to do. But *should* we? Is it morally OK to design children, much as you might design a new suit or a handbag? Is that a proper attitude to take towards another human being?

That is a question science can't help us with.

Still, even if science can't answer all our questions, the fact is it's an enormously powerful tool. It has changed our lives dramatically. That transformation has been almost entirely for the better.

Science and religion

As I say, the rise of science has involved quite a struggle. One of the most famous battles was over the theory that the Earth moves.

Back in the seventeenth century, the Catholic Church was

immensely powerful. It took the view that we inhabit a stationary Earth located at the centre of the universe, with everything – including the sun – revolving around us, like this.

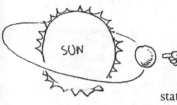

Certainly there are passages in the Bible that strongly suggest the Earth is stationary. Psalm 93.1 of the Bible says...

But then the scientists Copernicus and Galileo developed a scientific theory in which the Earth revolves around the sun. The Catholic Church condemned Galileo for claiming that his sun-centred model was true and imprisoned him in his own home until finally he agreed to withdraw his claim.

But Galileo was right: the Earth *does* move.

Interpreting the Bible

Of course, the vast majority of Christians now accept that Galileo was correct. So what do they say about passages such as Psalm 93.1?

They say that we should be careful about taking everything that the Bible says entirely at face value. To begin with, let's remember that while the Bible may be the word of God, it was written down by humans, and of course humans can and do make mistakes. Christians may also suggest that many of those parts of the Bible that *appear* to be contradicted by the findings of modern science have either been wrongly interpreted, or else were never meant to be taken literally. After all, the Psalms are poetry. People don't criticise the poet Wordsworth for writing 'I

wandered lonely as a cloud'
on the grounds that
clouds are incapable of
feeling emotions such as
loneliness.

Poetry isn't meant to
be interpreted entirely
literally. The same might
be said of the Bible.

Creationism

Now let's get back to pseudo-science: stuff that *looks* like science
but isn't. The example I am going to focus on in this chapter
involves *creationism*.

By creationism, I mean the view that the Biblical story of
creation is *literally* true. That, at least, is what most of those who
describe themselves as 'creationists' mean by the term.
Creationists believe that everything described in
Genesis – the first book of the Bible – *really
happened.*

So what does the Bible have to say
about creation? According to Genesis,
God created the universe, including
the Earth and all the different species
of plants and animals, over a period of
six days.

On day one, God created 'heaven
and earth' and night and day.

On day two, He made 'a firmament' which he called 'Heaven' (I'm not really sure what a firmament is). On day three, God created dry land with grass and trees. On the fourth day He created the Sun, Moon, planets and stars and on the fifth day He created fish and fowl.

And on the sixth day, God created cattle and other creatures that crawl on the dry land, including, finally, the first man – Adam – and woman – Eve. God commanded Adam and Eve to be fruitful and multiply and to rule over everything on Earth.

Creationists believe this story is no myth. As I say, they think it really happened. God created the universe and all living species in just six 24-hour days.

But when?

A six-thousand-year-old universe

According to most creationists, God made the universe about six thousand years ago. Creationists usually base their calculations of the age of the universe on the generations listed in the Bible (the passages that say Adam begat Seph who begat Enos and so on). In fact in 1650 James Ussher, an Anglican Bishop, calculated that the universe was created on 3rd October, 4004 years before the birth of Christ.

> GOD MADE THE UNIVERSE ON THE MORNING OF THE 3RD OF OCTOBER 4004 B.C.

The increasing popularity of creationism

Creationism is not just of historical interest. It is a living theory. In fact it has seen a vast surge in popularity over the last few decades.

True, in England, where I live, and in the rest of Europe, hardly anyone believes in creationism. But in the United States the situation is very different.

A recent poll conducted in the US indicated that *about 45 per cent of US citizens now believe in creationism.* They really believe that the universe, and all living species, were created in the same week less than ten thousand years ago.

So popular has creationism become that a university teacher from Tennessee recently wrote:

> *Medieval ideas that were killed stone dead by the rise of science three to four hundred years ago are not merely twitching; they are alive and well in our schools, colleges and universities.*

Is creationism scientific?

Why has creationism become so popular?

One of the main reasons is that people have been persuaded that creationism is *good science.*

In fact, in some states in the US, creationism is taught alongside evolution in biology classes. It is presented as an *equally respectable scientific theory.*

Even the current President of the United States, George W. Bush, believes both evolution and creationism should be taught in schools.

If many millions of Americans believe that creationism is scientifically respectable, then perhaps we should look at it a little more carefully. Maybe there is something to the claim that creationism is good science after all?

Let's find out.

The Big Bang/evolution theory

To start with, let's take a quick look at what the overwhelming majority of scientists now believe about how the universe started and how life emerged.

The universe, they say, started between ten and twenty billion years ago with the Big Bang, an unimaginably violent explosion in which matter, space and even time itself came into being.

A billion years is one thousand times a million years, which is itself one thousand times a thousand years. So ten billion years is a very long time indeed. It's hard to get a feel for just how long. Try the following little demonstration. Stand about twenty metres from a wall, pointing away from it, like so.

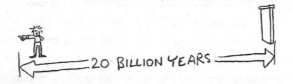

Now imagine that the wall is when the universe began and the tip of your finger is where we are now, with the twenty-billion-year history of the universe stretched out in between.

Then the distance between the tip of your finger and your nose – about a metre – represents *one* billion years. That means that one million years is one millimetre – about the thickness of the skin on the tip of your finger.

So how old is the Earth? Most scientists believe it's approximately four and a half billion years old. That's about four and a half metres back from the tip of your finger.

What of life? Scientists believe the first life-forms emerged on Earth some three and a half billion years ago. That's three and a half metres back from your fingertip.

A process of *evolution* then took place. The simplest life-forms very gradually evolved into slightly more complex life-forms, which in turn evolved into still more sophisticated forms of life. But it took a very long time for anything other than simple microscopic life-forms to appear. In fact the dinosaurs appeared

DINOSAURS
APPEAR

only some 230 million years ago: just a little way up your forearm.

And the first large mammals appeared only 65 million years ago: about where your finger joins your hand.

Modern man – *homo sapiens* – appeared perhaps only 200 thousand years ago: that's about one-fifth the thickness of the skin on the tip of your finger.

That gives you some sense of the age of the universe according to the overwhelming majority of scientists.

So where do creationists place the beginning of the universe? They say the universe is less then ten thousand years old. Ten thousand years is just *one hundredth* the depth of the skin on your fingertip.

You can now see that the difference in the age of the universe depending on whether you accept creationism or the Big Bang theory is *absolutely immense*: the difference between the ten to twenty metres stretched out behind you and one hundredth of the depth of skin on the tip of your finger!

As I say, the vast majority of scientists believe the Big Bang/evolution theory. Of course, they disagree about the details. For example, they disagree about *exactly* how evolution took place. And they argue over the *exact* age of the universe.

But that there was a Big Bang many billions of years ago and that life emerged and evolved over millions or billions of years is now accepted by the overwhelming majority of scientists.

Brad and Carol's discussion

Let's now take a closer look at why so many people believe that creationism is good science.

Meet Brad and Carol.

They're sitting in The Magic Café here in Oxford where I live. Brad is a visiting American student. He believes in creationism. Carol is a science student from England (she lives with Aisha – we met her in chapter one).

Carol believes that the universe started with the Big Bang billions of years ago and that life evolved gradually. She thinks creationism is a lot of unscientific claptrap. But Brad believes that creationism is just as good a scientific theory as Carol's Big Bang/evolution theory.

Let's see if we can figure out who is correct, and why.

Evidence against creationism

Carol: You believe the universe is only six thousand years old, that all living things were created at that time?

Brad: That's right.

Carol: Even the dinosaurs?

Brad: Yes.

Carol: So tyrannosaurus rex and the velociraptors roamed the Earth alongside man just six thousand years ago?

Brad: Yes.

Like most creationists, Brad doesn't deny dinosaurs existed. After all, we find their fossils beneath our feet. But of course, if

372

creationism is true, then they too must have been created just six thousand years ago, along with everything else.

Carol: But that's only *one and a half thousand years* before the Ancient Egyptian pyramid of Cheops was built.
Brad: True.
Carol: You're nuts!
Brad: Obviously you don't believe me. But don't be so quick to resort to insults. Tell me *why* you believe creationism is unscientific.

Carol now comes up with three pieces of evidence that she thinks conclusively show that creationism is false. Her first piece of evidence is the light coming from distant stars.

Light from distant galaxies
Carol: OK. Take, to begin with, the light and other emissions we observe coming from distant galaxies and other remote objects. These objects are so far away that it would take light millions or billions of

years to reach us. So we must see them as they were millions or
billions of years ago. See, the universe must be billions of years old!

Brad: I see your confusion. The universe is, in truth, only a few thousand
years old. But, when God created the universe, He created the light
you're referring to *on its way* to us.

THE EVENT WE ARE NOW WITNESSING THROUGH THE TELESCOPE ACTUALLY HAPPENED SIXTY MILLION YEARS AGO. IT HAS TAKEN THAT LONG FOR THE LIGHT TO GET HERE.

Brad is right: if God created the light quite close to the Earth, so
that it would take just six thousand years to get here, then the
universe could be just a few thousand years old.

Is God deceiving us?

But Carol thinks she has spotted a problem with Brad's reply.

Carol: But if God created the light *on its way*, then He's deceiving us, isn't
He?

Brad: Why?

Carol: Well, God is creating the *illusion* of a very old universe, isn't he?
Look, suppose we see a supernova explosion way off in deepest
space. It would take the light we see millions of years to get here
from that explosion, wouldn't it? Now, according to you, the light

we see *didn't* come from any supernova explosion! Actually, it was created *just six thousand years ago*, on its way to us. In fact, because the entire universe is only six thousand years old, then *the explosion we seem to see never really happened*!

Brad: That's all true.

Carol: But then God is deceiving us, isn't He? *He is making it look as if the universe is millions of years old, when it's not!* Its age is an illusion!

Brad: It's merely an illusion, yes.

Carol: But God is supposed to be *good*. Why would He go in for such deliberate deception? Why would He *deliberately* make it seem as if the universe is much older than it is? Why would he deliberately fool us into thinking the supernova explosion happened?

Brad still doesn't see why, by creating the light on its way to us, God would be deceiving us.

Brad: God isn't deliberately deceiving us. It's just that, because the universe and all living things were created fully-formed, that inevitably gives rise to the impression of a longer history. Take, for example, God's creation of Adam: the first man. God created Adam as an adult. But as adults grow up from children, the existence of Adam as a mature adult gives the impression of Adam being older – old enough to have had a childhood. Correct?

Carol: Well, I guess so.

Brad: Or take the existence of the first trees. They were created as mature, fully-grown trees. If Adam cuts down a tree it will turn out to have tree rings, just like any tree. Right?

Carol: I guess so.

Brad: But again, tree rings indicate age, don't they? They show a history of growth. So you see, by creating fully-grown trees, God would have created something that could easily be taken to be older than it really is. The same goes for the light rays that God created on its way to us. God doesn't *deliberately* deceive us. It's just that, because the universe was created fully-formed, it can inevitably give rise to the mistaken impression that it's older than it actually is.

Brad does appear to have dealt with Carol's first piece of evidence against creationism. So Carol tries a different approach.

Craters on the Moon

Carol: OK, here's *another* piece of evidence that the universe is much older than just a few thousand years. Take a look at the Moon and you will see that it's covered in craters.

These craters are caused by meteorite impacts, correct?

Brad: Yes.

Carol: There are countless thousands of craters, aren't there?

Brad: Certainly.

Carol: Yet meteorite impacts on the Moon are rare. The last recorded one was several hundreds of years ago. So the only way the Moon could have acquired that many craters is by being very old indeed.

Brad is ready for this argument.

Brad: Well, again, perhaps the Moon was created with its craters. I have already explained why that wouldn't mean that God is a deceiver.

Carol: Hmm.

Brad: But in any case other explanations are available. Perhaps, six thousand years ago, there was much more debris floating around in space. These space rocks were quickly drawn by gravity to objects like the Moon, causing lots of craters over a short time. Nowadays most of the debris is gone, which is why impacts are currently so rare.

Carol is finding Brad's answers hard to deal with. After all, if there was lots more space debris around six thousand years ago, that really would explain all those craters, wouldn't it?

The fossil record
So Carol moves on to her third piece of evidence.

Carol: What about the fossil record? Examination of the rock beneath our feet reveals strata or layers that have been laid down apparently over many millions of years. Fossils of long-dead creatures and plants can be found embedded in these strata. And you find different life-forms fossilized in the different levels. At the lowest levels, only simple creatures are found. Higher up you discover more complex forms, including the dinosaurs. Higher still you find the larger mammals. Only the most recently deposited layers reveal traces of man.

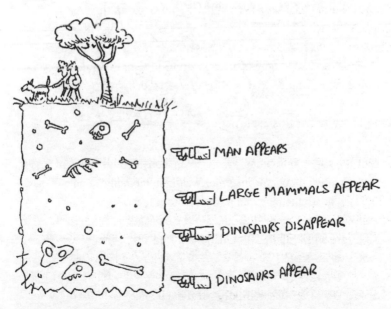

MAN APPEARS

LARGE MAMMALS APPEAR

DINOSAURS DISAPPEAR

DINOSAURS APPEAR

Brad: You're absolutely right: the fossils *are* ordered in that way.

Carol: Now this ordering of the fossil record tallies very well with the theory of evolution, but it seems to contradict the Biblical account on which all life-forms were produced more or less simultaneously less then ten thousand years ago.

Brad: Why do you say that?

Carol: Surely, if creationism was correct, we should expect to find examples of all the different life-forms muddled up throughout the rock layers – assuming, that is, that the few thousand years that have elapsed since creation are enough to allow rock layers even to form. For example, if man and all the other mammals lived along-side the dinosaurs, *there should be fossils of men and women, cows and pigs, elephants and giraffes and other large modern mammals muddled up with dinosaur fossils.*

But the fact is that today, even after millions upon millions of fossils have been dug up, not *one single* well-documented example of, say, a fossil of a large mammal in the dinosaur layers has ever been found. All we find in the dinasaur layer are small, squirrel-like mammals. How do you explain *that*?

Carol looks suitably satisfied with herself.

She thinks she has finally come up with concrete, irrefutable evidence that creationism is false.

Brad's flood theory
Yet Brad remains strangely unperturbed.

Brad: Actually, as a creationist, I *can* explain the fossil record. Quite easily. You see, we creationists believe in the Biblical Flood.
Carol: You mean, the flood on which Noah famously floated his ark?

Brad: Yes. That flood *really* happened. Everything described in the Bible *really happened*. Now, not surprisingly, the rains that caused the Biblical flood caused huge mud deposits.

GEE, THAT'S A LOT OF MUD.

GLOOP GLOOP

These mud deposits then solidified and turned into the rock layers we find beneath our feet. What you think of as layers of rock billions of years old are actually just mud deposits a few thousand years old.

Carol: But why do the fossils appear in the order they do?

Brad: Well, the reason one finds the larger, smarter mammals above dinosaurs, for example, is that the mammals are faster-moving and more intelligent than the cumbersome dinosaurs. When the flood came, the larger mammals ran to higher ground and drowned later.

So they got buried later. *That's* why they appear in the higher layers of mud.

This flood explanation of the fossil record is extremely popular among creationists – in fact almost all creationists now believe it. It's even taught in some American schools.

Carol is really beginning to struggle. She's becoming more and more irritated with Brad's replies. Every time Carol puts forward what she thinks is another solid bit of counter-evidence against creationism, it turns out Brad has yet another ingenious explanation up his sleeve. She feels as if she's being tied up in knots.

There are countless more pieces of counter-evidence that Carol *could* wheel out. But she's starting to suspect that Brad will somehow be able to explain them *all* away.

Why Brad thinks creationism is scientific

Brad sees that he is getting the better of the argument. So he sums up his position.

Brad: It seems pretty clear to me that your 'evidence' that the universe is millions or billions of years old is inconclusive.

Carol: Inconclusive?

Brad: Yes. It's becoming clear, isn't it, that my creationist theory is just as 'scientific' as your Big Bang/evolution theory? It's just as good a theory.

Carol: Why do you say that?

Brad: Well, scientists, I take it, use their five senses – the senses of sight, hearing, touch, smell and taste – to observe the world around them. And their job is to construct theories to *fit* and *explain* what they observe around them. Correct?

Carol: Yes.

Brad: Well, we have just seen that my creationist theory *does* fit what has been observed. It fits the evidence just as well as your Big Bang/evolution theory. As I have explained, it *does* tally with the fossil record. It *can* explain the existence of all those craters on the Moon. It *is* consistent with the existence of light from distant stars.

Brad looks triumphant.

Brad: So you see? *My creationist theory is just as scientific as yours!*

Is Brad correct? Is creationism really just as good a theory as the Big Bang/evolution alternative? After all, Brad's theory *does* fit the evidence.

Are dogs spies from the planet Venus?

Actually, Brad's theory isn't at all scientific. But why not? Why isn't creationism good science?

That's not quite so easy to explain.

Let's take a look at one of the problems with the claim that creationism is good science.

Suppose I tell you that dogs are spies from the planet Venus.

That's right, Fido here might look like a harmless pet, but he's actually a spy gathering information in preparation for an imminent Venusian attack.

Obviously, you don't believe me. But why not?

Well, doesn't all the evidence suggest that dogs are pretty stupid creatures incapable of such treachery? After all, they can't even talk, can they? And they have small brains, which suggest they are pretty dim. Nor do we find transmitters hidden about our houses by which our dogs might transmit their secret reports to Venus.

So surely, you would no doubt say, the evidence overwhelmingly supports the theory that dogs are affectionate and faithful pets, not spies from another world.

Defending the dogs–are–Venusian–spies theory

But hang on a moment. What if, in reply, I claim that while dogs' brains may be small, they're peculiarly efficient. In fact, I suggest, dogs are highly intelligent creatures which do possess language. It's just that they cunningly hide their intelligence and linguistic ability from us. And the reason we don't find their radio transmitters secreted about the house is that the transmitters are actually embedded in their brains.

RADIO TRANSMITTER

Now I have made my theory fit the evidence again! I have shown that all your counter-evidence actually fits in with my theory after all!

To this you might reply that an X-ray of a dog's head reveals no radio transmitter. Nor can we detect any transmission coming from their heads. And in any case, we know that Venus is a lifeless planet incapable of producing an invasion force.

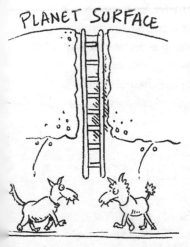

PLANET SURFACE

To which I might reply that dog transmitters are made out of organic material that resembles brain tissue, which is why they don't show up on X-rays or in dog autopsies. And dogs transmit via a mysterious medium we cannot yet understand or detect. And as a matter of fact Venus is inhabited. It's just that the Venusians live deep below the surface in secret bunkers.

That's why we don't know about them.

383

Notice that, yet again, by adding on a few additional claims, I have made my theory fit the evidence.

You can see how this rather silly game might continue. I can keep on protecting my weird theory about dogs being Venusian spies by constantly adding on new bits to deal with whatever evidence you might come up with.

So the interesting thing about my dogs-are-Venusian-spies theory is that I *can continue to make it fit and explain what has been observed.* I just need to keep on using my ingenuity to add on bits to deal with what might otherwise *seem* to be compelling counter-evidence. But if a good scientific theory is one which fits and explains what has been observed, then surely my theory that dogs are Venusian spies is just as "good" a theory as the common-sense theory that they are merely harmless pets, isn't it?

Reasoning close to madness

Of course not. Pretty clearly, the kind of reasoning that I am using to defend my bizarre theory about dogs is *not* scientific.

In fact you can see that *any* theory, no matter how utterly mad, can be protected in this way *for ever*, no matter how much evidence might be brought against it. If this was a scientifically respectable way of carrying on, then *all* theories would be equally scientifically respectable, including the theories that dogs are Venusian spies, that cheese is made of fairy dust…

...and that Mexicans are the secret rulers of the universe.

Interestingly, the kind of reasoning that I have been using to defend my dogs-are-Venusian-spies theory is symptomatic of certain sorts of mental illness, such as schizophrenia. It's exactly how schizophrenics defend their bizarre beliefs.

It is a form of reasoning that is, quite literally, close to madness. Yet it's exactly this sort of reasoning that Brad has been using to defend creationism. Brad has been playing much the same game that I played in defending my bizarre theory about dogs. Every time Carol comes up with a solid-looking bit of evidence

against creationism, Brad just adds a bit more on to his theory
to protect it.

What Brad is doing might look a bit like science. After all,
it's true that Brad is using his ingenuity to develop a theory that
continues to fit the evidence. But Brad's method is unscientific
(though of course he's not actually mad).

Confirming theories

Here's another very important difference
between creationism and the theory of
evolution.

> THE THEORY OF EVOLUTION IS STRONGLY CONFIRMED..

> BECAUSE IT MAKES A CLEAR AND PRECISE PREDICTION...

The theory of evolution is *strongly*
confirmed.

When is a theory strongly confirmed?

Well, to begin with, the theory has got to
make *predictions*. It has got to say what
we should expect to find when we
observe the world around us. And
these predictions must be clear and
precise.

Second, for a theory to be
strongly confirmed, the prediction
must be *bold*. That's to say, the
theory must predict something that
we wouldn't otherwise expect.

> A BOLD PREDICTION...

Here's an example. The theory of evolution predicts that, when we look under the ground, we will find the fossils of plants and animals arranged in a particular way throughout the rock layers. The lowest layers will have just simple organisms; higher up more complex life-forms will appear, and so on. The layers should show *evolutionary progression*. There should be absolutely no out-of-place fossils, such as a fossil of a man in one of the lowest layers. Not even *one*.

Now, if evolution *wasn't* true – if life on Earth *didn't* evolve – you really wouldn't expect this very precise ordering of fossils. In fact this sort of order would be pretty *unlikely* if evolution didn't take place.

So by predicting this precise order in the fossil record, the theory of evolution predicts *something we wouldn't expect otherwise.* That makes it a *bold* prediction.

Finally, in order for a theory to be strongly confirmed, the prediction must be *true.*

A PREDICTION THAT IS TRUE.

Even today, after many millions of fossils have been dug up, not *one single* example of an out-of-place fossil has ever been found. That *very strongly confirms the theory of evolution.*

Is creationism strongly confirmed?

So what about creationism. Is *that* strongly confirmed?

SO WHAT CLEAR, PRECISE AND BOLD PREDICTIONS DOES CREATIONISM MAKE?

ERR....

GENESIS IS TRUE

No, it isn't. For a start, let's ask what clear, precise and bold predictions creationism makes.

The answer appears to be: *none at all.*

Take, for example, the fossil record. What does creationism predict we should find?

387

Creationists are very vague about that. If the fossils were jumbled up in no particular order, they would say: 'See, that fits our theory!' But if the fossils are arranged in exactly the sort of way predicted by the theory of evolution, they say: 'But that fits our theory too!' They claim the flood explains the order of the fossils.

So it doesn't matter *what* we find: the creationists can say it fits their theory. That's because their theory doesn't take any risks with predictions. It makes no bold predictions. In fact it doesn't really predict anything at all.

But then it can never be strongly confirmed.

Why creationism isn't good science

So while creationism might *look* like good science, it isn't. In fact the kind of 'science' practised by creationists is really pseudo-science.

The trouble is, because most of us are very bad at spotting the difference between pseudo-science and the real thing, *lots* of people have been taken in.

True, no scientific theory is ever conclusively proved in the sense that it's proved beyond any possible doubt. There is always the *possibility* of error. But some theories are much better confirmed than others. The fact is that, while scientists might argue over the details, the theory that the universe is billions of years old with life having evolved from very primitive life-forms is *overwhelmingly* confirmed by the available evidence.

Creationism, on the other hand, is overwhelmingly discon-firmed. True, there's always the tiniest *possibility* of error. But it's hardly any more likely that it should turn out that the universe is actually only six thousand years old than it should turn out that the Sun goes round the Earth!

Creationism and Christianity

Of course, to say that creationism is false is not to say universe wasn't created by God. Perhaps it was. Even if we reject creationism, we can still be 'creationists' in that sense.

Many Christians are. They take the same view about the creation story in Genesis as they do about Psalm 93.1 – the Psalm that says that the Earth doesn't move. They may say that the Genesis story is simply a metaphor or myth. Or they may interpret the Genesis story in a way that makes it consistent with what science has discovered. For example, some Christians suggest that the six 'days' of creation shouldn't be understood as ordinary, 24-hour days, but 'days' lasting many millions of years.

So you can reject creationism while still remaining a Christian. Just as you can deny that the Earth is stationary while still remaining a Christian.

Spotting pseudo-science

We all know that science is pretty wonderful. We are impressed when something is described as 'scientifically proven', 'the latest scientific development' or 'recommended by leading scientists'.

But not everything that pretends to be scientific really is.

In this chapter we have looked at just one example of how people can be fooled into thinking that a theory is good science when it's not. But there are many other examples too. I'm sure you can think of some.

Philosophical Jargon

APARTHEID A system in which people of different races are segregated, usually because one race is felt to be superior to another. There was an apartheid system in South Africa until quite recently.

ARGUMENT In philosophy, an argument consists of one or more claims (often called *premises*) and a conclusion. The premises are supposed rationally to *support* the conclusion.

ASTROLOGY Astrologers claim that the arrangement of the heavenly bodies plays a role in determining what will happen on Earth. Many suppose that we can predict the future by looking at the stars.

ATOM A very, very small particle (though there are particles that are even smaller, particles out of which atoms are themselves made). Atoms group together to form MOLECULES. For example, a molecule of water is made up of two atoms of hydrogen and one of oxygen. Atoms are what all PHYSICAL OBJECTS (like peanuts, chairs, mountains and GALAXIES) are made up of.

 **BIG BANG** The huge explosion with which scientists suppose the PHYSICAL UNIVERSE began.

CELL All living things either are or are made up of tiny parts called cells. For example, your body is made out of many billions of cells. All cells are in turn made out of ATOMS and MOLECULES.

COMMON SENSE What most of us take to be just obvious.

COMPATIBILISM The view that DETERMINISM is compatible with FREE WILL.

CONFIRMED A claim is confirmed if there is some EVIDENCE (even if only a tiny bit) that is true.

CONTRADICTION A contradiction is a claim that says that something is true but also is not true.

COUNTER-EVIDENCE EVIDENCE against a claim.

CREATIONISM Usually, those who describe themselves as 'creationists' mean they believe that the account of creation in Genesis is really true: that the world and all species of life were created in just six days by God some time in the last ten thousand years or so. There was no BIG BANG and there has been no EVOLUTION of new species.

DETERMINISM The view that everything that happens in the PHYSICAL UNIVERSE is fixed in advance by the LAWS OF NATURE.

DISCONFIRMED A claim is disconfirmed if there is some EVIDENCE that it is false.

ELECTRON One of the tiny particles out of which ATOMS are made.

ESP Extra-Sensory Perception. Perception other than by the five usual senses of sight, taste, touch, smell and hearing. A sort of 'sixth sense'.

EVIDENCE Evidence is information that rationally supports a belief – makes it more likely to be true. For example, suppose I believe that someone is living in that cottage over there.

The fact that there is smoke coming from the chimney provides evidence that my belief is true.

EVOLUTION Species are supposed to evolve: they

gradually   change   and   adapt

over   many   generations.

FAITH To have faith is to believe even though there may be little if any REASON to believe.

FATALISM The view that what will happen to us is out of our control: it will happen no matter what we might do. So there is no point in our trying to prevent it from happening.

FREE WILL The ability to act freely. For example, I believe that I am now free either to scratch the top of my head or not.

There, I scratched my head. But I believe I was able not to scratch my head. I could have done otherwise. To believe in FREE WILL is to believe we can act freely.

GALAXY A huge cluster of STARS. There are about a million, million stars in our galaxy, the Milky Way.

GOD The SUPERNATURAL being that, according to Jews, Christians and Muslims, is all-powerful, all-knowing and all-good

HAEMORRHOIDS Also known as piles. A very painful condition of the bottom.

HEAVEN The wonderful, SUPERNATURAL place to which, according to many religions, we go when we die (at least if we have been good).

393

JUSTIFIED A belief is JUSTIFIED if there is good REASON to suppose that it is true ~ i.e. it is supported by good EVIDENCE and/or ARGUMENT.

KNOWLEDGE Just because you believe something doesn't mean that you know it. Your belief has got to be true. But even that isn't enough. Many philosophers would say that in order for a true belief to count as knowledge, you must also have some REASON to suppose your belief is true.

LAWS OF NATURE The laws of nature hold throughout the entire PHYSICAL UNIVERSE and determine how PHYSICAL MATTER and energy will behave.

LOGICAL/ILLOGICAL A claim is logical if it involves no logical CONTRADICTIONS. If it does, it is ILLOGICAL. An ARGUMENT is illogical if it doesn't support its conclusion.

MAMMAL A type of animal that suckles its young (that feeds its young using its breasts or mammary glands).

MATERIALISM The theory that there is only PHYSICAL MATTER: matter made out of ATOMS and MOLECULES.

MIND If you are conscious, are able to think, feel, have experiences, make decisions, and so on, then you have a mind (though not everything with a mind need have *all* these different PROPERTIES: minds can be unconscious, for example).

MOLECULE A tiny, invisible particle made out of ATOMS. Physical matter is made out of MOLECULES.

MORALITY Morality is concerned with right and wrong – with what we ought and ought not to do. For example, most of us believe that repaying one's debts is right and stealing is wrong.

NATURAL SELECTION The process by which EVOLUTION occurs. Natural selection is explained in chapter eight.

NEURONE A neurone is a type of CELL. It looks like this.

A NEURON

Neurones are what our brains are made out of. Each human brain is made up of about a million million neurones woven together to form a complex network.

OBSERVATION One observes by means of one's five senses: sight, hearing, touch, taste and smell.

OCKHAM'S RAZOR The philosophical principle that says that when one is faced with two theories each of which is otherwise equally well-supported by the EVIDENCE, one should always choose the *simpler* theory.

PARANORMAL Beyond the normal. For example, some believe that we have a sixth sense called ESP in addition to our normal five senses of sight, taste, touch, hearing and smell.

PHILOSOPHY The question: What is philosophy? is itself a philosophical question. Philosophers disagree over what philosophy is, exactly. In this book I have tried to give you a feel for what philosophy is by giving you examples of the kind of questions philosophers struggle with.

PHYSICAL WORLD/UNIVERSE/MATTER PHYSICAL MATTER is made out of ATOMS and MOLECULES. The physical universe is the universe we seem able to observe around us with our five senses. The only matter in the physical universe is PHYSICAL MATTER.

PLANET A planet is a large object circling a STAR. Unlike stars, planets don't give out any light of their own. The Earth is a planet.

PROPERTY Objects have properties. For example, my desk is an object that has the following properties: it is made of wood, it is brown and it weighs fifteen kilos.

PSEUDO-SCIENCE Something that *seems* like science, but isn't.

RATIONAL Supported by REASON and good ARGUMENT. JUSTIFIED.

REASON You and I can both REASON: we can think and work things out. We also talk about having a reason to believe something. A reason to believe is something that supports a belief, that makes the belief more likely to be true.

REINCARNATION If you believe in reincarnation you believe that after a person dies they can be reborn with a new body, perhaps even the body of a different sort of animal.

QUALITY See PROPERTY.

SCEPTICISM Sceptics claim that we don't know what we might think we know. For example, sceptics about the external world say that you have no KNOWLEDGE of the world around you.

SCIENCE System of knowledge arrived at by means of observation and experiment.

SOUL A SUPERNATURAL object made out of non-PHYSICAL MATTER: 'soul stuff'. A soul is capable of existing on its own quite independently of anything in the PHYSICAL UNIVERSE. According to those who believe in the existence of souls, it is your soul that thinks, feels, is conscious, has experiences, makes decisions, and so on.

STAR Large shining heavenly object. The nearest star to us is the sun. Stars are clustered together to form GALAXIES.

SUPERNATURAL Not part of the natural, PHYSICAL UNIVERSE

UNIVERSE See PHYSICAL UNIVERSE.

VEGETARIAN Someone who doesn't eat meat.

VEGAN Someone who doesn't eat any animal produce.

VIRTUAL ENVIRONMENT The environment to be found within a VIRTUAL REALITY.

VIRTUAL OBJECT An object found within a VIRTUAL ENVIRONMENT.

VIRTUAL REALITY A computer-generated reality, such as the kind of reality one finds in many computer games.